TE AO
HURIHURI

ASPECTS OF MAORITANGA

EDITED BY
MICHAEL KING

REED

This edition first published 1992 by Reed Books, a division of
Reed Publishing Group (NZ) Ltd, 39 Rawene Road,
Birkenhead, Auckland. Associated companies, branches and
representatives throughout the world.

ISBN 0 7900 0239 6

First published 1992
Reprinted 1993, 1994
Printed in Singapore

CONTENTS

Hei tohu aroha ki oku hoa kaumatua ki a Piri Poutapu
raua ko John Rangihau mo a raua tohutohu, manaaki,
atawhai i ahau.

Te Ao Hurihuri
te ao huri ai ki tona tauranga:
te ao rapu;
ko te huripoki e huri nei
i runga i te taumata o te kaha.

*Te Ao Hurihuri
is a world revolving:
a world that moves forward
to the place it came from;
a wheel that turns
on an axle of strength.*

CONTRIBUTORS

Ranginui Walker: Whakatohea; Associate Professor in Maori, Auckland University; columnist *New Zealand Listener* and *Metro* magazine; 15 years chairman of the Auckland District Maori Council; author of *Ka Whawhai Tonu Matou*.

Timoti Karetu: Tuhoe; Professor of Maori, University of Waikato; former chairman of the Maori Language Commission; prominent teacher and judge of Maori action song, and author of *Te Reo Rangatira*.

Api Mahuika: Ngati Porou; chairman New Zealand Maori Congress and Ngati Porou Runanga; former senior lecturer in Maori Studies, Massey University, and teacher at Victoria University and Correspondence School.

Douglas Sinclair: Ngai Tahu; former general practitioner, Hamilton; member of the Ngai Tahu Trust Board; president of the Tainui branch of Maori Graduates Association; died in Australia in 1984 while establishing Aboriginal health clinics.

Harry Dansey: Te Arawa and Ngati Tuwharetoa; former Race Relations Conciliator, journalist and artist; author of four books and one play; died in 1979.

Maori Marsden: Te Aupouri; a kaumatua for the Muriwhenua tribes and senior member of Anglican clergy; former Royal New Zealand Navy chaplain.

Wi Tarei: Ngati Awa; minister of the Ringatu Church; prominent Bay of Plenty social worker, member of Mapou Marae Committee; died in 1980.

Moana Raureti: Ngati Kahungunu; respected Wairoa kaumatua; former District Maori Welfare Officer, Hamilton, and active in 28 Maori Battalion Association.

Robert Mahuta: Tainui; director of the Centre for Maori Studies and Research, University of Waikato; member of Kahui Ariki, active in Tainui Trust Board, Waahi Marae Committee.

John Rangihau: Tuhoe; former Maori consultant, member of Tuhoe Trust Board, research fellow Centre for Maori Studies and Research, University of Waikato; District Maori Welfare Officer, Rotorua; died in 1987.

INTRODUCTION

IN THE 1990s there is scarcely anybody who would regard it as appropriate for a book such as this to be initiated and assembled by a Pakeha editor. The climate was very different in the 1970s, however, when *Te Ao Hurihuri* had its genesis.

At that time, other than on marae, there were few Maori voices heard in the public debate on the relevance and role of Maoritanga in the modern world. Most of the ground rules for the debate were set by politicians, educators or social scientists, and the argument was carried on in print *on behalf of Maori* by Pakeha.

From 1972 to 1974 I was involved in the making of a major series of television documentaries, *Tangata Whenua*. The impulse behind this project was the then novel notion that, in matters of Maori definition, Maori should speak for themselves. And so they did, with authority, eloquence and utter persuasiveness. It was while these programmes were in production that the publisher, Ann Mallinson, approached me and asked whether it might not be time to commission a book based on the same principle. My response was cautiously favourable, but I told her I would have to take soundings among Maori opinion leaders before I could commit myself to the idea.

And so I had discussions with John Rangihau, Piri Poutapu, Ngoi Pewhairangi, Harry Dansey, Ranginui Walker, Koro Dewes and Api Mahuika. Without exception they reacted to the idea with enthusiasm, and six of them wrote for the resulting book. My role as editor was to facilitate agreement about the content, commission essays, prod the authors into delivering manuscripts to a deadline, and to ensure that the contributions were comprehensible to a non-specialist Maori and Pakeha readership.

Thus was *Te Ao Hurihuri* conceived and – in 1975 – born, to some argument and some acclaim. Its purpose, in the words of my original introduction, was to 'convey information and feeling about the way in which Maori – as distinct from other ethnic groups in New Zealand – relate to one another and to the places in which they live and meet'. It would also demonstrate that Maori things 'can and should be written about by Maori participants rather than by Pakeha observers', and it would reveal to those who were not aware of it that Maori culture was not national and homogeneous, but tribally based.

Some reviewers criticised the fact that, apart from Ngoi Pewhairangi, the book had no female authors. I simply note here that women were asked to contribute but either declined to participate or failed to deliver their chapters.

The very considerable success of the book, in sales, and in its impact on national opinion-making, led to a companion volume, *Tihe Mauri Ora*, in 1978. Both books were in heavy demand for almost a decade and underwent several printings.

They were eventually allowed to go out of print in the mid-1980s because the then publisher, Longman Paul, believed that they had run their course. The world had moved on (te ao hurihuri indeed!), some of the authors were now deceased, and other books and other opinion leaders had emerged .The kinds of issues thrown up in *Te Ao Hurihuri* and *Tihe Mauri Ora* were now being discussed nationally, by Maori and Pakeha, as a matter of course. I agreed with this decision at the time.

It proved to be a mistake, however. Almost from the moment both books ceased to be available I was deluged with requests for them, especially for *Te Ao Hurihuri*. These appeals came from students, and from a large body of readers who were simply trying to build up a reputable library on things Maori. My own copies soon disappeared, lent to a chain of borrowers that became so long that it vanished into the mist of mythology. Photocopies of the chapters most in demand were soon in wide circulation, in total disregard for the conventions of copyright.

When Ian Watt approached me on behalf of Octopus Publishing and suggested that the books be brought back into print in a single-volume edition, I was receptive to the idea. We canvassed opinion among the contributors still living and most agreed. Some asked for the opportunity to revise their chapters, others were content for them to be reprinted as written, and several withdrew essays on the basis that the passage of time had outdated them.

I thank the living authors whose work does appear in this book for their cheerful cooperation – now and at the time the essays were originally commissioned – and I salute those who have passed over to Te Rerenga Wairua. Haere, e tuakana ma. Haere ki te Atua, haere ki te kainga.

Michael King

FOREWORD

LEARNING AND TAPU

WHEN YOU ARE DEALING with the knowledge of the past, you have to take it seriously. Otherwise you don't get inspiration or spiritual fertility from that knowledge. And if you ignore the tapu of sacred things, it can lead to sickness or even death.

I remember a boy stood up at a seminar I was at. He said he had in his possession books that had belonged to his ancestors and that had been handed down through his father to him. He didn't know how he should handle them. I stood up and replied to the speeches and I said to him, 'These books are valuable, they hold your whakapapa and your tapu. If you want to learn from them, take them away from food and clothing that belongs to women, to somewhere surrounded by nature. When there is just you and your books and nature you can recite and learn all those things. That way you can preserve the tapu that your ancestors have placed on those books. In time, you will find you will be inspired to carry on what they have left for you.'

Tapu has to be held in the highest esteem. You see in people, it is not in the hands: it is in the head, in the crown. In the old days, you could never touch the head. We take it seriously, knowing that it survives. In particular, it protects us from the temptations of the modern world. We may put on Pakeha clothes, we may eat Pakeha food. But deep inside we are Maori at heart and tapu will stay with us forever.

The handing down of knowledge by old people is a very difficult thing now. They have a look at their own children, perhaps the eldest son. If he is mature enough or interested enough in his Maori, he might become the repository. But a lot of people say no. They would sooner take a knowledge of their own traditions with them than pass them on to the present generation. They believe that if it goes out to another person outside the family, in a short time it will have dissolved, absorbed by all the other people who have access to it.

There is also a fear that by giving things out they could be commercialised. If this happens, they lose their sacredness, their fertility. They just become common. And knowledge that is profane has lost its life, lost its tapu.

– Te Uira Manihera, Tainui

WHEN YOU LEARN anything Maori, it has to be taken seriously. It involves the laws of tapu: genealogies, history, traditional knowledge, carving, preparing flax, in fact, nature itself. Tapu is something that teaches you how to respect the whole of nature, because Maori things involve the whole of nature.

Awareness of tapu associated with learning is something we grew up with. If you are born on a marae, there are certain qualities about you that are recognised by elders. They don't actually teach you. They select you and place you in a situation where you absorb knowledge. When you're asleep on your own, they're singing waiatas or reciting genealogies in the next room. As you're lying in the dark, you absorb everything that's going on. And before you realise what you're doing, you've learned how to recite too, or you've learned the words of a certain song. And this can go on for three or four years. But you don't realise that they're putting you into the situation to learn.

Suddenly, later, they take you to a meeting house and they recite these genealogies or sing these waiatas and deliberately forget a line. And you find yourself singing by yourself because you've recited and learned these things by heart. And you sing this line they've left out. And after a while they say to you 'Why don't you learn other songs or other genealogies?'

Then again you hesitate. You know the restrictions placed on these sorts of things. But they take you in hand. The tapu is so great they wouldn't take you in hand and teach you unless you yourself had done work in your own time and shown yourself able and suitable.

Nowadays, people raise the question about whether these things involving tapu should be taught in schools. Well, it's difficult. I wouldn't teach them. You see the way things are done in the classroom, teaching can become mechanical. And there are dangers. Take flax, for example. There are a lot of restrictions involved in flax work. The reason why old people hesitate to teach the young ones about this sort of work is because of the restrictions and tapu connected with it. If anyone learning breaks the rules connected with dyeing of flax, someone will have to suffer the consequences. Old people know that young people are inclined to break laws. So they are reticent to lay them down. There are certain ways of cutting flax, you see. You don't just go along and say 'I'll have this part because it's the best and the softest flax to work with'. You have to cut the flax that is really needed and in the way prescribed.

I'll give you an example of what can go wrong. We were preparing kiekie and had an old lady here teaching us how to do it. She even went into the bush with us to show the men how to cut the kiekie and strip them and bring them back here. This was my first experience of the tapu placed on this type of work. We went through the whole process of boiling the kiekie and that wasn't so tapu. But the dyeing was. It was placed in the mud for about two weeks and that old lady herself went on a trip to collect it. They brought the kiekie back here and found the dye hadn't gone through. The first words she uttered were that something had gone wrong or somebody had done wrong. 'There's nothing we can do about it. Someone will have to suffer the consequences,' she said. 'Someone will die because the dye hasn't been done properly and whoever placed it in the mud must have broken the law of tapu.' Two days after, the old lady died. This is the first time ever I'd known that tapu really had this effect. I believe in it now. This is the reason I don't like teaching tapu things. Because I know someone some time will break the rule. If you're making mats or preparing flax for weaving, you're not allowed to sleep with your husband for three nights. You're isolated from each other. He's not allowed in. I don't think it's wise to say to young folks 'Come here and learn this' and expect them to carry out these rules.

It's especially hard to communicate this sort of thing to a Pakeha, unless it's to one who lives on the marae and is brought up in this environment to see the values of Maori culture and the tapu placed on things. He's got to see it and see how Maoris suffer through the breaking of tapu connected with all the culture. Then he'll realise there is some value in tapu.

I know there are a lot of Pakehas who would love to learn, not only the language, but the Maori heart. And it's a thing one can never teach. Quite a number of Pakehas are sincere about it. This is part of the Maori they want to learn: respect for nature, respect for anything Maori, how they should come on to a marae, how they should come into a meeting house, and how to learn to speak like an orator. But anyone can speak on a marae once they've been shown the proper procedure. This is just scratching the surface. Maoritanga goes deeper than that and I don't think Pakehas are aware of this. They think that because they've been to university and studied the language and the culture, they've mastered it. To me listening, it sounds as if there is no depth there at all, especially as far as tapu is concerned. There is so much tapu connected with the whole culture and I don't think Pakehas can absorb it.

One thing hard for the Pakeha to understand is that our elders never allow us to sell any knowledge of anything Maori that is really tapu. To them it is priceless. Money can never buy knowledge and when they teach they will tell people: 'This knowledge I am passing over to you must never be sold.' This is how we get to know things. They're handed down from generation to generation and it becomes part of you. And this is the part of Maoritanga you can never teach. You know it's there all right, you've got it all there.

Some people, Maori and Pakeha, say 'Why don't those old people teach us how to do this?' But they don't realise it goes deeper. Only certain people can teach. It's like the Pakeha system. Only certain people can teach law, and certain people become statesmen. The same with the Maori. Only certain people, certain families, inherit these different aspects of our Maoritanga and are entitled to pass them on.

– Ngoi Pewhairangi, Ngati Porou

To PASS ON KNOWLEDGE, the main thing we have had to overcome is the conservative nature of Maori elders, particularly elders who have withdrawn as a result of pressure from the outside. This has been the case with my own tribe, Tuhoe. For a long time our elders tended to hold back from telling all they knew about our history.

I heard a young man say recently he was trying to equip himself so that when the time came for him to take his place on the marae he would have learned all the things required of him. Most people would support him in this. But he and others like him have to wait. You have to look at the old people's reasons for not passing things on to young people too soon, and the reasons for not allowing them to speak on the marae in front of their fathers.

I often speak of the mauri or the life force which Maoris give to many different things. We believe that every time you give of yourself you are starting to lose some of the aura, some of the life force, which you have for yourself. In the case of my son, if he starts to get up then he's drawing something from me and eventually I will be left an empty hulk. This is the real reason behind not allowing the young man to speak before the father dies. Because it is possible that he will take some of the mauri which rightly belongs to the father. And immediately you do this you start to take away all sorts of things from the father. Strange as it seems, I've seen it happen: a young man, a very aggressive young man, has carried on doing this in spite of cautions. And you can see the father dwindling in stature. Now the father seems to be hanging around at the back of the marae. He seems to be a person without any purpose: His son is taking the place the father should have.

However we have overcome much of the conservatism. I suspect the main reason is because within a period of something like three years, the elders who would have been the most difficult ones all passed away. It was obvious to the elders left behind that not one of them could say he was an expert on Tuhoe things. So they quickly realised they had to come together and pool their expertise so they could cover all aspects of Maoriness. Once they realised that, it was a short step to get them to understand that if they didn't do anything about passing all that material on, then their children could be left in the same position they had been, by people dying off quickly. When they accepted that, they were very receptive to the idea of setting up schools of learning for Tuhoe children.

These things are certainly not to be taken lightly. It's very difficult for me to be able to interpret in a way that the Pakeha mind can see. I talk about mauri and some people talk about tapu. Perhaps the words are interchangeable. If you apply this life force feeling to all things – inanimate and animate – and to concepts, and you give each concept a life of its own, you can see how difficult it appears for older people to be willing and available to give out information. They believe it is part of them, part of their own life force, and when they start shedding this they are giving away themselves. Only when they depart are they able to pass this whole thing through and give it a continuing aspect. Just as they are proud of being able to trace their genealogy backwards, in the same way they can continue to send the mauri of certain things forward and down to their children after death. They pick and choose from their children and if they have none, it is up to the person himself to pass information to one of his kinfolk. It's a very greyish area at the moment. There is no black and white as to how to do these things. But I have seen so many aspects of Maori life that are difficult to explain that I tend to withdraw and not say too much about them.

There are things you do for example on certain occasions, chants you use in certain circumstances. Unless you know what these circumstances are, you could mix them up and step over the area, which isn't done. In other words you could step on the mauri, on the prestige of other people. So the old people have to be fairly careful with knowledge and not use it indiscriminately. Maoris as travelled people are very sensitive to any derogatory remarks passed about their tribal backgrounds. And some of the chants are chants of derision directed at different tribes. You don't use these. This is the sort of thing I suspect is worrying people who are cautious and I can appreciate what they're talking about.

Generally the New Zealand public is very interested in things Maori and that's good. But in some cases they're so interested in advanced Maori they fail to realise that like getting a degree in any subject, you have to lead yourself up to University Entrance and BA and MA level to a doctorate. In some cases they want to get a doctorate in Maori things right away without going through the preliminary stages. In other words, people like to see and know about things in depth, without going through the whole process of learning, to allow them to appreciate it when they get the whole thing.

It worries me that everybody is getting on this bandwagon, but starting at the top, rather than coming through the ordinary ways that you should learn about any foreign language and customs. This is another reason why most of the old people face giving information with a certain amount of trepidation. Because they feel that people who want this information should come through other learning areas beforehand. One of the other things is that if the general New Zealand public clamours for this and wants to know about it at the top, then you're left with a number of people who have some knowledge at that level, but cannot explain why these things are being done.

I have been talking about such things as life force, aura, mystique, ethos, lifestyle. All this is bound up with the spirituality of the Maori world and the force this exerts on Maori things. It seems to me that people who want to enter this world need to enter it with a lot of respect and always be aware of these different life forces which are going on and which the Maori believes are part of his being. For some time in our own tribal set-up we have sensed that Pakeha values have slowly impinged on so many Maori aspects of life that we are now faced with a need to keep an area sacrosanct, an area where we can say these are the sorts of things which happen in this place. I'm referring to the marae, of course, but particularly to rural marae where our life still goes on and has dynamic existence. But also to urban marae where the urban sprawl has grown around them. They have an aura of their own too and there are a number throughout New Zealand. I believe this is where we should see that we don't step on the mauri of our people. So you set down rules of behaviour and protocol for these places. I believe the New Zealand public is aware that you do certain things only on a marae. And I also believe that if you tell them you do those things they will accept them in good faith, because they want to retain perhaps the last remnants of what they regard as the real Maori strength. Everywhere else outsiders have been coming in and participating in Maori life. So in this area you are able to say to people, 'It's good that everybody enters into the life of the Maori and knows what it's about. But there are certain places where you've got to be respectful, where you've got to realise that there is a spirituality about Maori things.' And this spirituality doesn't fit in with fast-changing Pakeha conditions.

– John Rangihau, Tuhoe

MARAE: A PLACE TO STAND

RANGINUI J. WALKER

Introduction

THE MARAE IS THE FOCAL POINT of Maori culture and communal activities. As an institution, its antecedents can be traced via the Cook Islands to the Society Islands, and ultimately right back to Samoa and Tonga. In Samoa, the marae was an open space of ground near the chief's house. It was a place of beauty, with well-kept grass and shaded by trees. Like the marae in New Zealand, it was the courtyard, the plaza and meeting-place near the chief's house. But unlike its New Zealand counterpart, formal ceremonies were conducted in the house instead of on the courtyard.[1] The Tongan marae was similar to that of Samoa. It was the village green, a place for social intercourse and open-air meetings. All secular activities were held there.[2]

In Tahiti, the marae was a specialised rectangular courtyard paved with stone or blocks of coral. At one end stood a raised rectangular platform or ahu. In some instances the ahu consisted of a stepped platform rather like an elongated low pyramid. At Papara on the west coast of Tahiti stood the marae of Mahai Atea which was recorded on Captain Cook's first voyage. Its base measured 120 feet by 80 feet. The ahu was 30 feet high.[3] The most renowned marae of all is Taputapuatea at Opoa on the island of Ra'iatea. It was known as an international marae because representatives from different islands met there periodically for instruction and edification. They brought presents and human sacrifices to the god Oro. These sacrifices from abroad gave the marae its name, Taputapuatea.[4]

Marae were located at coastal and inland sites and were associated with ari'i, the highest members of Tahitian society.[5] The paved courtyard was notable for a number of stone uprights which were thought to be backrests for ari'i.

Prominent marae were centres of ritual and ceremonial activity. These included the installation at the marae of fare atua (god house) and the display of the maro 'ura (red feather belt), the symbol of the ari'i.[6] Above all, the marae was used for the investiture of ari'i with the maro 'ura and the offering of human sacrifice to the god Oro.[7] Marae derived their mana and tapu from the bones of ari'i interred in the ahu and those of sacrificial victims under the pavement of the court. Taputapuatea at Ra'iatea is notable for the amount of bone fragments thrown up even today beside the burrows of land crabs around the precincts of the marae. While Taputapuatea is located among coconut palms fifty yards or so from the shoreline at Opoa, there are two smaller marae within fifty yards of each other right on the water's edge. The one on the left facing out to sea was a fisherman's marae and the other on the right a navigator's marae. The fisherman's marae was used by tahu'a (priests) to call fish to the passage in the reef, where they were taken by fishermen. The navigator's marae was used for rituals associated with voyages to other islands.

At Maeva, on the island of Huahine, along the shores of Lake Faunanui, are nineteen family marae restored by Sinoto, archaeologist of the Bishop Museum Honolulu. Those on the lagoon itself are associated with fishing and the operation of fish traps. The main marae, Mata'irea-rahi, located on the high ground above the lagoon, was the centre of the centralised government of Huahine. It unified the marae of the eight sons of Hotuhiva, the founding princess of Huahine from the ari'i line of Ra'iatea. There are eight backrests at Mata'irea-rahi for the chiefs of the eight districts.

In the Society Islands there are literally hundreds of marae which were used for different purposes. There were three classes of public marae: international marae, such as Taputapuatea, national, such as Mata'irea-rahi, and local ones. There were also five classes of domestic marae. There was the small private marae built on family land in memory of ancestors and used as a place of worship. Another class of marae was used for social purposes. Then there were the marae used by tahu'a, the priestly adepts of different specialties such as healing, canoe building, and fishing.[8]

In Rarotonga, villages were located along Te Ara-nui-a-Toi, a 22-mile long road which circled the island at the base of the mountains. The road was 12 feet wide and paved with blocks of lava and coral. Each hamlet along the road had its own marae, which consisted of rectangular stone platforms like the Tahitian marae with an ahu at one end. The two renowned marae on Rarotonga were Arai-te-tonga, which belonged to the Makea family, and Kauariki. The latter, which belonged to the Tinomana family, is at Arorangi. It was used for investitures and ceremonial sacrifices to the family gods.[9]

With the arrival of missionaries in the Society Islands and the transference of allegiance to the new God of the Europeans, marae fell into disuse. The paving stones of marae were in some instances quarried and put to other uses, such as building churches. In time, the church displaced the marae completely. In the Cook Islands the process of displacement of marae by churches was repeated. Marae were destroyed and carvings burned. With the appointment of Colonel W.E. Gudgeon after the turn of the century as New Zealand's first Resident Commissioner there, the ariki system was undermined as well. Gudgeon went so far as to lay down rules for the investiture of ariki, with the consequence today that contenders for titles resort to courts of law to adjudicate on succession.

The Marae in New Zealand

Despite the corrosive effect of missionaries on the culture of Maori society in New Zealand and the assimilationist policies of successive governors, the marae as an institution has persisted into the modern era. Today, the marae consists of the marae atea, the open space of ground, which serves as the ceremonial courtyard in front of the carved ancestral meeting house.

In pre-European times, the marae in front of the chief's house was the focal point of every permanently inhabited village. It was used daily by the people for many social purposes. It served as a rendezvous for hunting, fishing and war parties leaving the village. Returning expeditions were also met there before members dispersed to their own houses. People assembled in front of the chief's house for meetings of a secular nature. The marae in New Zealand differed from its counterpart in Tahiti in that religious rites were conducted by tohunga away from the marae at secluded tuahu or stone shrines. When a marae was not in use for formal meetings, children used it as their playground. Youths practised manly sports on the marae, such as wrestling, while adults spent many hours there just talking and passing the time of day. Every day, the marae served as a dining place, assembly point and seating place for the community.

When the chief of a community was ill and sensed the approach of death, he was brought out on to the marae to deliver his poroporoaki (farewell) and ohaki (dying speech) to the assembled tribe. The tangihanga (mourning ceremony) was also held on the marae and it culminated in the hakari (funerary feast). The hahunga, the ceremonial exhumation of bones, took place a year or so later. The bones of the chief, together with those of other dead ancestors, were welcomed back on the marae where they were wept over before final burial in a cave or some other secret place, such as a hollow tree deep in the forest. The significance of the marae in Maori society is neatly summarised by the eminent anthropologist Raymond Firth:

> The marae of a village was bound up with all the most vital happenings, with warm and kindly hospitality, with stately and dignified ceremonial, with the grouping of hosts and visitors in positions determined by etiquette and traditional procedure. This helps to account for the fact that to the native it was more than a simple open space in the village or a convenient assembly ground, and bore distinct social importance.[10]

Although it is not certain that a separate carved meeting house existed in every village in pre-European Maori society, the stories of mythology attest to folk memories of large houses in their Hawaiki homelands. One house was so large that it reputedly had ten fireplaces inside.[11] But there is a difference between myth and reality on the ground. The records of early navigators suggest that when they arrived there were no large buildings like the modern meeting house that is the focal point of the marae today. The largest houses they saw ranged from 10 to 33 feet in length, 5 to 10 feet wide and 6 to 8 feet high.[12] When the missionaries arrived in 1814, they were usually accommodated in the chief's house, which, at about 30 feet long, was the largest in the village. But the doorway was only 2 feet high and 18 inches wide. Illustrations by the artist Augustus Earle, who spent some months in New Zealand between 1827 and 1828, support these descriptions.[13]

The Wharepuni

The precursor of the meeting house was the wharepuni (sleeping house). The wharepuni was of a rectangular design with the side walls and roof extended at the front of the house to form a porch. This architectural form evolved in the colder climate of New Zealand and is found nowhere else in Polynesia. The porch provided an outdoor living space sheltered from southerly winds. The wharepuni as an architectural form appeared in the archaeological record at approximately the twelfth century.[14] By the fifteenth or sixteenth century, the wharepuni, such as the Makotukutuku house at Palliser Bay, was large enough to need two centre poles to bear the ridgepole. There were ten poupou, squared pillars, down the side of the house with notches at the top to fit the rafters.[15]

By the eighteenth century, the primary elements of the architectural design of the wharepuni, with decorative carvings on both interior walls and exterior pillars and bargeboards, were well established. One house seen by Captain Cook and Banks at Tolaga Bay was 30 feet long and had all the side posts carved.[16]

In traditional times, temporary guest-houses were built to accommodate large parties of visitors. In the traditions of the Tainui tribes, Turongo built a guesthouse to receive his bride Ruaputahanga and her entourage. But his house was too small, so the party was lodged with his brother Whatihua instead, who then won the bride for himself. This event occurred around 1500 AD.

In historic times, with the increase in the number of visiting Europeans, chiefs resorted to building houses solely to accommodate visitors. One house, built for Wakefield and his men of the New Zealand Company, was 50 feet long and 28 feet wide.[17] The introduction of iron tools had a remarkable effect on Maori architecture. Larger slabs of building timber could be worked and so buildings were upsized to emulate the large church halls built by missionaries. The art of carving also flourished in the decoration of chiefs' houses.

By the 1840s the houses of chiefs had doubled in size to 40 feet long, 15 feet wide and 12 feet high. Te Rangihaeata's house, Kaitangata, painted by Angas in 1844, is a prime example of a chief's house of the period. This house, in its architectural form and decoration, was one of the precursors of the modern meeting house. At the apex of the maihi (barge-boards) was a tekoteko (ancestral statue). Below it was a koruru, a head carved in naturalistic style and thought to represent Te Rangihaeata, who carved the house. The barge-boards were decorated only at the ends with the raparapa, the stylised representation of the fingers of the welcoming arms of the ancestor. The amo (pillars) bearing the maihi were fully carved. The window and door lintels were also carved. The poutokomanawa (central pillar bearing the ridgepole) was also carved in the human form of the tiki. The rafters were decorated with painted kowhaiwhai designs that drew their inspiration from the tendrils of the gourd and the pitau, the centre shoot of the tree fern.

The most exceptional house of this period was Te Hau-ki-Turanga, built by Raharuhi Rukupo. At a time of growing Pakeha influence in the land, Rukupo built the house in 1842 as both a cultural symbol and a political statement. The house represents the mana of the people of the district of Turanga (Poverty Bay). It is the prototype of the modern whare whakairo, the fully carved house decorated inside and out with ancestral carvings, tukutuku (decorative wall panels) and kowhaiwhai. This house, which is in the National Museum, is 55 feet long, 18 feet wide and 11 feet 7 inches high.[18] The kaupapa (conceptual design) of Rukupo's house functioned to conserve tribal history. To this end, 45 ancestors are carved on both the interior and exterior posts of the house and 15 on the rafters.

In Taranaki, tribal meetings were held to discuss growing Pakeha influence. Large houses on a scale not seen before in New Zealand were built for these assemblies. In 1853, the missionary Richard Taylor recorded a house measuring 90 feet long by 30 feet wide. It was named Taiporohenui, indicating that the tide of Pakeha settlement would be stopped.[19] This house, and Rukupo's Te-Hau-ki-Turanga, were symbolic political statements in relation to the invading culture of the Pakeha. They portended the clash of cultures in the Taranaki War, which broke out in 1860 and spread to the Waikato.

When the Waikato Land War ended in 1864, guerrilla resistance to Pakeha dominance was conducted from the interior of the Urewera against the settler government by the religious leader Te Kooti. In 1870 Te Kooti built a large house named Te Whai-a-te-motu (Pursuit of the Island) at Ruatahuna. It was used for meetings, church services and accommodation for his followers. The carvings of this house were not completed until 1888.[20]

In 1872, Te Kooti retired from the field of battle behind the aukati, the boundary line of the King Country. While there he built the carved house Te Tokanga-nui-a-noho at Te Kuiti. The kaupapa of the house stressed ancestral links between the East Coast and Tainui tribes. The inclusion of the canoe ancestors Hoturoa (Tainui), Tamatea (Takitimu), Tamatekapua (Te Arawa), Toroa (Mataatua) and Paikea of the Ngati Porou tribe, linked together Te Kooti's followers from different tribes.[21] This house was a political statement on the need for a pan-Maori identity to counter the dominance of the Pakeha. But Te Kooti's political views were not shared by Major Rapata Wahawaha, who fought on the Government's side against him and his Tuhoe allies to settle a tribal grudge.

Although Rapata Wahawaha was Te Kooti's relentless pursuer, essentially he shared the same cultural vision. He expressed that vision by building Porourangi, the ancestral house of Ngati Porou at Waiomatatini. The house, which was opened in 1888, consolidated all previous conceptual design elements concerning tribal identity and history. But it also had some innovative elements, such as the depiction of the human form in tukutuku panels. In 1907, Porourangi was moved by Apirana Ngata to higher ground away from the danger of floodwater. The refurbishing of the house marked the promotion by Ngata of the carved meeting house as the symbol of tribal mana and pride.

Ngata's interest in promoting the meeting house to strengthen Maori culture coincided with the Maori Councils Act 1900. The Act established village councils to attend to local affairs, such as sanitation, health, drainage and the provision of pure water supplies.[22] Ngata drafted the by-laws for the marae councils. These included the building of wooden floors in meeting houses, improved ventilation, and the prohibition of lighting fires in meeting houses unless chimneys were installed. There were to be proper arrangements for the disposal of refuse.[23] Marae reserves, which were gazetted by Order in Council, had to be enclosed by boundary fences capable of keeping out wandering stock. The Maori health officer, Dr Maui Pomare, and later Dr Peter Buck, worked with Ngata to promote the reforms under the new regulations.

The Cultural Renaissance

When Ngata became Minister of Maori Affairs he revived interest in the almost moribund art of carving by establishing the school of carving at Rotorua in 1928. In cooperation with the Waikato leader Te Puea, Ngata launched the cultural renaissance of the Maori at the opening of the meeting house Mahinarangi at Turangawaewae Marae the following year. Over 6,000 people from all tribes attended the opening.[24] The name Turangawaewae symbolised the footstool of the King Movement and a place to stand for all Maori. As a consequence of this hui, the spread of the cultural renaissance was assured as the different tribes returned home inspired to emulate what they had seen. Thereafter, tribes around the country began building carved houses or refurbishing old ones. Ngata's name is connected with a number of modern meeting houses, including the Treaty Memorial House at Waitangi, Tamatekapua at Rotorua, Wahiao at Whakarewarewa, Tukaki at Te Kaha and the carved memorial church at Tikitiki.

Essentially, a marae, with its ancestral house as the focal point, is the property of a kin group such as a hapu (sub-tribe), or an iwi (tribe). The meeting house is usually named after a founding ancestor of the tribe, who is depicted by the koruru, the carved face at the gable of the house. The house is conceptualised metaphorically as the ancestor and is accordingly referred to as the whare tipuna, the ancestral house. The maihi (barge-boards) represent the outstretched arms of the ancestor extending a welcome to guests. The tahuhu (ridgepole) is the backbone and the heke (rafters) the ribs. Thus, an assembly of the tribe in the house is said to be a meeting within the bosom of the ancestor. The porch is referred to as the roro (brain) of the ancestor. The kuwaha (mouth) is the doorway. It symbolises the transition from the outer world of light in the courtyard to the inner world of the spiritual realm inside the house. The carved poupou around the interior of the house represent the illustrious descendants of the founding ancestor, who uphold the mana of the tribe. Some carvings depict gods, such as Tane the procreator and legendary heroes such as Maui, as the forebears of the tribal ancestor. Thus the spiritual unity between gods, their descendants, human forebears and living people is reinforced.[25]

The decorative tukutuku reed panels between the carved posts are symbolic of human pursuits. The patiki (flounder) design represents weather forecasts, food, the bounty of the summer months and storage of the surplus. The poutama (stairway to heaven) design symbolises higher learning, advancement and success. The nihotaniwha (dragon's teeth) design represents the world of mythology, of fairies and make-believe. The kaokao (chevron) design represents arms, combat and readiness for war. Predictably, the roimata turuturu (flowing tears) pattern symbolises catastrophe and lamentation.[26]

The spatial arrangements and disposition of buildings on a marae are also symbolic and determined by the basic dichotomy in Maori life between the tapu (sacred) and noa (profane). The marae atea was the common domain of the tribe, and as such it was not tapu. All members of the tribe had turangawaewae or standing on the marae. It was the forum for open debate. But in practice, only the spokesmen for each whanau (extended family), usually the senior persons, exercised speaking rights. On ceremonial occasions only the senior kaumatua (elders) sat on the paepae (threshold of the house) to give the speeches of welcome on behalf of tangata whenua (people of the land) to manuhiri (guests). The paepae was tapu to men. Today, the paepae consists of a bench or sheltered seat off to one side of the meeting house. Some tribes, such as those of the Arawa confederation, do not permit women to speak on the marae. Although most tribes do not specifically prohibit women from speaking on the marae, the right to speak is rarely exercised by women. Only the most powerful and charismatic women have availed themselves of that right.

The meeting house, at the focal point of the marae from the entrance, is highly tapu in the sacred sense. Respect for the sanctity of the house is marked by the custom of removing shoes before entering, and by the prohibition of food inside. The house, with its carvings of gods, culture heroes and ancestors, is the analogue to a cathedral. It is the celestial realm, the domain of peace and harmony where the children of Tane (god of the forest) are said to be conjoined in Tane-piripiri.

Food is the antithesis of tapu, and consequently kauta (kitchens where food is prepared) are sited away from the meeting house. Similarly, there is a spatial separation between the dining-hall and the ancestral house. Toilet and ablution facilities are tapu in the unclean sense so they are spatially separated from the meeting house and the dining-hall as well.

As an institution, the marae is ideally suited for a community to arrive at decisions by consensus. Ancient aphorisms suggest that the democratic process was not served unless issues were discussed openly on the marae – 'kia whitikia e te ra, kia puhipuhia e te hau', to be shone on by the sun and blown about by the wind. The marae facilitates the process of decision-making by consensus. If matters under debate are not finished on the marae, then discussion continues in the house at night. The physical arrangement in the house, with bedding on the floor, is well suited to the prolonged discussions needed to reach consensus. Those who become tired simply fall asleep, to rejoin the debate later. Old people are particularly skilled at appearing to sleep while keeping their ears open in the long discussions that take place in the house. One aphorism asserts 'nga korero o runga o te marae, me whakatutuki ki roto i te whare', the discussions on the marae must be brought to a conclusion in the house. Thus, the meeting house, as the place where final decisions are made, complements the marae.

Marae Protocol

On formal occasions, the protocol of the marae is strictly determined by the dichotomy between tangata whenua (hosts) and manuhiri (visitors). When visitors who are strangers to a marae arrive, they are deemed to be waewae tapu (sacred feet), people who bring with them their own sanctity and ancestral spirits that might be inimical to the spirits and mauri (life force) of the tangata whenua. For this reason, visitors have to go through a highly formalised ritual welcome designed to decontaminate them of their alien tapu and negate any evil spiritual influences that might accompany them.

The ritual begins with the karanga, the melodic, high-pitched call of a woman signalling to the visitors to enter the marae. It is no accident that the first voice to be heard on the marae is that of a woman. She has the power of mana wahine to neutralise the tapu of the strangers. The manuhiri enter the marae with an answering call from one of their women, while a kaumatua chants a waerea, a protective incantation against local demons. The rest of the visitors enter in silence at a slow walk, silently paying homage to the dead. The visitors halt on the marae, keeping a discreet spatial separation between them and the tangata whenua, who are assembled in front of the meeting house. Both stand quietly for a short time paying homage to their mutual dead. The hosts then signal to the visitors to be seated.

The elders on the paepae open the mihi, the formal speeches of welcome. The orators follow a set pattern in their speeches. A speech begins with a tauparapara, a poetic chant of tribal composition with a spiritual or philosophic message. This is followed by a eulogy to the dead, which culminates in a reference to the separation between the living and the dead. The dead are exhorted to tread the broad path of Tane to the dwelling place of spirits. The living are then addressed directly and welcomed. Skilled orators recite their whakapapa (genealogy) in a manner that links them to the manuhiri, to make them feel welcome and at one with their hosts. The kaupapa, reason for the assembly, might be mentioned and the orator then concludes his speech with a waiata (song). The waiata removes the tapu from the elder's oration while standing on the marae and allows him to resume his place on the paepae. When the local elders finish their speeches they hand over the marae to the visitors to reply with their whaikorero. Whether or not a tribe adheres to the custom of paeke (one side speaking first) or tu atu tu mai (alternating speakers), it is usual for the number of speakers on each side to be matched.

When the speeches are finished, the space between hosts and guests is closed by the latter crossing the marae to whariru (shake hands) and hongi (press noses) with the tangata whenua. Guests and hosts are then able to mingle freely. Partaking of food in the dining hall completes the ritual decontamination of the tapu of the visitors. But if there is some residual evil influence that has not been exorcised by the rituals of welcome, it is negated when visitors enter the meeting house. On the inside lintel of the door is usually a carving of a female. Her genitals constitute the procreative power of mana wahine. Since mana wahine, in the person of Hinenuitepo, the goddess of death, killed Maui the demi-god, no demon can withstand that power.

Urban Marae

The carved houses built in the first stage of the cultural renaissance promoted by Ngata are symbols of tribal mana, and as such are located in tribal territory. After World War II, when 75 percent of the Maori population migrated to urban areas, the marae and meeting house as the most potent symbols of Maori identity and cultural pride were transplanted into towns and cities. This second stage of the renaissance is characterised by cultural adaptation and innovation.

In the first decade of the urban migration, the migrants were preoccupied with learning the necessary skills for survival in the urban milieu. This included taking regular employment, total commitment to the cash economy, and all that was entailed in meeting financial commitments to rent, rates, mortgage and time-payment. In the meantime, social and cultural needs were met by a number of ad-hoc strategies. Cultural clubs were formed for teaching action songs. Family bereavement clubs were formed for the purpose of assisting members to return the bodies of deceased kin to their home marae.[27] For friends and kin who were not able to accompany a body back to the marae for the tangi, the home of the deceased was turned into a mini-marae for them to pay their last respects before the body was taken home. The sitting-room cleared of furniture served as a meeting house for the lying in state. Temporary cooking facilities outdoors were set up to extend the traditional hospitality to mourners. Some families went so far as to erect garages on their lots to serve as dining-rooms for tangihanga (funerals).

In time, as the people put down roots in cities, they formed tribal and pan-tribal associations to build urban marae. The first traditional, kin-based marae to be opened in Auckland, in 1965 under the aegis of the Tainui tribes, was Te Puea in Mangere. This is a tangata whenua marae located in an urban centre encompassed by tribal boundaries. It consists of the full complex of marae, carved house, ablution block and dining-hall. The marae is built on seven acres of Maori land set aside from confiscation by the Government and held by a Waikato family. After the Surplus Lands Commission returned 4000 pounds to King Koroki, the King donated this money at the behest of the Maori community of Auckland to start the building fund for the project. The Maori committees of Onehunga, Mangere, and Ihumatao, together with the Waitemata Executive, spearheaded the fund-raising activities. As a consequence of tribal and pan-tribal cooperation, all tribes are entitled to use the marae. But it is tacitly understood that it is a Waikato marae. The three trustees are the Maori Queen and two members of the family that hold the land rights to the marae.

The other tangata whenua marae in Auckland is Orakei, belonging to the Ngati Whatua descendants of Tuperiri and Apihai Te Kawau. The marae had a chequered history arising out of the Government's designation of the marae as a facility for all the people of Auckland. In 1987 the Waitangi Tribunal recommended that the marae be returned to the control of Ngati Whatua. Two set-backs delayed the implementation of that recommendation. Early in 1990, the newly finished meeting house, Tumutumuwhenua, was consumed by fire. Then in November, the Labour government was swept out of office before enacting the Orakei Empowering Bill. In the meantime, the meeting house is being rebuilt, and life on the marae continues, with the Education Centre being used for administration and as a dining facility.

A variation on the traditional marae is the kin-based Mahurehure community centre at Point Chevalier in Auckland. The Mahurehure are a northern tribe with kinship links to Ngati Whatua, who are the tangata whenua of the Tamaki Isthmus. The centre consists of a general purpose hall and associated ablution block and cooking facilities. Although the usual marae activities such as tangi, receptions, fund-raising, church services and club functions are held there, the centre differs from what is normally understood to be a marae. The land on which the centre is located is not a marae reserve, nor is there a carved house and marae. Yet despite the absence of these traditional criteria, ideologically the centre is treated as a marae, a place for urban migrants to stand and fulfil their cultural needs.

The Tuhoe Benevolent Society is similar to Mahurehure, except that it consists

24

of members of a tribe from the Bay of Plenty with only a tenuous connection to Tamaki. As migrants into the district, the society sought permission from Ngati Whatua to establish a marae in their domain. In 1973, the Tuhoe people refurbished an old building in Panmure and converted it into a full marae complex named Tira Hou.

In Auckland's western districts of Te Atatu and Henderson, the large Maori community there formed a non-tribal committee to build a marae. The opening of the John Waititi Memorial Marae in 1980 represents an important departure from tradition, in the sense that it is not kin-based. Instead, the cohesion of its tangata whenua is derived from a growing pan-Maori sense of identity. This marae is marked by the dynamism of its leaders who, since its opening, established the first kohanga reo (language nest) in Auckland in 1982. Three years later the trustees opened the first kura kaupapa Maori (primary school based on the Maori language) in New Zealand.

Another alternative to the traditional marae is Te Unga Waka Community Centre in Manukau Road, built by the Auckland Maori Catholic Society in 1965. Although Te Unga Waka fulfills all the usual functions of a marae, it does not have an open space of ground for the marae atea. The facility consists of a general purpose hall, dining room, cooking facilities and ablution block. Te Unga Waka serves as an alternative model to the traditional kin-based marae. In this case, religious affiliation transcending tribal boundaries replaces kinship as the unifying principle for the tangata whenua of the centre.

The most recent marae innovation, which took on in the last decade or so, was the establishment of marae on the campuses of secondary schools and tertiary institutions. These facilities range from made-over prefabricated classrooms decorated with carvings to serve as meeting houses, to purpose-built, fully decorated houses with their own courtyard and associated dining and cooking facilities. Two of the finest examples of this type of marae are Te Herenga Waka at Victoria University in Wellington and Waipapa at Auckland University. These facilities are run by staff in Maori Studies Departments of the various institutions as adjuncts to their work in teaching language and culture to their students. The transplantation of meeting houses on to the campuses of schools and universities is a symbolic statement of the ethos of Maori society. They fulfil deeply felt needs for the maintenance of culture, assertion of identity, and resistance to assimilation.

Conclusion

The marae is an institution deeply rooted in the foundations of Maori culture. Its origins can be traced back in time to the first millenium via the Society Islands to Samoa and Tonga. While the marae is clearly a stable institution, it is not immutable. In New Zealand, the marae evolved over time in response to changing human needs. The paved courtyard of Eastern Polynesia was not replicated in

New Zealand. Instead, the marae reverted to the open space or courtyard in front of the chief's house, as in Samoa. The ahu also disappeared and in its stead religious rituals were conducted away from the marae at tuahu, simple stone shrines which had no resemblance to their Tahitian counterparts.

The wharepuni, originally a simple dwelling for sleeping in at night, or as shelter in the day from inclement weather, appeared in the second millenium. The largest wharepuni in pre-European times belonged to the chief, whose status was marked by decorative ancestral carvings on the house. Although large wharepuni were built in traditional times to accommodate visitors, they were not necessarily permanent features of every village.

With the coming of the Pakeha, the carved houses of chiefs increased in size from 20 to 40 feet and were more elaborately decorated. These houses, with Rukupo's house Te Hau-ki-Turanga setting the benchmark, were the precursors of the modern meeting house. During the Land Wars of the 1860s, meeting houses became symbols of pan-tribal resistance to Pakeha dominance. After the turn of the century, they became the focus of the cultural renaissance in the rural tribal hinterland. That renaissance was carried into towns and cities with the urban migration in the last three decades. The development of urban marae is marked by dynamic changes in their organisational base. Traditional, kin-based marae have been supplemented by church-based marae, secular, pan-tribal marae, and teaching-based, campus marae at secondary and tertiary institutions.

Urban marae, while fulfilling deeply felt spiritual and cultural needs of the Maori, are also potent symbolic statements of identity. The marae is an institution where any Maori has turangawaewae, standing, in relation to the dominant culture of the Pakeha. It proclaims New Zealand as a bicultural nation.

FOOTNOTES

1. S.P. Smith, *Journal of the Polynesian Society*, Vol. 7, p. 145.
2. Te Rangihiroa, op. cit., Vol. 44, p. 50.
3. S.P. Smith, op, cit., Vol. 7, p. 146.
4. Teuira Henry, op. cit., Vol. 21, p. 78.
5. Roger and Kaye Green, *New Zealand Journal of History*, Vol. 2, No. 1, p. 68.
6. Green, op. cit., p. 71.
7. Green, op. cit., pp. 72-74.
8. Teuira Henry 1912: 119.
9. S.P. Smith, *Journal of the Polynesian Society*, Vol. 7, p. 144.
10. R. Firth, 1959: 96.
11. Sir George Grey, 1956: 97.
12. L.M. Groube, 1964: 84.
13. A. Murray-Oliver, 1968: 47-48.
14. N.J. Prickett, 1979: 43.
15. J. Davidson, 1984: 155.
16. L.M. Groube, 1964: 85-86.

17. A. Salmond, 1975: 80.
18. T. Barrow, 1976: 33-35.
19. K. Sinclair, 1969: 85.
20. A. Taylor, 1988: 38.
21. E. Craig, 1972: 17-35.
22. R.J. Walker, 1990: 171.
23. R.J. Walker, 1990: 174.
24. M. King, 1977: 142.
25. P. Harrison, 1988: 1.
26. P. Taiapa, unpublished manuscript.
27. J. Metge, 1964: 65.

REFERENCES

T. Barrow, *A Guide to the Maori Meeting House Te Hau Ki Turanga*, National Museum, Wellington, 1976.
P.H. Buck, 'Material Representatives of Tongan and Samoan Gods', *Journal of the Polynesian Society*, Wellington, 1935.
E. Craig, *Sown in Blood Reaped in Harmony*, Te Kuiti Centennial Booklet, 1972.
J. Davidson, *The Prehistory of New Zealand*, Longman Paul, Auckland, 1984.
R. Firth, *Economics of the New Zealand Maori*, R.E. Owen, Government Printer, Wellington, 1959.
Roger and Kaye Green, 'Religious Structures (Marae) of the Windward Society Islands', in *The New Zealand Journal of History*, Vol. 2, No. 1, University of Auckland, 1968.
Sir G. Grey, *Polynesian Mythology*, Whitcombe & Tombs, Christchurch, 1956.
L.M. Groube, 'Settlement Patterns in Prehistoric New Zealand', unpublished M.A. thesis, University of Auckland, 1964.
P. Harrison, *Tane-nui-a-Rangi*, University of Auckland, 1988.
T. Henry, 'The Tahitian Versions of the Names Ra'iatea and Taputapuatea', *Journal of the Polynesian Society*, Vol. 21, Wellington, 1912.
Author unknown, *Ancient Tahiti*, Bishop Museum, Bulletin 48, Honolulu, 1985.
M. King, *Te Puea*, Hodder & Stoughton, Auckland, 1977.
J. Metge, *A New Maori Migration*, The Athlone Press, London, 1964.
A. Murray-Oliver, *Augustus Earle in New Zealand*, Whitcombe & Tombs, Christchurch, 1968.
N. Prickett, 'Prehistoric Occupation in the Moikau Valley', in B.F. & H.M. Leach (editors), *Prehistoric Man in Palliser Bay*, National Museum of New Zealand, Bulletin 21, Wellington, 1979.
A. Salmond, *Hui*, A.H. & A.W. Reed, Wellington, 1975.
K. Sinclair, 'He Tikanga Pakeke', in *The Feel of Truth*, edited by P. Munz, A.H. & A.W. Reed, Wellington, 1969.
S.P. Smith, 'Hawaiki the Whence of the Maori', *Journal of the Polynesian Society*, Vol. 7, Wellington, 1898.
A. Taylor, *Maori Folk Art*, Century Hutchinson, Auckland, 1988.
R.J. Walker, *Ka Whawhai Tonu Matou (Struggle Without End)*, Penguin Books, Auckland, 1990.

LANGUAGE AND PROTOCOL
OF THE MARAE

TIMOTI KARETU

BEFORE THE COMING OF THE PAKEHA to New Zealand with his superior technology, all literature in Maori was oral. Its transmission to succeeding generations was also oral and a great body of literature, which includes haka, waiata, tauparapara, karanga, poroporoaki, paki waitara, whakapapa, whakatauki and pepeha, was retained and learnt by each new generation. It is frequently claimed by those who do not know, that there is no literature in Maori and therefore the language is not worthy of study. Any person who had delved into things Maori however will appreciate just how absurd this attitude is when faced with the wealth of material that survives in the language from before the time of the written word.

Today, more material is being added to a large body of literature formerly retained in people's minds. In a number of instances it has been committed to paper for posterity. The School Publications branch of the Department of Education has produced a number of bulletins in the Maori language for use in schools. Many have been written by speakers of the language who made no recognition of the fact that people learning the language in schools were predominantly non-native speakers.

They wrote in a style and idiom suitable only for people with a very good command of the tongue. This series is called *Te Whare Kura*. In addition, there is a series of elementary readers in the language called *Te Tautoko*, intended as an adjunct to *Te Whare Kura*.

Magazines such as *Te Ao Hou,* published by the Department of Maori Affairs, provided further avenues for the written word, even though many of the articles were not in the vernacular. Such was the case, too, with *Te Maori*, a magazine published by the Maori Council. In 1973 a paper called *Rongo* appeared, published by Te Huinga Rangatahi o Aotearoa (formerly the Federation of Maori Students). It featured articles, not only in Maori, but also in the languages of other Pacific Islands such as Niue, Samoa, Tonga and Tokelau. Unfortunately, many of these magazines appeared only sporadically.

For a long time the only sources of written Maori to which students had easy access were *Nga Moteatea* in three volumes, *Nga Mahi a Nga Tupuna*, and the Holy Bible. *Nga Moteatea* is a collection of traditional songs compiled, edited and translated by the late Sir Apirana Ngata and Dr Pei Te Hurinui Jones. It was left to Dr Jones to complete the task because Sir Apirana died well before seeing the publication of Volumes 2 and 3. In 1990 Volume 4 of *Nga Moteatea*, edited by Dr Tamati Reedy, was published. It should be noted, however, that all the material in the four volumes are examples of oral literature which have been collected in book form to ensure that generations to come will have access to them.

Nga Mahi a Nga Tupuna is a collection of paki waitara, or legends, which were related orally to Sir George Grey, who arranged for their publication. A vague translation was made and published under the title of *Polynesian Mythology*.

With the paucity of written material that students could study, the Bible became very popular with examiners. The sections particularly favoured were the Beatitudes, the Song of Solomon and the Book of Job. The Bible is translated in a number of dialects and while the Maori in a number of instances was forced to fit the biblical context, it was and remains a good source for those wishing to improve their knowledge of the language, even if it is a little archaic. While it may not be part of oral Maori literature, as a guide to the use of the language it is quite valuable.

The wide field of oral literature is just beginning to be tapped by students of Maori and by families who have in their possession valuable manuscripts including whakapapa (genealogies) and often a great deal of valuable tribal history. These types of manuscripts have formed the basis for a number of publications on aspects of Maoritanga at present flooding the market.

But a far more substantial body of material is heard on the marae. It has not yet found its way into books and yet it is most worthy of the attention of people interested in probing the depths of Maoritanga and its underlying philosophies.

If we use the kawa o te marae (formal marae procedure) as our starting point, we shall see just how important oral literature is and how it is used. Let us assume we have been invited to a marae to attend a function as guests of that marae.

One must wait for the formal call of welcome or karanga of the host women before one may approach or enter the marae proper. It is in the karanga that one will hear much of the beauty of the language, and experience some of the most moving moments of Maori experience. It is the voice of the caller herself and what she says that arouses the emotions. Her first call will be something like this:

> Haere mai ra, e te manuhiri tuarangi e,
> Haere mai, haere mai.

> Welcome visitors from afar,
> Welcome, welcome.

This is a very formal call normally extended to people who are not from that marae. If however the visitors are from the host tribe, but from a different locality, then the karanga would be like this:

Haere mai ra, e te whanau e,
Haere mai, haere mai ra.

Welcome members of the family,
Welcome, welcome.

If the visitors are coming to a tangi, then the karanga would be different again. Let us assume the deceased is male. The karanga would be as follows:

Hoki wairua mai, e koro e,
Irunga i o hapu,
Haere mai, haere mai.

Return in spirit, sir,
With your sub-tribes,
Welcome, welcome.

The spirit of the deceased is asked to return to its people along with the visitors coming on to the marae to pay their respects.

These calls are not learnt from books but from listening to the women who know what to do. In this way they are transmitted orally to the next generation of women when it is their turn to assume the role.

The women of the party coming on to the marae then call in response to the karanga they have received. The first call of the visiting women should always be the call of farewell or poroporoaki to the dead, whether there is a corpse on the marae or not. It is customary to pay one's respects to the dead of the marae who have fallen since one was last there. If one has never been on that marae before, the first call of the visiting women should be an acknowledgement of the dead of that particular marae as well as of the dead that one brings with one 'on one's shoulders'. The first poroporoaki would be like this:

Haere atu ra nga mate o nga ra, o nga marama, o nga tau,
Haere atu ra, haere atu ra.

Farewell, to you, the dead of recent days, months and years,
Farewell, farewell.

If the visitors are coming to a tangi, then the first call would be a call of farewell to the deceased. If the corpse were a female, the call would be as:

Haere atu ra, e whae e,
Haere atu ra, haere atu ra.

Farewell to you, o mother,
Farewell, farewell.

The next call could be:

Takahia atu ra te ara whanui a Tane,
Ki te po uriuri, ki te po kerekere, e whae e,
Haere atu ra, haere atu ra.

Tread the broad pathway of Tane,
To the world of interminable darkness, of impenetrable dark-
ness.
Farewell, farewell.

The calls of the visitors should also acknowledge the calls of the host women
and a call to the living would follow:

Tena koutou nga kanohi ora,
O te hunga kua whetu rangitia i te ra nei e,
Tena koutou, tena koutou.

Greetings to you the living descendants
Of them who are as stars in the heavens,
Greetings, greetings.

It is customary also for the visitors to announce the reason for their visit in
their calls:

Tenei ra te whakaeke nei i runga i te aroha
Ki nga taonga a nga tipuna kua riro ki te po,
Karanga mai, karanga mai.

Here we are coming on to the marae
because of our great affection
For the customs and traditions of our departed ancestors,
Welcome us, welcome us.

The calls of both sides contain a wealth of meaning and knowledge. The
karanga and poroporoaki can be considered valid components of oral literature.

After the hosts and the visitors have finished their calling, a respectful silence
is observed in memory of the dead of both sides before the men take over and
the speechmaking or whaikorero begins. It is in the whaikorero that the tauparapara, waiata, whakatauki and haka come into their own. The basic format for a
whaikorero is:

Tauparapara
Mihi ki nga aitua, ki te hunga ora
Kaupapa
Waiata
Haka or pokeka.

The tauparapara is a formal introduction to a speech and can be performed as a haka, chanted or recited. Each tribe has its own tauparapara but many have become common property with the migration of people of all tribes to all parts of the country. A tauparapara can be used as an introduction of oneself to one's audience, should one not be known. A manawa wera of Tuhoe, for instance, ends with the line:

Ko te uri o 'Tuhoe moumou tangata ki te Po'.

I am a descendant of 'Tuhoe extravagant with human life'.

The audience is immediately informed that the speaker is of the Tuhoe tribe because of the extract from the pepeha which is,

Tuhoe moumou kai, moumou taonga, moumou tangata ki te Po

Tuhoe extravagant with food, with precious heirlooms, and with human life.

Most tauparapara begin with the words 'tihe mauri ora' which means, literally, the 'sneeze of life'. It serves the purpose of announcing 'Here I am. Listen to me. I am about to speak.' Since one is just beginning the whaikorero, it is appropriate to begin with these words. Some speakers also end their tauparapara with the words 'tihe mauri ora'.

In some tauparapara tribal areas are referred to, or well-known landmarks. In another Tuhoe tauparapara a number of tribes are referred to in these terms:

Ka mawhiti ra taku haere ki nga tihi tapu
Ki Maungapohatu, ki a Taiturakina
Kia titiro iho au ki Ruatahuna, ki Manawaru,
E ko Te Aitanga a Tuhoe-potiki
Noho ana au i te nohonga o te tipua
Tu ana au i Huiarau, ka tahuri ake au
Ki Nukutaurua, e ko Kahungunu
Ka tiawhe ra taku haere ki te pu o te tonga
Ki Kahuranaki, ki a Te Whatuiapiti.

I now leap on to the sacred mountain tops
To Maungapohatu where dwells Taiturakina

And look down at Ruatahuna and Manawaru
Where dwell the tribe of Tuhoe-potiki
And so I remain in the dwelling place of the god-like.
I stand on the summit of Huiarau and look towards
Nukutaurua, where dwells the tribe of Kahungunu.
I now move southwards to the giant of the south
To Kahuranaki, where dwells the tribe of Te Whatuiapiti.

This tauparapara goes on to name other tribes and their famous landmarks and
ends by returning to the territory of the tribe:

Ka hoki au ki te mauri o taku waka, o Mataatua.
Ki Putauaki, ko Ngati Awa,
Ki Tawhiuau ko Tangiharuru,
Ki te rae ra o Kohi ko Awatope,
Ko Te Manuka-tu-tahi ki Whakatane, ki a Apanui.
Ko te mauri i heria mai nei hei whakaoho i taku moe,
E ko, ko ia e ara e!

And so I return to the life-giving essence of my ancestral
canoe, Mataatua.
At Putauaki dwell the tribe of Ngati Awa,
At Tawhiuau dwells Tangiharuru,
At Kohi is Awatope,
At Whakatane are Manuka-tu-tahi and Apanui.
Thus the life-giving essence brought to arouse me from
my sleep,
And so I rise.

At this point the speaker stands up.

It is courteous to the host tribe for the visiting people to mention them in the
tauparapara or by using pepeha and whakatauki relevant to that tribe. The essential difference between pepeha and whakatauki is that a pepeha is a tribal saying
(that is, a saying about a tribe) and a whakatauki is a proverb or pithy saying. Both
are used liberally in whaikorero and are worthy of study in themselves because
they contain philosophies and wisdom of people long gone that still find application in the contemporary setting. But before discussing these, let us return to the
whaikorero.

Having completed his tauparapara, the speaker goes on to pay his respects in
words to the dead of the marae, having first acknowledged the meeting house and
the marae in these terms:

Te tipuna marae e takoto nei, tena koe,
Te tipuna whare e tu nei, tena koe.

The ancestral marae lying here, I greet you,
The ancestral house standing before me, I greet you.

It is in the acknowledgements to the dead and in laments composed for the dead that some of the most beautiful examples of the language are found:

Haere e hoki i runga i o koutou waka,
Ki Hawaiki-nui, ki Hawaiki-roa, ki Hawaiki-pamamao,
Ki Te Hono-i-wairua.

Go, return on your canoes,
To Great Hawaiki, to Long Hawaiki, to Hawaiki of the Great
Distance,
To the Gathering Place of the Spirits.

This would be the type of poroporoaki the speaker would make in his whaikorero. It could also be something like this:

Haere ki te kainga i tauiratia mai mo taua, mo te tangata,
Haere ki Paerau, ki te huinga o te kahurangi
Ka oti atu ai e.

Go to the home predestined for you and me, for mankind,
Go to Paerau, to the assembly of the illustrious
And there remain for all time.

The speaker then moves on to pay his respects to his hosts:

E aku rangatira e whakanui nei i a au,
Tena koutou, tena koutou, tena koutou.

You, my superiors, here bidding me welcome,
I salute you. Greetings.

And from here, he moves on to the kaupapa or basic theme of his whaikorero. This will depend on the occasion or the reason for his being on that particular marae.

At the conclusion of the whaikorero (or during it if the speaker wishes) comes the waiata. Waiata is the generic term for all traditional songs. It can be divided into four main categories:

Waiata tangi
Waiata aroha

Oriori

Patere.

The greater number of waiata fall into the waiata tangi category, songs of lament. In this genre also fall such songs as maimai, moteatea and apakura, although the latter word has a special meaning to Tuhoe. Apakura (or tangi whakahuahua) is used to refer to the heart-rending weeping of women who speak as they weep. It is because of this that the term has come to mean lament. The type of waiata depends on the occasion. In a lament by Harehare of Ngati Manawa, the opening lines are:

Kaore te mokemoke te tuohu noa nei e,
I te po roa e, i te po makariri e.
Tu mai, e tama, kia poipoia koe.

Loneliness will not leave me,
Not these long, not these cold nights.
Arise, my son, that I might once more caress you.

In a song which could well qualify as a waiata tangi, Mihi-ki-te-kapua of Tuhoe soliloquises on her fate when she is left alone on the shores of Lake Waikaremoana after all her family have grown up and left her. In her song she notes that even the mutton bird has a partner, whereas she is similar to the egg of a kiwi which has been laid at the base of the tawai tree. In the second stanza she goes on to say:

Noku koia te wareware te whai au i te tira haere
No Te Hirau whakangaro ana
Nga hiwi maunga ki Huiarau.
Kia ringihia ki te roimata
Ko te rere au ki Ngauemutu.

It was I who forgot to travel with the party
Of Te Hirau, which disappeared
Over the mountain ranges of Huiarau.
And so I spill my tears,
Just as the waters pour forth from the falls at Ngauemutu.

There is a poignancy about these words which makes the waiata a very appropriate one for singing on occasions of sadness. Other waiata may be songs like the following:

Whakarongo,
Whakarongo ra te taringa ki te hoko o te whenua e hau mai nei kei

Rotorua, hurihia,
Hurihia ra to kanohi ki Te Whaiti, ki Ruatahuna, ki
Maungapohatu, tikina,
Tikina ra moni a te Kawana kei te Peke o Niu Tireni,
he koronga,
He koronga no roto kia nohia nga whare tiketike o te rangatira.

Listen,
Listen to the sound of the land sales taking place at Rotorua
Turn your face to Te Whaiti, to Ruatahuna, to Maungapohatu,
Then fetch the money from the Bank of New Zealand
For I have a strong desire to reside in the storied buildings of
the wealthy.

This song would qualify for inclusion in the tangi section for it is one of lament by Tuhoe for the loss of their land. It is one of the more recent compositions with a traditional tune.

The use of transliterations in many of the best known waiata indicates that their composition dates from Pakeha contact. In the well-known lament of the Waikato tribes, a lament for a chief called Te Wano and composed for him by his cousin Rangiamoa, this is the opening line:

E pa to hau he wini raro

The composer has used the word 'wini' for 'wind' rather than the word 'hau', the original Maori word. This is also the case in the well-known love-song of Rihi Puhiwahine of Ngati Tuwharetoa for her cousin lover, Te Toko of Ngati Maniapoto. She too used a transliteration in preference to a genuine word.

Ko taku tau whanaunga no Toa i te tonga
No Mania i te uru, ka pea taua.

My loved relative is from Toa in the south,
Mania in the west, and so we are a pair.

She uses the word 'pea', a transliteration of the word 'pair', and later in the same song says:

Na Rangi mai ano nana i marena.

It was Rangi who married them.

Again she uses a transliteration – the word 'marena', a form of the word 'marry'. This is valid as 'poetic licence' as the composer probably felt the transliteration would scan better.

These, then, are some of the songs sung at the conclusion of the whaikorero. In these songs are found classical references to battles, to mythology, to the constellations of the heavens, and to events of interest to individual tribes.

In the Tuhoe lament for Te Maitaranui, killed by Tuakiaki at Te Reinga in the area occupied by the tribe of Ngati Kahungunu, is this reference:

I riro mai ai a Te Heketua, i mate ai Nuhaka.
Tona whakautu pahi ko Te Rama-apakura.
Haere ki roto o Te Mahia,
Mo Kahawai, mo Kauae-hurihia.

And so Te Heketua was obtained and Nuhaka overrun.
In exchange Te Rama-apakura was also received.
Then go on to Mahia,
And there obtain Kahawai and Kauae-hurihia.

All the names mentioned in this extract are greenstone patu given to Tuhoe by the chief Te Rakatau of Ngati Kahungunu as a peace offering. Unfortunately, the peace was not achieved.

It is for these reasons that waiata of all categories are worthy of study. They contain a wealth of historical and cultural information. Included in many of these waiata are pepeha and whakatauki quoted by the speaker at a time he considers appropriate to imply a great deal in a few words. For instance, if one were in the tribal territory of Ngati Tuwharetoa, one would include somewhere in one's whaikorero this pepeha:

Ko Tongariro te maunga,
Ko Taupo te moana,
Ko Tuwharetoa te iwi,
Ko Te Heuheu te tangata.

Tongariro is the mountain,
Taupo is the sea,
Tuwharetoa is the tribe,
Te Heuheu is the chief.

Another example of the pepeha is:

Arawa mangai nui.

Big mouthed Arawa.

Throughout Maoridom, the Arawa people of the Rotorua-Bay of Plenty area were regarded as eloquent and dynamic speakers on the marae. Even today the people of this tribe are regarded as the best exponents of the waiata.
Here is another pepeha:

> Waikato taniwha rau, he piko he taniwha, he piko he taniwha.
>
> Waikato of a hundred monsters, at each bend of the river a monster.

This pepeha is used here to refer to the great numbers of chiefs who formerly occupied the Waikato River.

Whakatauki are often quoted to sum up a situation or make a succinct point:

> He kokonga whare e kitea, he kokonga ngakau e kore e kitea.
>
> The corners of a house can be seen but the corners of the heart cannot.

This proverb is quoted to express gratitude. Here is another:

> Ahakoa iti, he pounamu.
>
> Although it is small, it is of greenstone.

Greenstone was very valuable to the Maori and hence the proverb indicates that things should not be reckoned by their size, but rather by the attitude which prompted their being given.

Whakatauki contain some of the most beautiful sayings in the language, such as:

> Hokia ki nga maunga kia purea koe e nga hau a Tawhiri-matea.
>
> Return to the mountains and there be cleansed by the winds of Tawhiri-matea.

This whakatauki says that one should return to one's own tribal area and there learn about oneself prior to going out into the world. Its basic philosophy is 'know then thyself'. The whakatauki cover the roles of men and women in society, the role of the chief, hospitality, gratitude, and in more recent times, the question of identity:

> Kia u, kia mau ki to Maoritanga.
>
> Cleave to and retain the very essence of being Maori.

Much of what our tipuna (ancestors) considered to be important is found in a study of both whakatauki and pepeha.

To return to the whaikorero. Once the speaker has concluded and sung his waiata, he should then perform a haka. The types of haka normally performed at this point are short but stirring, as in the following from Tuhoe:

Ki mai nei koe, e te iwi, kei a koe tonu te pito o te aroha.

You, the people, say that you are in full possession of affection.

For 'e te iwi', the speaker may substitute the name of a person or the name of a tribe, whichever is the more appropriate at the time. Haka, like waiata, contain a wealth of information worthy of study and appreciation.

Let us assume the speakers have concluded and the hosts and visitors have shaken hands and are now in the meeting house or dining room, where a great deal of socialising takes place. It is on these occasions one will hear the waiata-a-ringa or action song, an activity very much underestimated and unappreciated by those who do not know the language. In the waiata-a-ringa can be found some of the great beauty and versatility of the language, even though the form is a modern one.

It is probably because the waiata-a-ringa borrowed Pakeha tunes current at the time of their composition that they have been dismissed out of hand by those who have not considered the lyrics on their own as valid pieces of literature. It should be noted that with the exception of a very few songs, the Maori lyric is not a translation of the original. The tune has merely been employed to convey the composer's ideas to his audience. It would be well to look at a number of waiata-a-ringa and consider the lyric separately from the tune.

Perhaps the best known and best loved of all waiata-a-ringa is a composition by the late Tuini Ngawai of Ngati Porou entitled *Arohaina Mai.*

Arohaina mai, e te Kingi Nui,
Manaakitia ra o tamariki e,
Horahia mai ra te marie nui
Ki Te Hokowhitu-a-Tu Toa.

Have mercy, Great King,
Take care of thy children,
And let your great calm
Be spread over The Maori Battalion.

This was one of her many songs composed to farewell the Ngati Porou contingent of the Maori Battalion prior to their departure overseas in World War II. She was a prolific composer and her songs cover many themes:

Te matauranga o te Pakeha
He mea whakato hei tinanatanga mo wai ra?
Mo Hatana!
The education of the Pakeha
Was conceived and made manifest for whom?
For Satan!

The song concludes by saying that 'the education of the Pakeha' deadens Maori thought and kills Maori custom.

Many people would consider World War II to be the 'golden age' of the action song. But many waiata-a-ringa have been composed since the war. Competitions have helped to retain interest in the waiata-a-ringa as a living art form and to get the composer to try to compose his own tune rather than borrow one. The Tuhoe people have their own tribal competitions annually where members compete in waiata and haka which are Tuhoe in origin. This competition has also seen the composition of a number of waiata-a-ringa such as the following:

Nau mai ra e nga uri e,
I Turi-o-kahu, i Kuha-tarewa e
Ara te wai kauakau o nga tipuna
Te nohonga o Haumapuhia.

Welcome to you the descendants
From Turi-o-kahu, from Kuha-tarewa,
That is, from the lake where our ancestors once bathed,
The dwelling place of Haumapuhia.

These four lines convey a lot of interesting information. Turi-o-kahu is a little hill located at Kuha Pa, near Lake Waikaremoana, and is a symbol of the 'tatau pounamu' or ever-lasting peace between Ngati Kahungunu and Tuhoe. The lake referred to is Lake Waikaremoana and Haumapuhia is the taniwha who is credited with its formation. The song is one of many compositions of John Rangihau.

The following are lines from a waiata-a-ringa composed and dedicated to the people of Waikato. It was performed in 1974 at the annual conference of the Maori Women's Welfare League held in Hamilton:

E koro Tawhiao,
Hoki wairua mai ki runga i o marae e
Ki o koutou maunga karangaranga,
Ki Pirongia, ki Kakepuku, ki Karioi e,
Ki te maunga tapu, ki Taupiri e,
Ki te taumata okiokinga o te kahurangi.

O Tawhiao,
Return in spirit to your marae
And to your echoing mountains,
To Pirongia, to Kakepuku and to Karioi,
Return also to the sacred mountain, Taupiri,
On whose summit rest the illustrious.

The waiata-a-ringa has certainly enjoyed great popularity. It is sad that so many people who watch it performed cannot appreciate the beauty of the lyrics for themselves rather than just responding to a tune or, as often happens, dismissing the waiata-a-ringa merely because the tune is recognised. The waiata-a-ringa, like any other art form, does have its rubbish. But there are a great many songs which are worthy of study.

Those who oppose the introduction of Maori into school curricula, on the grounds that there is no literature, have not a leg to stand on. The language is rich in oral literature and the fact that is mainly oral does not make it less than literature. Because much of the beauty of the language is lost in translation, people should try to appreciate the work in the original form. The late Bruce Palmer, who edited the revised edition of *Nga Moteatea* Part I, said in the introduction to that volume:

> The difficulty of translating from one language to another is a truism that needs no stress. But one point should be remembered by all who read this volume. No matter how brilliant the translation, how apt the phrase or vivid the image, the English version is no substitute for the original Maori.

While it is not easy for everyone to understand the works in Maori, it is surely a desirable goal. The Maori language has much to offer the student, Maori or Pakeha, who cares to delve deeply and to discover for himself its beauty and the thought contained in the karanga, the poroporoaki, the tauparapara, the whaikorero, the waiata, the pepeha, the whakatauki, the haka and the waiata-a-ringa.

Whaia e koe te iti kahurangi;
Ki te tuohu koe me maunga teitei.

Pursue that which you cherish most dearly;
Should you have to give in,
Let it be only because of some insurmountable object.

LEADERSHIP: INHERITED AND ACHIEVED

API MAHUIKA

EARLY WRITERS ON THE MAORI devoted much time to discussions on leadership. Buck sums up the general consensus of these writers: 'Leadership at home and in foreign affairs was exercised by males, and primogeniture in the male line was the deciding factor in succession to chiefly rank.'[1]

As a criterion for leadership, Buck and others see primogeniture relating to the first-born male in any generation, and one's seniority being dependent upon the longest line one can trace through first-born males. Indeed, one writer[2] has said that when there were no males in a particular generation in a chiefly line, the first-born female was used as a 'male-substitute' in that particular genealogy. By definition, then, the hierarchical structure of leadership would always have a male at the apex.

If we examine the popularly defined elements of leadership in Maori society, the following points emerge:

· Leadership is the prerogative of males only;

· Leadership is determined by primogeniture which is based on male issue;

· If a female was the first-born she would relegate rights to leadership to her male relatives. She retained, however, deference due to her rank as a female ariki (first-born of a most senior family);

· Chieftainship and leadership in most cases went together.

These points have been reiterated *ad nauseum* in one way or another over the years and it is not my intention to present new arguments to support old themes. Rather, in the belief that tribal variations lie at the root of Maoritanga and give it its strength, I would like to suggest these points be used as the framework for further examination of the questions of chieftainship and leadership on a tribal basis. My approach has further been conditioned by the fact that using this framework to examine traditional leadership in my own tribe, Ngati Porou, I found significant differences in emphasis in the application of commonly accepted views. It may be that these cases are not exceptional to Ngati Porou. But the whole purpose of the approach is to provide a catalyst for others to cite their tribal experience.

Leadership and chieftainship will be looked at in the following contexts:

- Primogeniture and the Maori terminology associated with this;
- Achieved leadership;
- Mana and tapu;
- Marriage;
- Waiata, haka and whakatauki. The common factor linking these is the tribal whakapapa and its related traditions and history.

Primogeniture

The aristocracy in Maori society was the rangatira. The most senior member of this aristocracy, i.e. the first-born of the most senior family in society, was called the ariki. The most senior family was that which could trace its descent from the founding ancestor of the tribe or sub-tribe through as many first-born antecedents as possible in the chiefly genealogies.

The terms 'tuakana' and 'taina' were used to denote one's genealogical relationship to other members of the society. 'Tuakana' means the elder brother or male cousin of a male, or the elder sister or female cousin of a female. 'Taina' means the younger brother or male cousin of a male, or the younger sister or female cousin of a female.[3]

The following genealogical table of parents and offspring shows examples of tuakana and taina:[4]

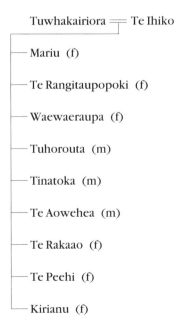

Tuwhakairiora == Te Ihiko

- Mariu (f)
- Te Rangitaupopoki (f)
- Waewaeraupa (f)
- Tuhorouta (m)
- Tinatoka (m)
- Te Aowehea (m)
- Te Rakaao (f)
- Te Peehi (f)
- Kirianu (f)

Mariu is tuakana to all her sisters, but the term is not applied to describe her relationship to her three brothers, Tuhorouta, Tinatoka and Te Aowehea. The only term one can use in this context is 'tuahine' which simply means 'sister', and which applies to all the sisters regardless of order of birth. Similarly, all the other female issue are taina to Mariu, whereas the male issue are simply 'tungane' or 'brothers'. Tuhorouta is tuakana to Tinatoka and Te Aowehea, Tinatoka is tuakana to Te Aowehea, and both Tinatoka and Te Aowehea are taina to Tuhorouta. Te Aowehea is taina to Tinatoka. But, once again, the only terms available to define their relationship to their sisters are tuahine and tungane.

Because the first-born child, Mariu, is female, 'the functioning position of ariki passed to the first-born male child'[5] in this case Tuhorouta. Further, according to the commonly accepted view, Tuhorouta would be used in preference to Mariu in establishing the eminence of a pedigree. Mariu is entitled to the term ariki, but Tuhorouta is referred to as the matamua (first-born male).[6]

Achieved Leadership

As stated, chieftainship is a birthright and the measure of chieftainship is the sum of a whakapapa. Leadership is the political functioning of chieftainship. Buck says, 'The first-born son inherited the power to rule . . . but his mana remained dormant within him . . . until it was given active expression on his father's death.'[7] The obvious corollary was that the power to rule remained forever dormant in a female first-born. This was not to overlook the acknowledged fact that women wielded much power and influence behind the scenes. Further, there were occasions when a taina chief became the effective leader of a tribe or sub-tribe. This was achieved through one or a combination of the following:

• By usurping leadership from a matamua or ariki who lacked the ability to lead;

• By migrating out of the tribal or sub-tribal territory and establishing a new group;

• By the equal allocation of certain areas within the tribal or sub-tribal territory to more than one heir;

• By marriage. It was possible for a taina chief to increase his mana considerably through marriage to a high-born woman, to the extent of becoming a recognised leader;

• By inheriting the mana of a taina ancestor who achieved leadership.

It is important to bear in mind that leadership in subsequent generations was still the prerogative of the descendants of the ariki or matamua lines and that the first-born son of a weak ariki or matamua could justly lay claim to the right to lead.

In other words, while a matamua may forfeit the right to lead, his chieftainship remains intact and is passed on to his descendants with its privileges and rights.

Mana and Tapu

The chiefs were imbued with the qualities of mana and tapu by reason of their exalted birth. According to Buck, 'The mana of a chief carries the meaning of power and prestige. Tapu is . . . a form of personal sanctity.' Both mana and tapu were viewed as coming from the gods. Further, the ariki was regarded as the taumata (the resting place of gods) and therefore the closest to the gods – hence his was the greatest mana and tapu in society.

Mana was inherited from one's father. However, it could be increased by the personal achievements of an individual rangatira. Expertise in a particular field such as war could greatly add to a chief's stature and hence to his mana and to that of his descendants. The son of a chief inherited from his father the mana of his ancestors as well as that his father acquired. The mana of the chief gave him the authority to control and direct the activities of the tribe or sub-tribe. This power to direct human activity was called mana tangata. There is also mana whenua which is the power to claim a territory defined by one's ancestry, with the right to rule this territory and hold it in trust for the tribe or sub-tribe.

Tapu was inherited in the same way as mana, and because of his tapu, a chief was regarded with a respect amounting to awe and dread. So great was this tapu that some chiefs, just by sitting in a particular place, automatically caused that place to become tapu. The violation of a chief's tapu usually resulted in death.

Marriage

The norm was that marriage should be between people of equal status. This was important, not only in terms of personal mana, but also for the perpetuation of the mana of a particular line. However, as noted, it was possible to increase mana by marrying someone genealogically senior. Marriage was generally endogamous, that is, within the hapu or sub-tribe. In Ngati Porou, first-cousin marriages were not uncommon in pre-European times, such was the degree of 'in-marriage'. There is a saying, 'E moe i to tuahine (tungane) kia heke te toto ko korua tonu.' (Marry your sister (brother) so that if blood is to be shared, it is only your own.) This suggests that the situation was not peculiar to Ngati Porou. The inference is that if the 'blood' was 'shared' among close kin, the unity of the hapu would not be jeopardised.

In the cases where marriage was exogamous, that is, outside the hapu, it was usually for a political end. It was not uncommon for marriages to be arranged between high-born members of different hapu to give strength to an alliance between the two groups. Occasionally, such marriages were inter-tribal.

Whichever the case, it was usual for the wife to reside with the husband's kin group. This is in keeping with the view that mana came from one's father and seniority came from male ancestors.

Waiata, Haka and Whakatauki

For a study of leadership, oral literature is important because its conventions and symbols convey the status of people mentioned in them. They provide clues as to how people were regarded by society. Many of them rely on material from whakapapa and tribal history for their effect. They may be defined as follows:

- Waiata is the term applied to oral poetry and song literature. They may be chanted, shouted or recited. There are four categories of waiata:
Waiata aroha or love ditties;
Waiata tangi or laments for the dead;
Oriori or lullabies, specifically to instruct a young child about who he is;
Patere or songs of abuse.
- Haka are also song literature, but are performed with actions. There are two categories:
Haka tuna or war haka, performed by men;
Haka taparahi or ceremonial haka, performed by men or women.
Both types may contain elements of the patere.
- Whakatauki are proverbs.

Traditional Leadership: Ngati Porou Case

As I stated at the beginning, when I applied accepted 'rules' of leadership to Ngati Porou I found that there were some important differences in emphasis. These relate almost exclusively to the status of women in the tribe. This situation has been observed by other writers. Metge says, 'Women are frequently recognised as kaumatua[8] in their own right among the East Coast tribes.'[9] Buck says, 'In rare instances, a female ariki, such as the famous Hinematioro of Ngati Porou, was raised to queenly pomp and power by her people.' And Best notes, 'It occasionally happened that a well-born woman attained a high position in a tribe, owing to special qualities of mind and heart. Thus Hinematioro, grandmother of Te Kani[10] . . . was the most important person of the Ngati Porou tribe in her time.'[11] However, none of these writers has looked at the question in depth and they have therefore drawn the conclusion that such women are exceptions to the rule of male leadership. A study of tribal whakapapa and tradition reveal that this is not the case. How, then, do women fit into the 'model' of leadership?

Primogeniture: If one considers the concepts associated with the principle of primogeniture – tuakana, taina, and matamua – one finds that in Ngati Porou

46

these terms are used regardless of sex. If we return to the genealogy given earlier, the following would apply:

• Mariu is tuakana to all her brothers as well as her sisters. Similarly, both Te Rangitaupopoki and Waewaeraupa are tuakana to the three male children;
• All the children after Mariu are, therefore, taina to her;
• Mariu is both ariki and matamua.

In my own lifetime, my father has used the term tuakana to describe my relationship with the daughters of his elder sister (they being tuakana).

Further, if one accepts that a male was always at the apex of the whakapapa, then it follows that a hapu or tribe should bear the name of a man, although 'occasionally a woman became the founding ancestress of a clan, as in the case of one named Ngati Hinepare.'[12] In Ngati Porou one finds that more of the senior subtribes are named after women than men: Te Aitanga-a-Mate (Whareponga); Te Whanau-a-Hinerupe (Waiapu Valley); Te Whanau-a-Hinepare (North Waiapu and probably the 'Ngati Hinepare' of the above); Te Whanau-a-Hineauta (Tikapa); Te Whanau-a-Hinetapora (Mangahanea and Tuparoa); Te Whanau-a-Ruataupare (Tokomaru Bay); Te Whanau-a-Iritekura (Waipiro Bay); Te Whanau-a-Rakairoa (Waiapu Valley); Te Whanau-a-Hinematioro (Tolaga Bay); Te Whanau-a-Uepohatu (Ruatoria and Tuparoa); Te Whanau-a-Tapuhi (Te Araroa and Tikitiki).

In addition to these surviving hapu, there were hapu, such as Ngati Ruawaipu, Te Wahine-iti and Ngati Hinekehu, which have been absorbed into the others. It further follows that if one wanted to establish status in any of these hapu, one would trace a line of descent from the woman who gives her name to the hapu. In Ngati Porou, this was done by tracing descent from the founding ancestor through as many first-born issue as possible, regardless of their sex. Indeed, the late Arnold Reedy[13] said, 'Remove our female genealogies and our genealogies will be made common.' Certainly one's rank in society is not dependent on what Firth called the ability to trace it 'through as long and unbroken a male line as possible'.

The question arises whether the women who gave their names to hapu were actually leaders in the political sphere and not just chieftainesses or figureheads. The comments already made about Hinematioro indicate that these women were more than figureheads. It is further supported by the following story.

After the battle known as 'Te roro huka tai' (The scattering of human brains like the foam of the sea) where the great warrior leader, Tuwhakairiora, avenged the death of his grandfather at the hands of the Ngati Ruanuku people, he said to his niece Iritekura, 'E noho ki Waikawa hei tiaki i nga pungarehu a o tungane.' (Stay at Waikawa to guard the conquered remains of your male relatives.) Iritekura was recognised as leader when Te Atau, one of the warrior chiefs and few survivors of the battle, said to his fellow tribesmen, 'Haere mai, haere ki te wahine urukehu ra kia ora ai koutou.' (Come, go to that fair-headed woman, that you may be spared.) This acknowledged her as their new leader.

I think the fact that women in Ngati Porou have the right to speak on the marae indicates they were leaders in the fullest sense. If one accepts the marae as the centre of tribal affairs where the political fate of the tribe is decided, then to deny women the right to speak would support the view that they were figureheads. In recent times, women have also been accorded the right to speak on behalf of the tribe outside the tribal area. At the Waitangi celebrations in 1934, Sir Apirana Ngata asked my father to speak on behalf of Ngati Porou. But my father replied that Materoa Reedy[14] was to speak, which she did.

Another story concerns the Whanau-a-Apanui chieftainess, Mihi Kotukutuku Stirling. In her lifetime she was the acknowledged leader of the tribe. In 1917, when the son of Tiweka Anarau died, Whanau-a-Apanui went to Rotorua. When Mita Taupopoki, a chief of Te Arawa, was speaking, an Omaio rangatira, Timutima Tawhai, was asked who was going to reply, because Te Arawa do not allow women to speak on their marae. Timutima replied, 'Ana ra te upoko ariki e noho mai na,' (Yonder sits the paramount ariki) and he pointed to Mihi. True to form Mihi stood up, the first time a woman had stood to speak on an Arawa marae. Immediately, Mita Taupopoki stood up and demanded that Mihi sit down. Mihi replied, 'Kaore koe e tau hei korero ki au. Ana aku tungane, ma ratou te koreroko ki a au. O makawe hina na i puta ake i konei!' (You have no right to speak to me. There are my male relatives sitting there, let them speak to me. Your mop of grey hair came from here!) She punctuated her remarks by pointing between her thighs! There was silence and she was allowed to continue her speech.

When Mihi Kotukutuku died, Te Arawa came in force to pay their respects to her and one of their speakers said, 'Kaitoa koe kia, mate atu, te wahine takatakahi i nga ture o Te Arawa.' (Serves you right that you have died, you disrespected Arawa custom.) This was a direct reference to the earlier incident and while such a remark might be construed as disrespectful, it was part of the tangi and a sign of their respect for her. This was a measure of her leadership.

All this should not be taken as an indication that male leaders were not important in Ngati Porou, because they were; there were many more male leaders than female. But it does show that more than one or two exceptional women became acknowledged leaders.

Achieved Leadership: If we return to the list of hapu named after women, we find that a number of these women were not, in fact, first-born children.

In the following genealogy, it can be seen that Hinerupe was taina to her two sisters, Te Aopare and Tamateakui. The three girls were the 'toasting' girls of the tribe. Early in life they displayed outstanding personal qualities fitting them for leadership. Of the three, however, it was Hinerupe who stood out and it was she who became the acknowledged leader of the people and founded the hapu which still exists today.

Hinerupe's sisters also recognised her greater ability and voluntarily surrendered to her lands under their power, making her territory very extensive. There is a saying which indicates the extent of her boundaries: 'Mai i te moana tae noa atu ki te ao parauri.' (From the sea to as far as the eye can see.)

By surrendering their territory to Hinerupe, her sisters also forfeited their right to the mana tangata so that Hinerupe assumed political leadership over the whole territory.

Genealogy: Hinerupe

Porourangi

Hau

Tuere

Rongomaikairae

Whatiuaroa

Uekaiahu

Uetaha

Te Aopare   Tamateakui   Hinerupe

The chieftainess, Hinetapora, was another who was not first-born, yet she was probably the most important leader of her time.

49

Genealogy: Hinetapora

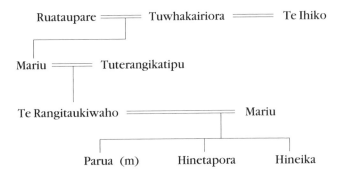

Maori Land Court records[15] reveal that both Parua and Hinetapora grew up at Uawa (Tolaga Bay). When Hinetapora was a young woman, the eldest son of the great warrior chief, Umuariki, came to get her as a wife for his taina, Te Rangikaputua. They settled at Horoera where Hinetapora's parents were living. So far I have been unable to determine when and why Hinetapora moved to the Ruatoria area[16] where the Whanau-a-Hinetapora is. But the records show that her father, Te Rangitaukiwaho, was 'sacked' from Horoera. He heard the people saying, 'Ka nui te marino o te moana' (How calm the sea is) and he knew the people wanted him to leave. He left to return to Tokomaru Bay and died at sea. Perhaps it was as a result of this that Hinetapora also left Horoera. Whatever the reason, her importance is not in doubt.

When Hinetapora was an old woman, she was killed by the Whanau-a-Apanui chief Tamahae, who cut off her head and held it aloft for all to see. When he was scorned for killing an old woman, he replied, 'Ka nui tenei. He kotahi ia, he mano kei raro.' (She is enough. Although there is only one of her, she represents thousands.) This was the final indication of her prestige. Here, then, is a case of a woman achieving power through migration in spite of her taina birth.

Hinepare was another of taina birth who was a strong leader in her time. Hinepare's mother, Te Aokairau, recognised that three of her children, Putaanga, Huanga and Hinepare, had leadership abilities and she divided her territory among them. Putaanga ruled in the area known as Poroporo Valley, Huanga to the south, and Hinepare in North Waiapu. To this day the people in the Poroporo Valley are known as Te Whanau-a-Putaanga, while the Whanau-a-Hinepare is found at Rangitukia.

Genealogy: Hinepare

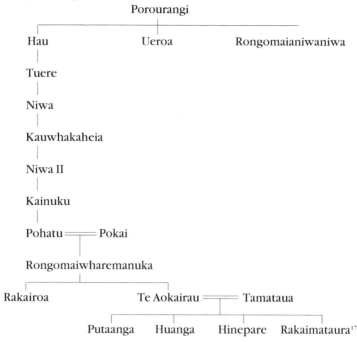

Putaanga achieved fame as a warrior and the strength of Hinepare's rule is indicated by the following story. When Kokere's pa was threatened by Tamahae, Tamokai said to him, 'Haere taua ki Waiapu ki tatara e maru ana . . .' (Let us go to Waiapu where there are many people to help us.) The leader of the people at Waiapu was Hinepare.

The classic example of a taina chief increasing his status through marriage to a high-born woman is that of Tuwhakairiora, possibly the greatest warrior chief of Ngati Porou. Tuwhakairiora's marriage was, in fact, his launching pad. Through his wife, he was able to acquire access to large tracts of land and gained for himself the pa called Okauwharetoa, on the south bank of the Awatere River, formerly Ruataupare's pa.

It was Ruataupare, though, who was acknowledged leader of the people in Hicks Bay and Te Araroa. And it wasn't until Tuwhakairiora proved himself such an outstanding leader in war that he was able to usurp her authority. His mana was such that he was able to pass it on to his children and his line is still one of the most prestigious in Ngati Porou.

It is interesting to note that Ruataupare was aware very early in her marriage that her position was in jeopardy because of the great ability displayed by her husband. The people in the area were known as Te Whanau-a-Ruataupare. But after

51

several victories Tuwhakairiora was heralded into the village by the people and his band of warriors was given the title Te Whanau-a-Tuwhakairiora. This annoyed Ruataupare so much that when her husband approached her to retire with him, she said, 'Haere ki taku taina ki a Te Ihiko, kia kiia ai koe he rangatira.' (Go to my younger relative Te Ihiko, that you may rightly be called a chief.) This, of course, was a great insult to Tu. Ruataupare was saying that by having intercourse with Te Ihiko, who was his tuakana, he would achieve chiefly status. This put into poor repute the status Tuwhakairiora had gained as a warrior.

Ruataupare's insult backfired. Tu accepted her challenge and took Te Ihiko as his second wife. In order to preserve her name, Ruataupare left the area, settling at Tokomaru Bay where she founded another sub-tribe, Te Whanau-a-Ruataupare, which exists to this day and is senior sub-tribe in the area.

The principal example of a woman succeeding to the mana of a taina chief or chieftainess is that of the daughter of Hinerupe, Te Aotaihi. The late Pine Taiapa (a leading tribal historian who died in 1972) said the two daughters of Hinerupe, Te Aotaihi and Te Atahaia, became the 'parekereke' (nursery) for the chiefly lines of Ngati Porou. The eldest girl, Te Aotaihi, became the leader of Te Whanau-a-Hinerupe after her mother and held a position of respect and awe comparable to that which Te Kani-a-Takirau was to occupy. She received the first fruits of every food, as Te Kani did in his time, this in spite of the fact that her husband, Tuterangiwhiu, was her genealogical senior, a son of Tuwhakairiora and Ruataupare and himself a great warrior.

The story of Te Aotaihi is also connected with the founding of the Whanau-a-Tapuhi. When Hinematioro returned to Te Araroa to visit the village of her ancestor, Tuwhakairiora, she was accorded the kind of welcome reserved only for the noblest. In her reply to the speeches of welcome, Hinematioro asked, 'Ko wai te puhi o te karaka a Tu?' (Who is the plume of the karaka tree of Tu?) The obvious answer would have been, 'Ko koe!' (It is you.) But a younger woman, Tapuhi, replied, 'Ko au.' (It is I.) Her claim was based on the rule of tuakana and taina, as can be seen from the genealogy.

Genealogy: Tapuhi and Hinematioro

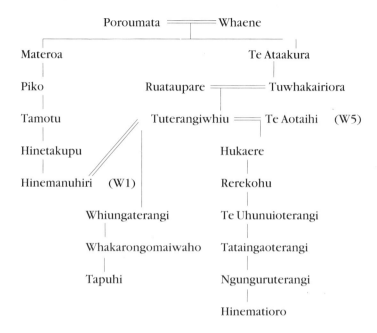

Not only was Tapuhi able to claim seniority through the relationship of the two sisters, Materoa and Te Ataakura, but also through her ancestress, Hinemanuhiri, who was the first wife of Tuterangiwhiu, whereas Hinematioro's ancestress, Te Aotaihi, was his fifth wife.

Hinematioro recognised her claim and returned to Tolaga Bay. Tapuhi assumed the role of leader at Te Araroa and she formed her own sub-tribe which to this day is known as the Whanau-a-Tapuhi.

Mana and Tapu: What I have already had to say about primogeniture and achieved leadership is enough to indicate the power and prestige that many woman leaders in Ngati Porou had. But the following accounts will reinforce this.

Hineauta was a chieftainess of the Tikapa and Te Horo district where the Whanau-a-Hineauta is today. Most of the senior lines in the tribe converge on her. She is referred to as a 'queen' by her people and her tapu was so great that she never walked anywhere, but was amohia ai (borne on a litter). This way she did not make the ground on which she walked tapu.

The second story is also about her. The Whanau-a-Pokai chief, Whakanehu, planned to attack the people at Tikapa. But they got wind of his plans and brought Hineauta to Tikapa. When Whakanehu arrived, Hineauta was sitting in front of the meeting house and just the sight of her was enough to deter Whakanehu's attack. In this context, Hineauta was the protector of her people, so great was her mana and tapu. Whakanehu was not prepared to take the responsibility for her death.

Hapu Membership: I shall look briefly at the question of hapu membership and how it is determined. Firth (and others) acknowledge that a choice exists as to whether a person belonged to his mother's or father's hapu. But, he says, because of the political role of men, the choice was biased in the father's favour and 'claims to group membership were determined primarily by residence'. Firth further says the element of choice available to any one person 'did not entitle his descendants to perpetual membership of all such groups'. In other words, the decision of a particular individual about where he wished to exercise his mana whenua during his lifetime restricted the hapu membership of his descendants.

On my own tribal evidence, I would suggest that, while mana whenua was restricted in traditional society by the physical impossibility of living in too many places at once, one's mana tangata was not so restricted, and rank and right to belong to any group remained intact as long as one could establish the genealogical link. This would suggest that it was the knowledge of one's mana tangata that was the limiting factor, not the exercise of one's mana whenua. Obviously, in the case of a chief or chieftainess, once the mana tangata was established, he or she could lay claim to the mana whenua.

The case of Ruataupare is one in point. Her choice of Tokomaru Bay as a place to settle was not accidental. She was able to establish her genealogical link with the Ngati Ira and Wahine-iti people in the area and was accepted on this basis, although the claim to membership had not been 'validated by social action' (Firth) for a number of generations.

Once Ruataupare's mana tangata was recognised, it was only a question of time before she acquired the mana whenua, such was the quality of her leadership. This she passed on to her daughters and it is still held by the Whanau-a-Ruataupare. Further, as the above case and others indicate, I would suggest the element of choice lay not so much in what hapu one wanted to belong to, but in which one a person wished to live. And the consanguineal tie was never made 'invalid' as long as one could establish it existed.

Genealogy: Ruataupare

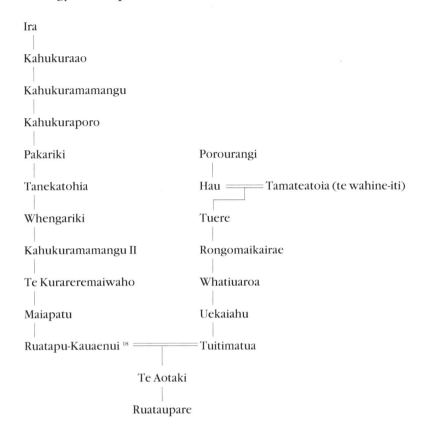

Ira
|
Kahukuraao
|
Kahukuramamangu
|
Kahukuraporo
|
Pakariki   Porourangi
| |
Tanekatohia   Hau ═══ Tamateatoia (te wahine-iti)
|
Whengariki   Tuere
| |
Kahukuramamangu II   Rongomaikairae
| |
Te Kurareremaiwaho   Whatiuaroa
| |
Maiapatu   Uekaiahu
| |
Ruatapu-Kauaenui [18] ═══ Tuitimatua
|
Te Aotaki
|
Ruataupare

This, of course, raises the question as to whether the commonly accepted view that land claims grew cold (mataotao) when not exercised is correct. There are two points to be made here. First, traditional land was not held by individuals but in trust by the chief (mana whenua) and the idea of 'land claims' as such is a post-European one. Second, I would argue that one's right to reside in a particular area never grew mataotao because, if one could establish the genealogical link, the right to occupy and use the land was accepted.

I agree with Firth that with the advent of modern communications the 'ambilateral character of the hapu system . . . has been strengthened'. But, on the strength of my own tribal experience and that of my fellows, I disagree that 'in such cases the effective kin are a relatively small group and use kin ties for individual purposes or for local association rather than for membership of corporate descent groups'.

If one considers the marae situation, here we have a piece of land collectively owned by a hapu and anyone who can establish his membership of that hapu through his genealogy can claim to be a tangata whenua or man of the land. This approximates the traditional situation.

One last point: I have established the importance of women in the genealogies of Ngati Porou and as leaders. It follows that it was by no means a foregone conclusion that the choice of group residence was biased in the father's favour. In fact, traditional evidence points almost to a bias in the opposite direction (i.e. in the mother's favour), so widespread was the practice of settling on one's mother's claims even when one's father was a prominent chief. There were even cases of a chief being content to settle on his wife's interests – as in the case of Te Aohore and his wife Rakairoa.

Rakairoa inherited the land on both sides of the Waiapu River from Reporoa to Te Ahikouka and Ngata says it was on her 'rights in the Waiapu Valley her husband, Te Aohore, was content to rest'. This is in spite of the fact that Te Aohore was from the senior Porourangi line, being a descendant of Rakaipo, the eldest child of Hau and Tamateatoia.

Marriage: The generally accepted 'rules' in regard to marriage apply within Ngati Porou. Marriage was generally between two people of equal status. Not only were there marriages between first cousins, but also between uncle and niece and aunt and nephew. Such cases are not isolated ones, as a detailed study of tribal genealogies has shown. On this basis, it would seem that marriage was, in the main, endogamous, for the sake of perpetuating the line. It is interesting to note that, as far as I can establish, there was no Maori word meaning 'incest' in pre-European days.

There are numerous cases of exogamous marriages at the rangatira level and, as already observed, they were principally for political ends to strengthen alliances between two hapu. And, as noted in the section on mana and tapu, residence was quite often in the wife's hapu – as in the case of Ruataupare and Tuwhakairiora and Hinerupe and Hukarere.

Two marriages stand out among those which were made for the purpose of political alliance. They are those of Ngunguruterangi and Tanetokorangi, and of Uhengaparaoa to Rakaipikirarunga and his brother, Mokaiaporou.

Ngunguruterangi's great-grandfather, Rerekohu, had insulted the chief Konohi, Ponapatukia and others as they travelled to Te Whanau-a-Apanui to avenge the death of Hinetapora at the hands of Tamahae. When Konohi returned, Rerekohu had to think of a way to appease him and he used Ngunguruterangi as a peace offering. She was given to Konohi's grandson, Tanetokorangi, as a wife and from this union came Hinematioro.

Uhengaparaoa was a descendant of Muriwai[19] and a granddaughter of the Opotiki chief Uekahikatea. Uekahikatea was slain and when his death remained unavenged, a call went out for an avenging party, which was answered by the chief, Tamahinengaro. When he and his taua (war party) had accomplished their mission, the Opotiki people made a number of gifts to Tamahinengaro in gratitude, and Uhengaparaoa was the *pièce de résistance*. She brought into Ngati Porou chiefly blood from the leaders of Mataatua.

Genealogy: Uhengaparaoa

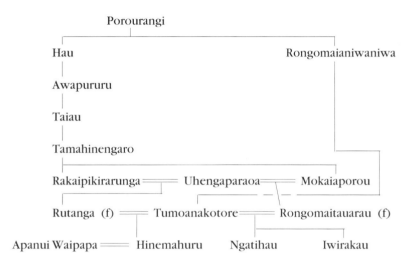

From Uhengaparaoa's marriage came Rutanga and from her marriage the wife of Apanui Waipapa, founding ancestor of Te Whanau-a-Apanui. When Rakaipikirarunga died, Mokaiaporou took Uhengaparaoa as his wife and from this union came the mother of Ngatihau, Rongomaitauarau.

Waiata, Haka and Whakatauki: There are many examples in oral literature which indicate a person's rank and I have space to give but a few of the better known. A common practice in Ngati Porou is to identify people as the children of their mother as an indication of their rank:
'Katahi hanga e nga kuri paka a Uetuhiao, me te manu e pokaia ana.' (There you are, you brown-skinned dogs of Uetuhiao, huddled together like wood pigeons.) Uetuhiao was the mother of the three brothers, Kuku, Korohau and Rongotangatake. The comment was made by the Whanau-a-Apanui chief, Taniwha, when he came across them after they had been slain in battle. 'Nga kuri paka' has passed into Ngati Porou usage to identify this line.
'E akiaki ana te whero o te tama a Te Atahaia.' (How explosive is the backside of Te Atahaia's son) – a retort from Tamahae to the chief, Makahuri, Te Atahaia being Makahuri's mother.
'Penei au i haere mai koe, te tama a Whakaroro, ki te tono i a au mau, kaore i

haere mai koe ki tono i a au ma te Kawhiu paua o Tokoroa nei.' (I thought that you, the son of Whakaroro, came here to ask my hand in marriage to you, but alas, you have come here to seek me for this paua diver of Tokoroa.) This was the response of Hinetapora to Taputerakahia when he came to get her as a wife for his brother Te Rangikaputua. Whakaroro was a high-born chieftainess and Hinetapora considered Taputerakahia would be more worthy of her rank than Te Rangikaputua, the son of Uepare, the second wife of the two boys' father, Umuariki. He had taken Uepare as his second wife after he had seen her paua diving. The descendants of Te Rangikaputua are still known as 'Nga kawhiu paua o Tokoroa' but it is no longer used in a demeaning sense. Hinetapora and Te Rangikaputua did marry.

'Ko te tumu herenga waka.' (The stake to which the canoe is tied.) This proverb indicates the influence and the reliability of a notable chief and was used by Pine Taiapa to describe the chieftainesses, Ruataupare and Hinerupe.

'Haere mai ki Hikurangi, te maunga kua tauria e te huka.' (Come to Hikurangi, the mountain on which rests the snow.) These words were used by Te Aotaki, the father of Ruataupare, when Tuwhakairiora was welcomed to Okauwharetoa and were a reference to Ruataupare's nobility, and follows the practice, in Ngati Porou and in other tribal areas, of comparing powerful chiefs with sacred mountains.

In the same way, waiata were used to indicate a person's rank. Hinekitawhiti composed such a song (an oriori) for her granddaughter. The song opens:

> Kia tapu ra koe na Tuariki
> Kia tapu ra koe na Porouhorea . . .
>
> You are the tapu descendant of Tuariki
> You are the tapu descendant of Porouhorea . . .

The song tells the young child she has inherited her tapu from her ancestors, Tuariki and Porouhorea, and that this tapu is very great. It goes on to exhort her not to 'descend too near to common places . . .' and to 'let only your younger relative be free from restriction'. The song links the child with other leaders and chiefs:

> . . . e rapa e hine i Te Kauwhau mua i a Hinemakaho
> Hai a Hinerautu, hai a Tikitikiorangi,
> Hai kona ra korua.
>
> . . . for the maiden seeks the first-born line from Hinemakaho
> Such as Hinerautu and Tikitikiorangi,
> And there you will be with your elder.

What the song does, in its totality, is establish for the young child just who she is and gives her links to all the hapu she can claim title to. In this particular part she is advised to seek the first-born line from Hinemakaho as the measure of her nobility. Hinemakaho was the elder sister of Poroumata and 'her descendants became incorporated with and supplied the chiefs and leaders for a section of Te Wahine-iti'.

There are many more examples to draw upon, but I think I have made my point that a valuable clue as to a person's rank and whakapapa can be gained from a close study of waiata, haka and whakatauki.

Contemporary Leadership

I have dwelt at length on the traditional situation in Ngati Porou because it is this which makes me who and what I am today. I have long felt that the commonly accepted views about leadership were frustratingly unsatisfactory in doing this. In discussing leadership in the immediate post-European and contemporary periods, I will also confine my remarks principally to Ngati Porou because I am not an authority on other tribal areas. Other writers have described the general situation and one study in particular[20] has looked at the situation in another specific tribal area.

In addition to the traditional determinants of chieftainship and leadership, the factors which have altered the flavour of leadership in post-European times are Pakeha education, religion and law, and the money economy. In the traditional system, the whare wananga was the educational institution. In the main it was the preserve of those of high rank and it was here that the history of the tribe, religion, whakapapa and so on were taught. The training ground for the young chiefs was the marae and whare runanga.

Both the priestly tohunga and the ariki were most senior in society. Indeed there were some religious rituals which could be performed only by the ariki, he being the most tapu and the closest to the gods.

The new whare wananga in the immediate post-European period was Te Aute College. It was here that the boys of chiefly rank were sent to acquire 'te matauranga o te Pakeha' (Pakeha wisdom) and they were later looked to for tribal leadership and to guide the people in their relationships with the Pakeha. At Te Aute they were 'nourished on the classics and the ideals of religion and service' (Winiata). Those who were selected to become the new religious tohunga were sent to Te Raukahikatea Theological College at Gisborne to learn the doctrines and dogmas of the new religion.

When the new priests returned to the tribe to teach and preach the new religion, they commanded the respect of the people because of their rank and status. It was also because of this that they were able to insist that people attend services and in their time these clergy filled their churches with people. They did not condemn Maori practices out of hand, but effected a balance between the two – the old traditional beliefs and the new Pakeha ones – and because they were educated in both they were able to reconcile the old with the Gospel.

Inevitably conflict arose because Pakeha clergy, the majority of whom remained unenlightened on things Maori, considered their Maori counterparts were condoning 'heathen' practices. Like the Pharisees, too many Pakeha clergy were concerned with the letter of the law and not its spirit. I refer here particularly to the Anglican Church, as this was the denomination which had the strongest hold on the East Coast. What wasn't realised was that many of these so-called 'heathen' practices were tenable according to the Gospel.

The second field of conflict lay in the status of the Maori clergy in the Church at large (here again I speak of the Anglican Church). I am convinced that the Maori clergy in the Anglican Church have always been the poor relations – a necessary evil to facilitate the conversion of 'heathens' to a civilised religion, and, later, to ensure continued allegiance to the faith, particularly financial. In the early days, the rank and status of the Maori clergyman within his own tribe was almost completely disregarded. In the new religious milieu, the traditional rangatira were subservient to a Pakeha chief elected to his position by the church hierarchy. One could argue that this position approximates that of the ariki in traditional society being replaced by a more capable taina. However what was usurped in the traditional case was the ariki's right to rule or lead, not his mana and tapu. The new priestly tohunga lost both to his adopted church.

The position of the Bishop of Aotearoa shows clearly the 'poor relation' status of the Maori clergy in the Anglican Church. Ngata originally mooted the idea of a Maori bishop in the belief that he would be a unifying influence in Maori society at large. But the Bishop of Aotearoa has never enjoyed more than suffragan status. He did not even have a vote in the General Synod of the Church, neither was he a full bishop,[21] making a mockery of Ngata's original ideal. While individual Bishops of Aotearoa have used their position to influence an issue in Maoridom at large (notably Bishop Panapa at the time of the 1960 proposed All Black tour of South Africa), none of the incumbents to date[22] has been a unifying force.

The educated rangatira provided the bridge between the traditional society and the new Pakeha one. Leaders such as Ngata were tenacious in holding on to the old Maori values while taking up the tools offered them by Pakeha knowledge and technology. It is beyond the scope of this exercise to go into how they did this in detail, but they left behind them a legacy of improved health conditions in Maori communities, the Maori land incorporation system, and many new marae and whare runanga in which 'the traditional and the modern were blended to create physical symbols of tribal cohesion, and to strengthen tribal pride and morale' (Winiata). They stood in two worlds; they represented the Maori to the European, while at the same time speaking to the Maori for the European.

The contemporary educated leader's role has not changed significantly. Many Maori communities still look to those with higher education for guidance and advice in coping with the modern world. The most important change is that most of the educated leaders are forced by the economics of providing for their families to live outside the rural traditionally orientated communities, returning when time allows and for important social occasions like tangihanga and tribal hui. In this way they live and work in a largely Pakeha world, but return to their marae when needed. In Ngati Porou at least, this homing instinct is strongest among those who are members of the rangatira class (in the same way as Ngata was in his time) and their rangatiraship and leadership is acknowledged in the community, even though they are absent for much of the year. In this respect, I disagree with Winiata who says that 'the responsibilities formerly exercised by the rangatira have now been assumed by the kaumatua'. In Ngati Porou, the term is still used and the traditional concomitants of leadership and responsibility still apply. What is more, these are recognised by the kaumatua who acknowledge their genealogical mana as well as looking to them for advice on European affairs. On the obverse side, these educated rangatira respect the kaumatua as their elders, and in many cases because of their knowledge of tribal kawa and history.

Neither do I subscribe to the view that present leadership is achieved rather than ascribed, at least certainly not in Ngati Porou. Here families like Reedy, Dewes, Kaa, Karaka, Kohere, Mahuika and Ngata, families which belong to the rangatira, have ensured that at least one of its sons has received the full benefit of Pakeha education because these are the families from which leadership is expected. In other words, Pakeha education is another preparation for leadership in the tribal situation, regardless of what they may achieve in the wider community. This would suggest that the traditional determinants of leadership are still relevant and important today, together with the changes wrought by the need to adjust to the wider community and the demands of modern life. Also, as in traditional times, where a rangatira lacks ability, his leadership role will be filled by another.

When this happens, as in the case of Ngata, it is still usual for them to seek the approval and consult with their tuakana before acting on their ideas. Indeed, this was partly the reason for Ngata's success in the tribal situation. Although he came from the senior whakapapa of the tribe, he was not the most senior in society. By acknowledging his tuakana, he was able to use them to his own advantage by winning their support before he went to the tribe as a whole.

The rangatira are still emerging strongly as leaders. Among my own sub-tribe in Waiapu we have the Weka, Green, Manuel and other families taking their rightful place in the leadership of their people. These people come from the same whakapapa as the other senior families of Ngati Porou.

In war, it was also to the rangatira class that people turned for leadership. In the early days of European contact, a number of rangatira from Ngati Porou became 'loyalists' fighting with the British army in the belief that this was the only way to ensure retention of their lands. They were mindful of what had happened in Taranaki and Waikato after the land wars. The most famous of these leaders was Major Ropata Wahawaha, a grand-uncle of Ngata.

During World War II, Ngata insisted that the officers of the 28th Maori Battalion be selected on a tribal basis and that these officers be of the rangatira class. When 'C' Company was commanded by officers from other tribes, that loyalty was not automatic, almost to the point of revolt on one occasion. Ngata intervened, the company command was changed to one from the rangatira line of Ngati Porou, and the revolt was averted. It has been shown in retrospect that 'C' Company performed best under officers drawn from the rangatira of the tribe. Thus leaders like Lt. M. Ngarimu V.C. and Colonel P. Awatere came from the senior ranks of Ngati Porou (the former being a nephew of Materoa Reedy).

On the home front it was women like Mihi Kotukutuku Stirling, Materoa Reedy, Merekaraka Waititi and others who were busy organising. Such women were used by Ngata because of their mana and influence, in the same way that he used the older generation of male rangatira as recruitment officers. These women, along with rangatira like Putiputi Haerewa, Hariata Turei, Te Aorere Haig, Tangipo Mahuika and Materoa Taare, were the last of the female leaders cast in the traditional ilk – steeped in tribal history and kawa, who spoke on the marae and were looked to for tribal leadership. The female rangatira of the tribe have not taken the same advantage of Pakeha education as their male counterparts, though many have been sent away to Maori Church Schools. Nonetheless, particularly through involvement with the Maori Women's Welfare League, these women are still looked to for leadership and are still able to exert this leadership on the marae when the need arises. The mana of their whakapapa is recognised by all.

Some of Ngati Porou's senior families have lost their leadership role to other families on the grounds that they lacked the ability to provide effective leadership. However, as in the traditional case, their mana as rangatira remains intact. The loss of leadership is by no means permanent, for it can be regained in the future by those who possess and exercise the ability and wisdom required of a leader.

In the discussion on traditional leadership, I argued that one's right to reside in a particular area never grew cold or mataotao because evidence in Ngati Porou oral tradition indicates that once a person established their genealogical link with a particular hapu, the right to occupy and use the land persisted. While the individualising of land ownership has altered the character of hapu membership, I believe that today one can still belong to several hapu at the same time and exercise rights on the marae (now the symbol of land) of all hapu to which one can establish membership. This is manifested by what happens frequently at tangi: various hapu members attend and often quite heated debate can take place as to where the deceased should be taken for burial – in this hapu territory or that – even though that person may only have exercised his or her right in one particular hapu in his lifetime.

This, then, is the Ngati Porou position on tribal and hapu leadership. I hope that what I have noted will excite further debate on the whole question of leadership in Maori society and, more particularly, provide a stimulus to others to examine and put forth their tribal experience. I hope they would do this not only in terms of leadership, but in the whole sphere of tribal tradition so that the real essence of Maoritanga will be preserved and grow.

FOOTNOTES
1. Buck 1962: 343.
2. Hugh Kawharu.
3. H.W. Williams, *A Dictionary of the Maori Language*.
4. Ngata 1943: Whakapapa tables p. 47.
5. Buck 1947: 345.
6. H.W. Williams, *A Dictionary of the Maori Language*.
7. Buck 1947: 346.
8. Kaumatua – elder, regardless of rank, age being determined by general age of group; waha korero or speaker, regardless of age; sometimes used in sense of rangatira or leader; in Ngati Porou is synonymous with pakeke.
9. Metge 1967: 158.
10. Te Kani – Te Kani a Takirau.
11. Best 1924: Vol. 1, 353.
12. Best 1924: Vol. 1.
13. Arnold Reedy was an acknowledged expert on Ngati Porou history and tradition.
14. Mother of Arnold Reedy and an acknowledged leader in Ngati Porou.
15. Settlement of the Poroporo Blocks, 20 May 1915, evidence given by Paora Haenga.
16. Hinetapora's right to move to Ruatoria is not in dispute, since she had the right to change her area of domicile to those areas where she was able to assert her genealogical connections, in this case, through her great grandmother, Ruataupare.
17. These four children are represented on the amo of the Rongomaianiwaniwa meeting house at Tikitiki.
18. Genealogy from Ira to Ruatapu given by author's grandfather, Nepia Mahuika.
19. Muriwai was the sister of Toroa, captain of the Mataatua canoe.
20. Maharaia Winiata, *The Changing Role of the Leader in Maori Society*.
21. In 1978 the Bishop of Aotearoa was made a full bishop and given a vote in the General Synod.
22. The present incumbent, Whakahuihui Vercoe, is the fourth.

LAND: MAORI VIEW AND EUROPEAN RESPONSE

DOUGLAS SINCLAIR

Ma te wahine ka tupu ai te hanga nei, e tangata,
Ma te whenua ka whai oranga ai.
Whai hoki, ki te tangohia to wahine e te tangata ke,
Ka ngau te pouri ki roto i a koe.
Na, ki te tangohia te whenua e te tangata ke,
Ka tapu to pouri ano.
Ko nga putake enei o te whawhai.
Koia i kiia ai
He wahine, he oneone, i ngaro ai te tangata.

Woman alone gives birth to mankind,
Land alone gives man his sustenance.
No man will lightly accept the loss of
His beloved wife, nor that of his sacred land.
It is said truly that man's destroying passions
Are the love of his wife and love of his land.

The Maori loved his land and identified with it. His close, spiritual relationship with the land stemmed from his traditional concept of the basic origin of mankind deriving from the loving union of the earthmother, Papa-tu-a-nuku, with the sky-father, Rangi-nui-tu-nei. The union was bountiful, and by a series of semi-evolutionary processes, the heavens were filled with their hosts of gods and attendant spirits. Eventually, the terrestrial world was populated by gods and myriads of vassal spirits and animate creatures.

The Maori of old accepted the responsibilities of his supernatural ancestry that made him guardian priest of the deities that controlled the relationships among the human, animal, vegetable, insect, reptile, fish, bird, mineral and spirit worlds. It was because of these ancestral and spiritual relationships that the Maori fished, hunted, and cultivated only to the degree necessary to secure his well-being. It was inconceivable for him to develop senseless exploitation of the environment to the degree required by the so-called civilised world. There were also opposing good and bad influences which had to be mastered, and due attention had to be paid to occult phenomena, astronomy and probably some form of astrology.

The great number of Maori place names that have survived commemorate a mass of long-remembered history, mythology and imagery that illustrates the close relationship maintained with the land. Every natural feature bore names that spanned long centuries of Maori occupation. The primeval ruptures of the landscape were named to identify the titanic feats of gods themselves. The dominant geological features recalled the strength of the supermen of old like Paoa, Rongokako and Rakaihautu. The long summer days with their hours of twilight at Murihiku and Rakiura were a daily tribute to the magic of Maui, the greatest demigod of all. The never-ending list of names remains a record of the passage of generations of men and women, identifying and preserving scenes of wars, stratagems, turmoil, peace, achievement and failure. They begin with birth itself and end in death, but always demonstrate the renewing cycle of life.

The land was regarded as the sacred trust and asset of people as a whole. Laws of tapu were invoked only to protect well-defined areas of land, lakes, rivers, waterways, or stretches of the seaside from human exploitation or defilement. Tapu would be applied for periods adequate to preserve or recover the sanctity of the soil or water. There were special cases when the presence of a burial ground, a malign taniwha, or some major infringement of a tapu, would result in the declaration of a specific area as a permanent wahi tapu, or sacred place. Each tribe would have its own sacred place where the mauri or talisman of the tribe was hidden, dating back to the arrival of the original tribal canoe from Hawaiki.

The great forests, Te Waonui o Tane, were nurtured as the principal source of food, medicine and timber for weapons, houses and ocean-going canoes. The giant totara grew tall, straight and wide in a slow-growing life span that was disturbed only by songs of the tui, kaka and bellbird in the day and the call of the owl and kiwi at night. The forests teemed with birds and insects, the trunks of the forest giants were laced with long creepers bursting into sprays of epiphytes, lichens draped themselves from the branches, and at their feet the forest carpet was rich with fern. The hills were hidden in a cover of never-ending green. Nowhere did the death of a tree leave a hillside scarred by erosion. At the edges of the forest the smaller hills were thick with fern. The root of the fern was gathered daily and was the most important staple. Others were cured berries from karaka groves, the kiore (rat) snared along the trails, the flesh of the pukeko from the edges of swamps, and the meat of weka flushed from shelter in shrubby grasslands.

Te Ika-a-Maui, the North Island, was aptly named. The fish lay stranded forever, its sides lapped by the ocean of Kiwa and its rugged surface covered with bush and grass kept verdant by rainfall. The swamps provided flax, eels and fish. The lakes, rivers and estuaries yielded fowl and more fish, and provided an important means of transport by canoe. The sandy stretches of beach harboured an abundance of shellfish, and sea food along the whole length of the coastline led to the proverbial reference to the basket of Tangaroa. The beds of pipi and tuatua all bore names, as did paua beds and mussel reefs. The enormous crayfish warrens, or rua koura, carried names and many were celebrated in history. The fishing grounds for the warehou, moki, tamure, maomao and hapuku were all known, and their sites fixed by carefully recording the tohu, or co-ordinating points.

The ancient Maori, in common with his Polynesian cousins, never progressed beyond Stone Age culture in terms of material development. But the skill and artistry achieved in wood and hard jade from West Coast rivers was comparable to the mastery displayed by the Chinese and the Central American Indians, who had the benefit of centuries of traditional carving and great advances in technology. The Maori worked a wide range of materials with stone and bone tools. The moa and the whale provided ivory for weapons and ornaments. Basalt around the eroded cones of long extinct volcanoes was selected for toughness and was fashioned into thousands of sinkers, drills and pounds. Superior pieces were made into beautiful but deadly patu onewa, or short hand clubs. Adzes of an infinite variety were fashioned from common greywacke. The argillite from D'Urville Island was the source of the distinctive hog-backed adzes of the moa hunters.

The most prized weapons, adzes and ornaments were made from jade. The sacred greenstone lurked in the waters of the Arahura and Teramakau Rivers, or spilled out of craggy cliffs high in the ranges beyond. The green and blue translucent tangiwai lay at the foot of the cliffs close to the headlands at Milford Sound, awaiting annual visits of Ngai Tahu craftsmen seeking the choicest specimens for their art. They had nothing but the most primitive of tools: sandstone, sand, water, pumice, shells and a simple wooden drill with a variety of stone drill points. But the world recognises the perfection in any well-made tiki that continues to defy the best of modern artisans.

The favoured cultivations, or mara, such as those perpetuated in the classical lullaby 'Popo', grew kumara crops for hundreds of years. Rongomaraeroa, the god of the cultivated foods, was a bountiful god to those who followed ancient rituals and traditions.

The mortal remains of countless generations of ancestors of the Maori were laid to rest in the bosom of the earth mother, secure in her sacred caves, sandhills and the other hidden places on tribal lands. There they remained to bind the glories of the past to the present. At the same time they presented their challenge to the tribe to maintain its integrity in the interests of generations to come.

Customary Title or Papa Tipu

The Maori system of land ownership worked in the best interests of the people and the land. The whole land mass was subdivided into distinct regions, with carefully defined borders occupied by individual tribes. The groupings of these regions were related to the areas chosen for settlement by the crews of the original canoes from Hawaiki.

It is convenient to regard the long period of settlement in two main epochs. The first was that of the pre-fleet period, and the second the fleet era. The pre-fleet settlers made their landfall somewhere between 500 and 800 A.D. Landings continued from Hawaiki, and possibly from other sources until 1350 A.D., the suggested time of arrival of the largest number of canoes with a common background in Hawaiki within the lifetime of a single generation.

The pre-fleet people discovered most of the natural resources of the country, laid the basis of land tenure, gave the countryside most place-names, and developed the basis of the material culture by exploiting mineral deposits. They left traces of their occupation through the land in caches of moahunter adzes from the North Cape to the Bluff. They formed tribes and sub-tribes and the land was divided into power groupings. This was important because later astute fleet leaders made early alliances with local chieftain classes, and in most cases succeeded in taking over the pre-fleet tribes completely and regrouping them according to dispersion from their own canoes. Many important Maori Land Court cases, where there were strong challenges to land rights of the fleet descendants, were finally won by taking the claims right back to original alliances with the pre-fleet occupants.

The ancient Maori held title to his land under a variety of headings.

Right of Discovery or Whenua Kite Hou

The first Maori arrivals established their claims to chosen areas by invoking rights of personal discovery and formal appropriation. The pattern of tribal dispersal based on lands settled and claimed by early navigators became apparent and the tribal boundaries clearly defined.

Every inch of New Zealand became subject to the claims of tribes and related hapus, with occasional instances of individual claims. Every block of land was named and carefully delineated by natural boundaries and topographical features. On occasion, stone or wooden markers (pou rahui) were used and protected by strict tapu. Every natural feature of the land bore names that spanned long centuries of occupation. The ability to recite long and complex lists of place-names enclosing the blocks, together with the traditional account of the food-gathering places, battles and fate of those who fought them on the land, the siting of the cemeteries and who lay in them, the genealogies of descent from the main tribal founders, the fate of internal disputes of ownership, all these were remembered by family leaders and passed from generation to generation. This knowledge was important, as customary title to every block of Maori land involved claims by right of descent and occupation.

Right of Occupation or Ahi Ka

If a Maori could prove land had been continuously occupied by successive and numerous generations of ancestors right down to himself, it was said he had kept his ancestral flame alive on the land. He had maintained his occupation against all comers and the successful dispersal of other claimants strengthened the ties. His title was that of the long burning fire, 'ahi ka roa'.

The longer the land remained in the undisturbed possession of the claimant, the stronger the claim. The Native Land Court established 1840 as the prime year for evidence of occupation. The evidence of undisturbed and exclusive use of cultivations or mara, as well as that of cemeteries or urupa, also confirmed rights of occupation. Similar rights were adduced from evidence recording the use of hunting and fishing grounds.

If a Maori left the district and neither he nor his descendants returned for at least three generations, the rights of occupation would be lost. If a woman left her fireside to marry outside the tribe it was said that her fire had become an unstable, or wandering one, 'ahi tere'. If she or her children returned, then the ancestral fire was regarded as rekindled. By this act the claim had been restored. If the fire not rekindled by grandchildren, then the claim was considered to have become cold or 'ahi mataotao'. If a person tried to revive some long lost and irretrievable claim that had been allowed to go cold he or she would be regarded as a 'mataotao'.

If a person came and squatted upon a piece of land without any title of occupation or ancestry, this occupation could convey no rights. This would be termed squatting, or 'kore take'.

Right of Conquest or Take Raupatu

Considerable areas of land could be won or lost in battle. This was not important on a national scale because tribal alliances would bring extra pressures into play if serious distortions were threatened as the result of some tribe or hapu having more than a modicum of success in battle.

Any claim to the ownership of land by conquest alone carried no real rights of ownership, unless succeeded by active secure occupation. If the battle was merely a skirmish carried out by a raiding party, which withdrew from the scene of victory, no permanent rights of ownership resulted.

Right of Gift or Take Tuku

Such claims were difficult to uphold unless the person making the gift was recognised as having the power to make it. The right to gift land was rarely made on an individual basis. Land might be gifted by a chief or a lesser person, but only in the interests, and with the consent and oversight, of the tribe or hapu.

Right of Deathbed Deposition or Take Ohaki

This claim was the same as that exercised under the claim by gift or 'take tuku', except that the gift was made by a person near death. The chief of a large tribe would often find he had several sons who would war together unless a fair allocation of the tribal land was made before his death. Some sons might have to leave the district and resume the interests they held from other antecedents, such as mothers or grandparents.

Law of Compensation for Misbehaviour or Muru

Any Maori who transgressed tribal law or tapu could be forcibly dispossessed of his land, canoes, valuables and food stores. No one was exempt, not even chiefs, and this law was often executed summarily and efficiently to punish acts of carelessness or disobedience, such as responsibility for the deaths of children by fire or drowning.

Customary Land or Whenua Tipu

Customary land is that which has never been put through a Maori Land Court to have the native title extinguished by sale to Europeans, or by transfer to European title. Today, Maori land held under customary title has all but disappeared from the New Zealand scene. The legal description of this class of land is in the Maori Affairs Act, 1953, and is defined there as land vested in the Crown, held by Maori or the descendants of Maori, under the customs and usages of the Maori people.

The Benefits of Customary Title

Maori customary title exerted a stabilising force on the ownership and use of land. The land could only be owned by those who actually lived on it. The land had to be physically occupied or worked by hunting, fishing or cropping, and all other claimants had to be resisted successfully. Those that let their fires become cold lost their rights permanently after a lapse of more than one or two generations. This strengthened ownership bonds among tribes and hapu who formed an integrated community ready to defend their lands. All members of such a community were ready to join in the communal activities necessary for the common good, such as hunting, cropping, cooking, weaving mats and clothes, as well as preparing and maintaining their fortified pa with adequate stores of food and water to guard against all contingencies.

There were no problems of absentee owners nor of excessive fragmentation of interests caused by overpopulation. The system worked admirably. There was no basis for its overthrow until a means of adaptation had been found that would be in tune with changing needs rather than the unbridled demands for land fostered by later European administrations.

The Introduction of Crown Title

So the whole country was held by tribes under customary title. The Treaty of Waitangi in 1840 was notable in that it confirmed customary title but immediately initiated action for destroying it in favour of the colonists' wants.

The first legal machinery set up to convert customary title to European title was direct purchase by Crown negotiation. Lieutenant-Governor William Hobson's massive purchases of land in Auckland for a mere pittance were the first indication of the English government's amoral sense of responsibility for the welfare of their newly acquired subjects. The failure of interested missionaries to give the Maori a true picture of the deeper implications of the treaty was equally reprehensible. The relaxation of Crown purchase by Governor Robert FitzRoy had disastrous effects, as butchers and speculators surged forward to rape the rest of the valuable land around Auckland.

Maori resistance to these speculative and profitable purchases by the Crown was soon aroused. Successive governors, however, were able to maintain the division among tribal leaders who were never given information revealing the true state of affairs, nor were they adequately appraised of the intentions of the colonists for total ownership of the land. The lack of communication among themselves and with the administration made Maori leaders easy victims. The governors bought off potential leaders with small annual grants and sinecures, and refused to promote any sort of political machinery which would enable the Maori to have an informed say in the development of the colony.

The eventual defeat of the Maori proved a more costly undertaking than that envisaged by the hawks from Taranaki and elsewhere, and unforeseen compromises were made which delayed the complete transfer of the country into European hands. It was eventually discovered that legal appropriation of Maori land was cheaper than fighting. Legislation was quickly implemented which neglected or over-rode safeguards written into the Maori version of the Treaty of Waitangi. Land purchase officers were sent into disaffected and loyal Maori districts and succeeded in bullying tribes into leasing or selling practically the whole of their heritage. The European lessees quickly set to work and by every unsavoury machination (including waving money and bottles at the more susceptible) succeeded in disrupting the tribal tenure of centuries. Legislation was bent in every possible way to facilitate rapid transfer of land to European applicants.

The situation became so acute that in 1929 the Department of Maori Affairs (then called Native Affairs) was forced to alter its chief function as a land purchase agency for Europeans to that of nominal trustee and developer of the few remaining acres of Maori land. Much of it was by then worthless residue and unfit for development.

The result is that today only a few pockets of customary land have escaped the vigilance of earlier land purchase officers, speculators and Maori claimants alike.

The last reliable figures available are in a report placed before the House of Parliament in 1919:

Papa tipu or customary lands left:	15,975	acres
Leased to Europeans:	3,103,812	
Held by Maori owners:	1,888,201	
	5,007,988	

Background to the Treaty of Waitangi

New Zealand may be regarded as the last important land mass to be subjected successfully to colonisation on the traditional European pattern.

By the 1830s British settlers were strongly entrenched in thriving colonies in the Americas, South Africa, Australia and Canada. The success of these colonies was built on ruthless exploitation and extermination of the indigenous inhabitants. Britain's methods differed little from the equally repressive methods employed by other great colonising powers, Spain, Holland, Portugal and France. In the 1830s a new factor had to be considered, however, because British humanitarianism and evangelical opinion was a force at home and abroad.

It is likely that Edward Gibbon Wakefield deferred to this force when he framed his own system of colonisation. He was mainly concerned to promote controlled settlement overseas by Europeans. But he broke new ground when he announced his novel and important concession to the interests of the Maori. A policy of tenths, he said, would form a valuable asset for the Maori, and would help to reclaim them from barbarism. The policy would reserve a balloted one-tenth of all land purchased by colonists for the indigenous inhabitants, to be governed by chiefs with official backing.

Wakefield had access to numerous accounts from missionaries, traders and travellers, as well as first-hand information offered to the House of Commons about the state of the aborigines of New Zealand. He must have known that such a warlike race as the Maori would not readily permit the introduction of a scheme which cut across their land usage customs and would disinherit the great majority to the advantage of the chieftain minority. The Maori were unlikely to rid themselves so quickly of the practices of centuries of occupation. They would not lightly suffer themselves to be removed from tribal holdings to such alien and tapu regions as they might receive by ballot.

New Theories

The terrible social conditions that existed in Britain in the mid-1830s created an ideal environment for Edward Gibbon Wakefield to air his new theories of colonisation. The New Zealand Association was formed in 1837 to obtain a charter from the Crown to colonise the country. The association attracted men of wealth and culture who were motivated by philanthropic principles as well as economic motives. If New Zealand were established as a British possession where the unemployed could find work and opportunity, then it was likely the country would attract a reasonable investment of British capital.

The colonial secretary, Lord Glenelg, offered the association a charter similar to those granted to the companies which had founded the 13 great colonies in America. But he made his proposition dependent upon the company forming itself into a joint-stock one with a fixed sum of subscribed capital. The company was opposed to the joint-stock company principle, holding that its motives were selfless and designed to promote the case for the colonisation of New Zealand.

It is strange that this association with its avowed humanitarian concern for the welfare of the Maori should run into very strenuous opposition from the strongholds of the humanitarian movement in England. The new humanitarianism was led by Quakers and Methodists. The Quakers believed in the fundamental equality of all men. The Evangelists, with Dandeson Coates as the permanent secretary of the London Missionary Society, were in close contact with missionaries in the field. The society declared itself in opposition to the association's colonisation in the interests of the Maori who were alleged to be making fair progress in religious improvement and civilisation, but whose lot could rapidly degenerate to the fate of other uncivilised peoples subjected to the processes of colonisation.

Even at this time a growing band of sealers, whalers, escaped convicts, traders, missionaries and farmers were actively establishing a pattern of settlement favoured by the Maori people in most areas, tolerated in others and suffered by those in smaller and more defenceless ones in the remoter parts of the South Island. By and large, the speed of progress was under the control of affected tribes and was largely in their interests.

Lord Glenelg and his permanent under-secretary, James Stephens, were convinced that as British settlers were already established in New Zealand, it was inevitable that colonisation would continue. Stephens believed extermination of the Maori would follow in the way it had in similar circumstances in other countries.

In 1838 the association became a company. Many of the idealistic philanthropists withdrew, but the required capital was subscribed. It was at this stage that the New Zealand Company lost its semi-philanthropic outlook and became a strictly commercial concern. The business of the company, promoting the organised settlement of New Zealand, was fully dependent on its ability to purchase land at a ridiculously low price from the Maori in New Zealand, then sell it for a 'fair' or high price in Britain. This was the accepted rationale for the existence of previous chartered companies. The New Zealand Company was no different. The rights of the indigenous people were of secondary consideration to those of shareholders and settlers, and the land was often sold in Britain before it had been purchased in New Zealand. Nor were there any adequate safeguards for the rights of the indigenous peoples whose lands and customs were being trampled on in the same old fashion of imperial colonisation.

It was at this juncture that the New Zealand Company was acutely embarrassed by the fall of Lord Glenelg. His successor, Lord Normanby, sent an official letter to the company dated 11 March 1839 in which he repudiated the promise of the charter. From this time the company received no further encouragement from the colonial secretary. Undaunted, the company pressed on with its plans, which were now altered to send agents to New Zealand and set up a system of government independent of the Crown. It is certain that they knew this was the only way to force the hand of government to intervene in New Zealand and ratify their ventures.

As soon as the colonial secretary knew the New Zealand Company was committed to such an irregular undertaking, he was forced to advise the following course of action:

- A consul would be established in New Zealand whose first duty would be to secure the cession of sovereignty from the chiefs;
- All territory so ceded would be annexed to the colony of New South Wales;
- The consul would then hold the rank of lieutenant-governor with the authority to preserve law and order within the country.

By this time the *Tory*, a clipper brig of some 400 tons, had left Plymouth on 12 May 1839. She was the pioneer ship of the New Zealand Company's fleet and carried a full cargo of trade goods with which Colonel William Wakefield ('Wideawake', as the Maori were later to call him) hoped to barter for extensive lands that would ensure the financial success of his company.

The New Zealand Company Makes Land Purchases

The *Tory* made its landfall at Queen Charlotte Sound on 17 August 1839. Within the space of three months Colonel Wakefield concluded negotiations for his three major land purchases in both islands on behalf of the New Zealand Company. The following is an extract from the deed of sale completed at Queen Charlotte Sound on 18 November 1938:

> Know all men, by these presents, that we the undersigned chiefs of Ngati Awa residing in Queen Charlotte Sound and other places on both sides of Cook Strait in New Zealand, have this day sold our rights, claims, titles and interest in all the lands, islands, tenements, woods, bays, harbours, rivers, streams and creeks within certain boundaries unto William Wakefield, Esq. in trust for the Governors, Directors and Shareholders of the New Zealand Land Company of London.

The boundaries of this remarkable deed took in the whole of the South Island above the 43rd degree south (which runs from Omihi across to Arthur's Pass, on to Whataroa and ends at Okarito on the West Coast, some 20 miles below Hokitika). They also took in all other lands on the northern shore of Cook Strait bounded on the north-east by a direct line drawn from the southern head of the river at Mokau . . .

> . . . and the New Zealand Company agrees that a portion of the land ceded to them, suitable and sufficient for the residence and proper maintenance of the said chiefs, their tribes and families, will be reserved by the said Governors of the New Zealand Company, and held in trust by them for the benefit of the said chiefs, their families, tribes and successors for ever.

A quantity of trade goods was set out as the principal inducement to the Maori to sell. But it is probable that the 31 muskets and supplies of gunpowder were the irresistible factor which clinched the transactions at Kapiti, Wellington, Wanganui, and later in Taranaki.

By some quirk of fate, Wakefield found the Ngati Awa at a time when they considered themselves in desperate need for guns. The old alliance of Ngati Awa with Ngati Toa and Ngati Raukawa under the volatile leadership of Te Rauparaha and Te Rangihaeata had long worn thin. And the constant and petty annoyances between them were being read as possible heralds of the onset of war. There was still a shortage of land and the expeditions led by Te Puoho and Te Whatanui into the South Island and Hawke's Bay had failed. Te Puni and Te Wharepouri, chiefs of Ngati Awa, saw Wakefield and his people as a bulwark to defend the remnants of their tribal land.

If Colonel Wakefield's purchases at Wellington, Wanganui and elsewhere are seen to have been irregular, it must be conceded that the European colonists of his era had been conditioned by centuries of experience to accept such acts as necessary prerequisites for successful colonisation.

Hobson's Instructions

When Captain Hobson left England in the HMS *Druid* he was armed with a series of instructions from colonial secretary Lord Normanby. The imperial policy so meticulously outlined in these instructions exemplified the best of contemporary humanitarianism, which was a great advance on previous attitudes to indigenous peoples. The following extracts are indicative of the humanitarian policy soon to be swamped by the commercial policy of the businessmen of London:

The increase in national wealth and power promised by the acquisition of New Zealand would be a most inadequate compensation for the injury which must be inflicted on this kingdom itself by embarking in a measure essentially unjust, and too fraught with calamity to a numerous and inoffensive people whose title to the soil, and to the sovereignty of New Zealand is indisputable . . .

It further appears that extensive cessions of land have been obtained from the natives, and that several hundred persons have recently sailed from this country to occupy and cultivate those lands . . . it can no longer be doubted that an extensive settlement of British subjects will be rapidly established in New Zealand, and that unless protected and restrained by the necessary institutions, they will repeat unchecked in that quarter of the globe the same process of war and spoilation under which uncivilised tribes have almost unvariably disappeared.

. . . The Queen . . . disclaims for herself and her subjects every pretension to seize on the Islands of New Zealand, or to govern them as a part of the Dominions of Great Britain unless the free intelligent consent of the natives, expressed according to their established usages, shall first be obtained.

. . . The chiefs should be included, if possible, to contract with you . . . that henceforth no lands shall be ceded, either gratuitously or otherwise, except to the Crown of Great Britain.

Hobson Lands and Prepares the Treaty

Captain Hobson landed in Sydney, late in December 1839. He was quite happy to meet the deputation of New Zealand landholders who wasted no time waiting on him. He encouraged them to occupy their lands and proceed with improvements.

The governor of New South Wales, Sir George Gipps, made no secret of his aversion to the activities of local merchant speculators in New Zealand and on 15 January 1840 he issued three proclamations which extended the boundaries of New South Wales to New Zealand, proclaimed Captain Hobson Lieutenant-Governor of New Zealand and called upon all British subjects to aid and assist him, and put an end to the speculation in New Zealand lands being carried on in Sydney.

The *Herald*, a frigate of 20 guns, brought Hudson to New Zealand, and on the morning of 29 January entered the Bay of Islands. As soon as the *Herald* lay at anchor she was boarded by Mr James Busby (British resident) and three missionaries. Mr William Colenso was given the task of printing on the Church Missionary Society press a number of circular letters to the chiefs, inviting them to meet Captain Hobson at Mr Busby's residence at Waitangi, and informing them that he had been sent by the Queen of England to be governor of New Zealand.

The same afternoon Hobson, accompanied by Captain Nias and the *Herald*'s officers, landed on Kororareka beach and walked to the church where he read his Letters Patent to the gathering. He then read out Sir George Gipps' proclamations. British subjects were now subject to the Crown and no land claims in New Zealand would become valid unless ratified by a grant from the Crown.

The invitation received by Tamati Waka Nene is preserved in the Auckland Museum and the following text comes from it:

> . . . Tenei ano taku ki a koe; na, tenei ano tetahi kaipuke manawa kua u mai nei, me tetahi Rangatira ano kei runga, no te Kuini o Ingarani ia, hei Kawana hoki mo tatou.

> This is another letter to you. A Man-o-War has arrived here, bearing on board a chief who has been sent by the Queen of England to be a governor for us.

The resident magistrate, Busby, was comfortably settled in New Zealand, and involved in massive land claims. He and CMS missionary Henry Williams, were the two men the Maori were most dependent on for a realistic interpretation of the benefits and disadvantages of the Treaty of Waitangi. They were both out of favour with the vigorous New Zealand Company and their backers in the British Government. Their standing was no better with the Sydney merchants who glibly claimed most of the country on the basis of paltry cash sums paid to odd Maori visiting their city.

Williams and Busby understood better than most the implications of the Treaty. They knew that only the Crown of England could confirm titles to their land claims. It should have been axiomatic that the Church and the servants of the state should never have been given the liberty to become involved in land dealings with primitive peoples. The question of self-interest should never have intruded, no matter how remotely, into the decisions of advisers. With Busby and Williams, self-interest was certainly a factor.

They were well informed about the unsettled political position back home in England, where the sympathetic stand taken by Normanby could easily be reversed by another Lord John Russell. They alone knew the contents of Normanby's instructions to Hobson. They knew the attitude of previous governors of New South Wales to what the governors were pleased to call 'the non-existent' rights of savages to their native lands, and that the governor of New South Wales would have precedence over Hobson so long as he was merely a lieutenant-governor. They knew also that it was proposed to subject all land purchases to an investigation by a special land commissioner, and further, that all purchases in excess of 2,640 acres would probably be denied them or vested in the Crown. In their case, such an investigation under a friendly governor might prove less traumatic. There was even the possibility that a benevolent governor might make large tracts of the best land available to them by way of grants or cheap purchases. It would appear that the rights of the Maori to their land were more in jeopardy than those of Europeans friendly to the new establishment.

There were many other imponderables. They knew there would be a contest for power by the growing settlements around Wellington, where local leaders would be seeking influence to the advantage of the New Zealand Company. There was always the possibility that Hobson could come under the domination of the company. Williams had seen the vast disruption of Maori society in the Cook Strait regions as the tribes there retreated or contracted before the advance of the grand plan of settlement of the New Zealand Company.

No one knew better than Busby and Williams the true order of Maori aspirations about the rate and final extent of European settlement: the Maori were anxious to promote the increase of European settlement, but only at a rate they could contain without risk of domination or subjugation. They were committed to friendship and they had already established a system of intermarriage. They had not been granted enough time to free themselves from their dependence on missionaries for their schools and religious indoctrination. They were anxious for the trade and technological training introduced by Marsden's guests in Sydney, some had travelled the world with the whalers, and there was an awareness of the benefits of prosperity based on peace, trade and cultural development. They had become accustomed to trading in land, but only the chiefs and people of the Ngati Awa, Toa and Raukawa tribes about Wellington had begun to feel the effects of dispossession resulting from massive land-sharking by the New Zealand Company.

The Maori in 1840 was ready for the benefits of the white man's civilisation, but he was ill-equipped for survival in direct competition with the settlers who now had the might of Britain behind them. The Maori needed a king, but the genius of Hongi and Te Rauparaha was for destruction without the saving grace of unity as an eventual objective. The lack of unity and inter-tribal communication were well understood by Hobson, who was prepared to undertake the piecemeal pacification of the country. The Maori divisiveness was the factor that loomed large in his calculations, and he knew time was on his side.

There is very little evidence of the manner in which Maori leaders of the day assessed their situation. But the fact that they seemed prepared to take the advice of Williams and Busby indicates that they were given scant time and little real information upon which to base a useful evaluation. The accounts handed down to us show a complete lack of appreciation of the real issues behind the signing of the Treaty of Waitangi.

The Treaty is Drafted and Translated

Hobson's ill health left him dependent principally upon Busby and Williams to complete his own draft of the projected treaty. The names J.R. Clendon and the Reverends A. Brown and R. Taylor were also involved. Busby completed his task by revising all that he thought might arouse Maori opposition in the original draft by Hobson. His efforts were complemented by the Williams translation, which omitted from the Maori text any further material that might still upset the chiefs. The result was an almost incomprehensible rendition of the important passages and, even more important, quite misleading versions of key phrases. The poor standard of printing by the Paihia press served only to aggravate the position.

The following is a reproduction of the English and Maori texts of the Preamble:

> Her Majesty Victoria, Queen of the United Kingdom of Great Britain and Ireland, regarding with her Royal favour the Native chiefs and tribes in New Zealand, and anxious to protect their just rights and property, and to secure to them the enjoyment of peace and good order, has deemed it necessary in consequence of the great numbers of Her Majesty's subjects who have already settled in New Zealand, and the rapid extension of emigration both from Europe and Australia which is still in progress, to constitute and appoint a functionary properly authorised to treat with the aborigines of New Zealand for the recognition of Her Majesty's sovereign authority over the whole or any part of these islands.

> Her Majesty, therefore, being desirous to establish a settled form of Civil Government with a view to avert the evil consequences which must result from the absence of the necessary laws and institutions, alike to the native population and to her subjects, has been graciously pleased to empower and authorise me, William Hobson, a Captain in Her Majesty's Royal Navy, Consul and Lieutenant-Governor of such parts of New Zealand as maybe, or hereafter shall be ceded to Her Majesty, to invite the confederate and independent chiefs of New Zealand to concur in the following articles and conditions.

> Ko, Wikitoria, te Kuini o Ingarani i tana mahara atawai ki nga Rangatira me nga hapu, o Nu Tirani, i tana hiahia hoki kia tohungia ki a ratou o ratou rangatiratanga, me to ratou whenua, a kia mau tonu hoki te Rongo ki a ratou me te ata noho hoki kau [kua] wakaaro ia he mea tike [tika] kia tukua mai tetahi Rangatira hei kai wakarite ki nga tangata Maori o Nu Tirani. Kia wakaaetia e nga Rangatira Maori te Kawanatanga o te Kuini ki nga wahi katoa o te wenua hei [nei] me nga motu. Na te mea hoki he tokomaha ke nga

tangata o tona iwi kua noho ki tenei wenua, a e haere mai nei.

Na, ko te Kuini e hiahia ana kia wakaritea te Kawangatanga, kia kaua ai nga kino e puta mai ki te tangata Maori ki te Pakeha e noho ture kore ana. Na, kau [kua] pai te Kuini kia tukua a hau [ahau] a Wiremu Hopihona, he Kapitana i te Roiara Nawi, hei Kawana mo nga wahi katoa o Nu Tirani, e tukua aianei amua atu ki te Kuini e mea atu ana ia ki nga Rangatira o te wakaminenga o nga hapu o Nu Tirani me era Rangatira atu enei ture ka korerotia nei.

Apart from the oversimplification and abbreviation of the English text in the Maori translation, as well as numerous printing errors, the preamble is most remarkable for what it does not say and the major obligations it avoids so adroitly. Hobson felt he had to strike while the iron was hot and was given every help by the missionaries. The Maori were novices, babes in the woods, when it came to matching the diplomatic genius of the English.

All they had to do was to sit on the fence and bargain with Hobson for such things that would have been the natural objective of less naive people: first, an equal share of legislative control; second, an equal share in the profits accruing from the sale of lands to be spent in furthering Maori education, health and technology; third, an equal say in the policy of land purchases on behalf of the new colony; fourth, the creation of European spheres of interest and Maori spheres under the common legislature subject to the governor, and retention of Maori language, land and customs in the tribal regions; with the final objective of ultimate amalgamation in one bicultural society. Hobson and the missionaries would probably have attempted the old and tried ploy of dividing the loyalties of the Maori. But the structure, once erected, would have been hard to destroy by constitutional means.

The Maori lost their one and only chance of constitutional equality by frittering away their meetings discussing red herring bait instead of getting down to the real business of the day: getting together and taking a real part in the structuring of a New Zealand legislature.

First Article of the Treaty

The chiefs of the Confederation of the united tribes of New Zealand, and the separate and independent chiefs who have not become members of the Confederation, cede to Her Majesty the Queen of England, absolutely and without reservation, all the rights and powers of sovereignty which the said confederation or individual chiefs, respectively exercise or possess, or may be supposed to exercise, over their respective territories as the sole sovereigns thereof.

Ko nga Rangatira o te Wakaminenga, nga Rangatira katoa hoki, kihai i uru ki taua Wakaminenga, ka tuku rawa atu ki te Kuini o Ingarani ake tonu atu te Kawangatanga katoa o o ratou wenua.

The precise translation back into English of the Maori interpretation of the First Article provides an excellent example of the devices employed to deceive Maori about the intent of the Crown challenge to their traditional rights to so-called waste lands, once there was a legal basis to supplant the authority of chiefs. The challenge is seen in the phrase: 'or be supposed to exercise'.

Such a translation would read:

> The chiefs of the Confederation, and the rest of all the chiefs as well who have not become members of the Confederation have truly given to the Queen of England forever the governorship over all of their lands.

Second Article

> Her Majesty, the Queen of England, confirms and guarantees to the chiefs and tribes of New Zealand, and to the respective families and individuals thereof, the full, exclusive, and undisturbed possession of their properties which they may collectively or individually possess, so long as it is their wish to retain the same in their possession; but the chiefs of the united tribes and the individual chiefs yield to Her Majesty the exclusive right of pre-emption over such lands as the proprietors thereof may be disposed to alienate, at such prices as may be agreed upon between the respective proprietors and persons appointed by Her Majesty to treat with them in that behalf.

> Ko te Kuini o Ingarani ka wakarite ka wakaae ki nga Rangitira, ki nga hapu, ki nga tangata katoa o Nu Tirani, te tino me o ratou taonga katoa.

> Literal translation: The Queen of England accepts the principle that the chiefs, sub-tribes and all the inhabitants of New Zealand shall exercise complete dominion over all their lands, houses and goods.

> Otiia ko nga Rangatira o te Wakaminenga me nga Rangitira katoa atu, ka tuku ki te Kuini te hokonga o era wahi wenua e pai ai te tangata nona te wenua, ki te ritenga o te utu e wakaritea ai e ratou ko te kai hoko e meatia nei e te Kuini hei kai hoko mona.

> Literal translation: However the chiefs of the Confederation and the rest of the chiefs, give to the Queen the right to buy those lands

they are happy to sell, and the price shall be arranged between them and a land purchase officer appointed by the Queen.

The inadequacies of the Maori interpretation cannot be construed as other than deliberate. This version had the effect of lulling Maori into a false sense of security because it emphasised security of tenure for their lands, houses and goods. There are several other semi-official translations of the Treaty which mention fisheries as another sacrosanct reserve, and no doubt the Maori read this into the Treaty too. But he was to find he was very much mistaken in this as in other rights he fondly imagined were preserved.

The extreme brevity of the Maori version would arouse suspicions in the minds of a more sophisticated people. But these were effectively smoothed over by the missionaries. The use of the word 'Rangatiratanga' in the Maori sense implied a degree of retention of administrative control on the part of the Maori of their lands. But what it amounted to was official neglect of Maori welfare until such time as the Crown was in a position to undertake purchase of more Maori land for the settlers.

The second half of the Second Article in English defines clearly the principle of pre-emption. But the all-important element of compulsion is side-stepped in the Maori version. Any hint of a total embargo on land sales to anyone other than the Crown would have rapidly alienated the chiefs and so this was carefully omitted. It is true that the Maori would have found himself swamped with advice from all sides of the spectrum of interest, disinterest and self-interest. The short time of debate left the Maori with little recourse but to depend upon the advice of those who seemed to be most dependable. They were soon to learn the double standards of the new society.

Third Article

In consideration thereof Her Majesty, the Queen of England, extends to the natives of New Zealand her Royal protection, and imparts to them all the rights and privileges of British subjects.

Hei wakaritenga mai hoki tenei mo te wakaaetanga ki te Kawanatanga o te Kuini. Ka tiakina e te Kuini o Ingarani nga tangata Maori katoa o Nu Tirani. Kua tukua ki a ratou nga tikanga katoa rite tahi ki ana mea ki nga tangata o Ingarani.

Literal translation: In fulfilment hereof of the agreement to accept the sovereignty of the Queen, the Queen will take care of all the Maori people of New Zealand. She extends to them the same rights and privileges enjoyed by Englishmen.

These were rare and fine words which granted full British citizenship to the Maori. They were not worth the paper they were written on for many many years. Hobson knew full well there was no way of honouring them in the foreseeable future. At that very time, the New Zealand Company (both at Port Nicholson and in the British Parliament) was gathering support for legislation that would negate the promises to respect Maori land interests and to deny effective citizenship to the Maori until they ceased to be an effective force in their own land. Imperialism thrived on broken promises and New Zealand was no exception. The Maori joined the ranks of the Empire's millions of second-class citizens. They had the use of the courts in which to be tried for crimes. The same courts rapidly divested them of their lands. They paid a large share of the taxes and received a pittance for their own welfare. They could fight for the Crown, but they were to be denied the right to vote for nearly 30 years.

Results

A review of the negative benefits to the Maori of the right of pre-emption is instructive. Maori who were induced to sell land to the Crown soon found the strict monopoly had greatly depressed the price of their land. They would only be paid a ridiculous fraction of the true market value. The Crown would then resell the land at infinitely greater prices to willing settlers, who would then resell it themselves for even greater prices. They were aware that the government was almost entirely dependent upon this source of revenue for its existence.

Hobson's first choice of a site for his new capital was the Bay of Islands. He paid £15,000 for it, but soon had to abandon it as unsuitable. He accepted the advice of Williams and moved his capital to Auckland, purchasing that magnificent site for goods and money worth a trifling sum. The Maori believed they were in for a great boom in the value of their waste lands. But Hobson's purchases rapidly disillusioned them. It was the governor who profited from the land boom, not the Maori vendors, who rapidly found their lands shrinking and slipping from their grasp. In 1841 the government sold by auction some 44 acres which fetched £24,275. Some months later £7/10/- a foot was being paid for choice city frontages. The situation was only a little better when Governor Robert FitzRoy later revoked the pre-emptive clause and opened the remaining lands around the city to the rapacity of business and tradesmen. In one stroke of the pen he created the basis of the fortunes of many established merchant families and pushed local Maori into fringe ghettos on the outskirts of the town.

The validity of land purchases was subjected by Hobson to investigation by the first commissioner of land claims, Mr William Spain, who had received his appointment from Lord John Russell, now colonial secretary in London.

Mr Spain and his 'Sub-Protector of Aborigines' exposed many irregularities in the procurement of deeds of sale by agents of the New Zealand Company. But they did little else about them. The court took on the appearance of a 'kangaroo' one as the commissioner was content to confirm irregular purchases, with the equally irregular contingency added that token awards should be made to native owners who were either absent at the time of sales or had refused to participate in them.

The appointment of Mr Spain did nothing to lessen the difficulties of the Maori. There was no regard for the true value of the land, no provision of adequate reserves for the tribes, and considerable disturbance of their traditional way of life. The powers of the court were further abused in that owners who were objectors to the inclusion of their lands in sales were literally forced to accept minimal-sized reserves and trifling cash payments in compensation. Continual pressure was exerted by colonists to have Maori settlements destroyed (with eventual success around the Wellington city and Ngauranga areas).

The system of tenths was allowed to lapse as soon as the New Zealand Company saw it need not be held by a complaisant governor to its original undertaking. However the Ngai Tahu were divested by Govenor Grey through the New Zealand Company of some three million acres of reserves when oral promises to honour the system of reserving a tenth of the land sold, in perpetuity, for Maori vendors, were not written into the deeds of purchase.

There is an endless repetition of similar events in both islands which establish not only the lack of protection offered the Maori in the Treaty, but the immediate intent to operate the administrative powers conveyed in the Treaty to the absolute detriment of the Maori people.

Nor is there any doubt that Hobson and the missionaries fully understood the implications of the obligations inherent in the proper observance of the Treaty. There is little evidence that there was any great intent to honour them to the letter and it appears that the whole affair was merely one of a customary expedient used to secure a legal foothold in the country, which would then be opened up for exploitation.

The principal factor was the settlers' limitless greed for cheap Maori land which inevitably brought about reaction and war. The Maori were both losers and the winners. They emerged unscathed morally, depressed materially, but still resilient enough to make slow progress. The odds are that the Maori renaissance in population, education, cultural development and material progress over the next 20 years will be felt throughout the whole of the land and will create a kind of reverse culture shock.

Passages from the Treaty of Waitangi reproduced by permission of New Zealand National Archives.

LAND SINCE THE TREATY

DOUGLAS SINCLAIR

WHEN THE FIRST NEW ZEALAND COMPANY SETTLERS arrived at Port Nicholson in 1840 they were a chosen band of men and women, well equipped and fully prepared to face the challenge of life in an alien but bountiful homeland. They were determined to succeed, but confident that the culture, institutions, and power of the British Empire must prevail over their Maori adversaries. They were determined to gain control of land, ruthless in their dealings with those who opposed them, critical of those who were not for them, and quite ready to set aside their allegiance to the Crown, if by doing so they would be better able to get on with the business of good colonisation and settlement of the vast spaces that awaited them. Most important of all, they were well led.

The success of Lieutenant-Governor Hobson in securing the cession of the Treaty of Waitangi was a great disappointment to the settlers and they did not trouble to disguise their opposition to the Second Article which affirmed the Maori title to lands until such time as they were willing to sell. They knew that Colonial Secretary Lord Normanby had the New Zealand Company in mind when he instructed Hobson to secure the right of purchase of all Maori land for the Crown alone. This meant they would not be able to deal directly with Maori for the sale or lease of land. They would have to wait until the Crown purchased it and then bid for it at special auctions. At the very least, there would be a minimum price they would be forced to pay the governor. Worse still, all the lands claimed to have been purchased before 1840 would have to be subjected to a special land claim. This meant none of the settlers would gain a legal title to the land they had purchased in good faith from the company until that company's massive claims of some 20 million acres had been scrutinised and approved by the special Land Court to be set up by Land Commissioner William Spain in 1842.

Hobson moved quickly to allay any fears they might have had. The settlers were to be allowed to continue in possession of land that they held and that was not the subject of dispute by native claimants. The company was not to occupy any further land until titles had been resolved. Reserves had been made for the natives, and cash compensation paid wherever required. In the meantime the rights of the natives to their unsold lands, their gardens, and their cemeteries had to be respected. As for the Maori, they were anxious to see Europeans settle amongst them, they freely acknowledged certain areas as sold, and they were content to see the settlers remain on agreed lands, having every confidence in the decision to be given by Mr Spain.

One major change had taken place, however. Hobson had been appointed by the humanitarian Lord Normanby, under whose instructions the Treaty had been drafted, and he had openly displayed his intentions to see the provisions of the Second Article honoured. He had allowed the settlers to remain on all the undisputed lands only while they awaited the outcome of the Land Claims Court of Mr Spain. The eclipse of Normanby's government in 1840 brought important friends of the company to power. Lord John Russell, new secretary of state for the colonies, was quick to award the New Zealand Company a Royal Charter of Colonisation and, more important, he made a huge grant of land to the company on the basis of the expenditure they had incurred in actual colonisation, about £200,000. The company was authorised to select this land from any situation within the area of their unproved claims.

Hobson was quite unequal to the new situation. He weakly offered land around Auckland for the new settlement that Russell had sanctioned, but Wakefield might as well have been governor himself. The new batch of settlers were sent to Nelson and Hobson was invited to shift his capital to Wellington. Hobson refused but bowed to superiors at home, and buried his principles. He withdrew to Auckland, and offered no serious opposition to the company. He died in Auckland on 10 September 1842.

Colonel William Wakefield was well aware that his purchases were the subject of dispute by the Maori in many areas, the more important being at Wairau, the Hutt, Porirua, Wanganui and Taranaki. His immediate problem lay with the fertile plains at Wairau where his purchase was strongly contested by Te Rauparaha and Te Rangihaeata. He felt he had the measure of the two chiefs and was inclined to push the issue to a conclusion. The decision to do so was a rash one. He had merely to wait an extra month or two and doubtless the decision of the land commissioner would have gone in his favour. It is possible he thought his claim would be improved if he could prove settlers were in occupancy. The rationalisation was that the chiefs would be readily appeased by a token cash compensation and the provision of a few small reserves.

Wakefield committed himself to offensive action. He sent his surveyors into the Wairau with the inevitable result that they were obstructed in their work and their hut burned at the order of the two chiefs. Wakefield had obtained his excuse for action. He procured a writ for arson from the police magistrate at Nelson and set out with 30 men armed with company guns to arrest Te Rauparaha. The old chief was found at Tuamarina, but he was not overawed by the show of force and refused to be arrested. Thompson endeavoured to execute his warrant, but a mêlée ensued, a chieftainess was shot down and the scuffle became a massacre. Colonel Wakefield, the magistrate and 20 others died. The rest escaped to Nelson.

This encounter was a curtain-raiser to the troubles the Maori had brought upon themselves by allowing themselves to be rushed into signing a treaty with a foreign power that used treaties as instruments to assume sovereignty and eventually further the interests of their own commercial and military development. The Treaty was not an instrument of security for the Maori but one for the security of the settlers.

Trouble in the Hutt

The settler-Maori disputes in the Hutt Valley arose from the fact that when Colonel Wakefield purchased the whole of Port Nicholson harbour and the surrounding lands from Ngati Awa chiefs Te Wharepouri, Te Puni and Ngatata, he did not mind that they did not own most of the land nominated. He had been appraised of the true status of the land by whalers in Queen Charlotte Sound. But he was confident of his ability to meet the challenges of the proper owners at a more convenient time. The land in the Hutt Valley belonged by right of conquest to Te Rauparaha and Te Rangihaeata along with Ngati Rangatahi of Wanganui who had built up strong rights of occupation.

Wakefield attempted to open the area for settlement. Attempts were made to get the Maori to surrender their lands in return for a small cash compensation and move outside the company's area of occupation. The pressure exerted by the company on Ngati Tama at Kaiwharawhara had finally caused their chief Taringa Kuri to accept Ngati Rangatahi's invitation to share their land in the Hutt. This additional influx increased the risks of racial conflict, arousing the feelings of the settlers who were grimly awaiting the day they could safely assume control of 'their' land.

Hobson had made an attempt to preserve the rights of the Maori provided for in his treaty, but gave way to Wakefield's claim that the guarantees were no longer acceptable in the light of the new powers vested in the company by the British government. He agreed the Crown should waive its right of pre-emption to certain lands for which the company would receive grants on the basis of valid purchases. The change in attitude made the company's victory complete, and a further concession was wrung from Hobson (September 1841) that he would permit the company to induce the natives who lived within the limits of the claims to move elsewhere.

The title to the Hutt Valley was decided by Mr Spain in April 1843, the court having begun its work in May 1842. The rights of Ngati Rangatahi were disregarded, except for the doubtful privilege of their being allowed to plant and harvest a final year's crops, after which they would be required to leave the Hutt. Te Rauparaha was a party to this agreement, but Te Rangihaeata was opposed to the dispossession of his old ally. The fate of Taringa Kuri affected Te Rauparaha because of his old alliance with Ngati Tama. The situation was at a stalemate when Governor George Grey appeared on the scene in 1845. He overrode Governor FitzRoy's award of pa and gardens and the old ploy of offering minimal compensation cash grants. Governor Grey was a determined man. He declared martial law and ordered the Maori out of the valley. The Maori evacuated the valley in mid-February 1846, and the settlers moved in behind them, only to find the Maori had moved into the surrounding hills and were reappearing on the land. Grey's troops looted and burned the deserted pa and ravaged the burial grounds.

The Wellington area was brought under lawful control by Grey within a reasonably short time. Ngati Rangatahi had fled to Te Rangihaeata's pa at Pauatahanui, but this was abandoned after Grey took Te Rauparaha prisoner by stealth in the early dawn from his pa. Grey had already built a military road from Wellington to Porirua, and Te Rangihaeata was attacked, pursued, and forced to find refuge in difficult swampy country near Levin. Te Rangihaeata made his peace the following year with the governor at Otaki. Te Rauparaha did not survive his imprisonment long. It is worth noting that no charges were ever brought against him.

Taranaki: The Beginning of the End

When the settlers took their places in the first full legislature, the new General Assembly, in May 1854 they found they had to raise money to pay for land claims of the New Zealand Company amounting to £200,000 and £180,000 to be used for the purchase of native lands. By this time large-scale purchases by Grey had exhausted the supply of lands held by weaker tribes which had been fair game for appropriation. These tribes were beginning to link together in self defence to protect their remaining lands. The Land Purchase Department had been forced to follow the traditional Maori custom of communal rights to land. This meant no Maori could sell his own individual piece. It was impossible for a block of land to be sold piecemeal without the consent of the whole of the owners. Finally, the completion of the sale hinged upon the will of the tribal chief who could (and often did) veto a proposed sale. It is apparent that many sales were transacted with little regard for this custom or for the rights of absent owners. But Chief Land Commissioner Donald McLean and Judge Fenton were ready to make more of the difficulties than the advantages of this system. In 1858 they were determined to exploit a new method of land purchase that would destroy the traditional right of veto and thereby unlock the waiting millions of acres for European exploitation.

In 1858 Governor Thomas Gore Browne, the Native Minister C.W. Richmond, and Mr McLean met chiefs at Waitara. In the face of the opposition of the principal chief Wiremu Kingi and the tribal council, the governor accepted the offer of land by the sub-chief Teira. The government planned to push the Maori past the limits of endurance into open rebellion and did all they could to force the Maori to a war in which there could be but one ending. Teira was paid £100 in November 1859 and on 20 February 1860 surveyors were sent on to the Waitara block, where they were obstructed by women. In the middle of March, however, the first shots of the so-called Maori War were fired from British guns. The government had built up their forces to the necessary strength and they had found an appropriate case on which to base a final military solution to the problem of limited access to Maori land.

The military situation at Waitara was allowed to drift into a series of skirmishes at Mahoetahi, Matarikoriko and Huirangi, relieved by several sharp reverses inflicted from Waikato. Ultimatums were sent to the Taranaki chiefs offering peace on the condition that they accepted the principle of the individualisation of land titles, and the Waikato were asked to give up the King Movement (which they had formed to protect their land and identity) and allow roads to be built through their lands. The penalty for non-compliance was to be the forfeiture of their lands.

The stage was set for the return of Sir George Grey. He offered peace and a comprehensive system of self-government for the Maori while he carefully set his military force into the most favourable dispositions to attack. When the troops did move, the outcome was in no doubt. The immediate prize of war was several millions of acres of land confiscated under the New Zealand Settlements Bill, which approved the confiscation of the whole of any district where considerable numbers of natives were believed to be in rebellion. The accompanying Suppression of Rebellion Bill enabled suspect rebels to be detained without trial and killed if necessary without the need for a proclamation of martial law.

Under the confiscation scheme, some 1,202,172 acres were taken initially from Waikato. This comprised the fertile lands between the Waikato and Waipa rivers. Some 314,262 acres were subsequently returned, but very little was to survive the rapacity of the land purchase agents and speculators. The same pattern followed in Taranaki where 1,275,000 acres were confiscated, of which 256,000 acres were returned and 557,000 purchased. Some 290,000 acres were confiscated at Tauranga, and even though 244,000 acres were returned, most were quickly resumed by land purchase agents. At Opotiki, a total of 448,000 acres was taken and 230,600 acres returned. Further confiscations extended to the Gisborne and Wairoa districts.

The importance of the confiscations was that vast areas of lightly occupied and desirable Maori land were opened to European settlement, leaving only the less fertile areas as places where the old form of Maori life could continue to survive. It did not really matter how much land was returned to the Maori because they were all reclaimed by the land purchase agents who were able to bully every tribe into submitting to their demands. The activities of the land purchase officers were so successful that one wonders why the settlers should have resorted to an expensive war which laid the basis of our national debt.

Hawke's Bay and the Wairarapa contain some of the best grazing land in the country and it was here that Donald McLean made his name as a land purchase officer and proud possessor of one of the finest estates in the country, which he called Maraekakaho. The first block purchased by him was the Ahuriri block which extended from the Tutaekuri River mouth, inland to the upper Mohaka and on to Titiokura, the summit of the ranges. The price: £1000. The first Waipukurau block was acquired on the same day, 4 November 1851, for the sum of £1800.

Governor Grey travelled throughout the Ngati Kahungunu territory of Hawke's Bay and the Wairarapa in 1853, exerting his personal influence on the people there. The Hon. J.D. Ormond, M.P. accompanied McLean and the governor. He described the expedition as a procession from Lake Wairarapa to Napier along which the Maori made arrangements to sell their lands. The official party was accompanied by an accountant with two packhorses carrying a large sum of gold and silver as payment for the purchases. Squatters met on the way were illegally renting their lands from the Maori. The chiefs were actually receiving more in rents from the squatters than they were to receive in final payment from the governor, who glibly told them of the great advantages that would come from the increase in settlement, and the value that eventual transfer of their remaining lands to Crown title would confer.

Grey was pursuing his policy of buying in advance of European settlement. It had the effect of increasing prices of land. Over half a million acres were sold in the Wairarapa on this occasion. McLean, Ormond and some fifty or so other landholders (who were known to the Maori as the Forty Thieves) had possession of nearly four million acres of land. There is no wonder that there was disaffection among the Hawke's Bay Maori because of rapacious purchasing led by the governor himself. James Cowan dutifully records the depth and extent of McLean's activities in his spheres of land purchase agent, Maori expert and Native Minister in the House. Cowan did not dwell on the fact that the official record of the department's land purchase activities (the Maori Deeds of Land Purchases in the North Island of New Zealand, ed. H.H. Turton, 2 vols., Wellington, 1877-8) was never released to the public because of the fear that the purchases would become the subject of acrimonious dispute. Perhaps the real merit of the policy of manipulative purchasing, confiscation and cultural suppression was best seen in the halcyon days before the turn of the century when land holdings of the members of both houses of the legislature amounted to several millions of acres.

The Land Court Blow

The only unbroken promise in the Treaty of Waitangi was that the Queen would assume the sovereignty of New Zealand. That same sovereignty was used most effectively to destroy the promises of equality and security. The principal vehicle for the suppression of Maori potential was the manipulation of the law, beginning with the weaknesses and evasion inherent in the Treaty itself. This evasive element was expanded in the Land Claims Ordinance (No. 1 1841) which constituted the whole land of the colony as the demesne of the Crown, subject to certain rights (or uncertain rights) of the natives. This meant that the normal privileges of the Crown would obtain the whole of the land, but would have to yield to customary title and usages in areas which were then quite well known.

If the authorities were unwilling to concede these areas, they were also quite unable to resist the Crown's appetite for the rivers, lakes, estuaries, sea coast, fishing grounds, and the Maori definition of 'mahinga kai' which included not only fixed works like gardens, eel weirs, fishing easements, but also the karaka groves, fern root gathering places, weka, pigeon and rat hunting and preserves, mutton bird islands, shellfish and deep sea and coastal fishing grounds.

The first blow for the extension of the Crown's sovereignty into Maori customary ownership was mounted in the 1846 Constitution Act which had to be suspended by Governor Grey to avoid open war at the time. This meant the whole concept of the transfer of the English Crown's feudal rights to New Zealand had to be deferred. The waste lands of the Maori were safe and so were the other aspects of Maori customary title, until such time as a war of conquest was won.

The land wars were not a war of conquest in that the greater part of the Maori people supported the Crown to assert its sovereignty to rule in accordance with the obligations of the Treaty of Waitangi, and to permit the freedom of trade and intercourse between the two races. The question whether the Crown was not honouring its obligations was another matter altogether. The obligations remained and could not be obscured by manipulations of the law, except, of course, by the specific permission of the Maori people or by the mutual agreement of both races.

The Constitution of 1852, in Clause LXXXI, upheld the maintenance of Maori customary usage . . . 'and whereas it may be expedient that the laws, customs, and usages of the aboriginal or native inhabitants of New Zealand, so far as they are not repugnant to the general principles of humanity, should for the present time be maintained for the government of themselves, in all their relations to and dealings with each other, and that particular districts should be set apart within such laws, customs or usages so observed.' It is amazing how the learned judges shortly to administer the law in the new land and other courts were able to evade the ready evidence of continuing application of Maori customary usage until the customary title had been extinguished.

In 1844, as noted, FitzRoy waived the Crown's sole right to buy land. The effects were both good and bad. Maori land suddenly had an improved market value, which was better than the pegged prices for sales forced by the government land purchase agents on to their unwilling prey. (This had forced them finally into land leaguing which was considered a crime by the authorities.)

In 1846 the pre-emptive right was restored by Grey, and the Native Lands Purchase Ordinance was passed to prevent sheep squatters from the illegal practice of negotiating directly with Maori chiefs for their leases and sales. The practice was forbidden officially but was still widely observed, particularly in the peaceful Ngati Kahungunu territories that stretched from Wairarapa to Hawke's Bay, and also in the Manawatu.

In 1858, the New Zealand Parliament passed a Territorial Rights Bill designed to abolish the right of pre-emption and permit direct purchasing of land from the Maori owners. The bill was vetoed by the British government.

In 1862, however, the imperial government approved the Native Land Act (in direct contravention of the Treaty of Waitangi) whereby the customary usages protecting the communal use and chieftain supervision of tribal lands were swept away by the machinations of a special court that was to examine customary titles of Maori land. The court was also to award the certificate of title to the owners who were then allowed to treat with Europeans for the lease or sale of the block. The Native Minister of the time, F.D. Bell, said the Act 'would strike at the very root of the agitation by which many of the tribes had been seduced from their allegiances to the Crown'. The preamble said the Act would give 'better effect to the Treaty of Waitangi', by providing the first franchise qualification that the administration was willing to recognise, namely, the possession of registered titles to land worth £50 freehold or £10 leasehold, or the occupation of a house worth £10 in the town, or £5 in the country. This was, however, merely another promise.

The 1865 Native Land Act set up the Native Land Court as the instrument of the individualisation of the customary communal Maori land titles. The court was presided over by the European judge who had the assistance of two Maori assessors. The judge heard the evidence of the tribal or hapu groups establishing their ownership under the accepted tenets of customary title. Where there was no disagreement, the judge had merely to confirm the lists of ownership handed in to him by the representatives of the various tribal or hapu groups. The principal pattern followed was that each hapu group or tribe endeavoured to set up either an ancestor who was known and recognised as having the dominion of the block, or other relatives associated with the block. In those days the Maori were very knowledgeable about their traditions and it was difficult to falsify evidence that would not be opposed by all.

The problem arose when ownership was complicated by recurring conquests, alternating periods of occupation, and the emergence of Maori with more knowledge and ability in the traditional lore who were ready to turn their knowledge to personal gain at the expense of their relatives. These people made a practice of turning up at every sitting of the land courts and worming their way into ownership because the judges themselves were incompetent and inconsistent in the assessment of material evidence. The fallibility of the judicial system which was set the task of rushing the title investigations through the courts to release the lands to the waiting speculators created chaos out of the orderly system of customary ownership.

Very few of the traditional Maori blocks were independent units for tribal survival and the pressure was always exerted upon the most fertile areas to be dealt with first and sold or leased over the heads and needs of the tribe as a single communal unit. The result was that the hapu were forced to give up their traditional way of life and congregate in little ghettos on remaining lands near large sheep stations run by the new occupants, or near the roads and small hotel stores where they soon came to depend on the odd jobs that came their way and ready credit for flour, blankets and liquor. Every time they could not meet their debts, the station owners, hotel keepers and storemen obtained another signature to whittle away their lands. These men had every faith that their system would not let them down, even if the practice happened to be illegal, and their faith was richly vindicated in 1894 with the passage of the Validation (of invalid sales) Act. Once the squatter or new arrival was confirmed in his lease, this was the standard method of securing the freehold at minimal cost. The court has always been reluctant to submit its mistakes to reinvestigation by virtue of its stated belief that more injustice would be caused by readjustment than was warranted by the original mistakes.

The 1865 Act was subject to many abuses which were the direct result of the new practice of limiting the names on the certificate of title to ten only, despite the fact that hundreds of other owners entitled to shares had all their rights vested in the dispositions made by the ten trustees. This situation was scarcely relieved by the amendment of 1867 which secured the inclusion of the names of all the owners in the title. However, in 1873 the Native Lands Act required that no alienation by sale or lease could proceed without the consent of all owners.

An excellent example of the malpractices of the times was the sale of the Umutaroroa Block in the Rangitane district. This block was an area of land within a much larger block of 250,000 acres which was sold to the Crown in 1870. There were only ten names on the certificate of title, as trustees for the rest of the Rangitane tribe, numbering about 200. The owners who had sold the main block to the Crown at a minimal price were required to repurchase the Umutaroroa Block back from the Crown at 1/6d an acre in order to be able to secure it as a tribal reserve forever. The title included a restriction on alienation, except with the consent of the Governor-General. A man called Smith was able to induce the ten grantees in the title to apply to get the restriction removed before the rest of the owners were able to get their names finally admitted to the title. The restriction of alienations was removed and the trustees sold the land to Smith who, with another speculator named Cadman, sold the land for up to £5 an acre.

In 1886 the Native Land Administration Act was the first conscientious attempt of government to hold the flood of sales and give the Maori an effective say in the disposal of their lands. This Act was hurriedly repealed following a change of ministry.

In 1891 the Native Land Law Commission offered frank criticism of native land legislation initiated by the 1862 Native Land Act, and the irregularities fostered as a consequence. In 1892 the West Coast Settlement Reserves Act stabilised the few remaining reserves in the Taranaki district but in doing so, vested them forever in the hands of European farmers. Seddon came to power following the death of the liberal Ballance. His own liberal policies were to gain world renown, and he rapidly became a popular and powerful politician. He restored the pre-emptive right of the Crown and the release of further millions of acres of Maori land were an important factor in his steady consolidation of power. This was the last massive inroad into the dwindling millions of acres of Maori reserves. Seddon obtained the land very cheaply because his forceful use of the pre-emptive right had the desired effect of greatly reducing the price of Maori land.

In 1900 the Maori Lands Administration Act was organised by Sir James Carroll who was able to stop the official government policy of progressive land purchases, and who shifted the emphasis to the leasing of Maori lands. The 1905 Maori Land Act was another milestone. It made limited amounts of state funds available to assist Maori farmers. These funds were increased in 1906 and 1908. In 1907 the Stout Ngata Commission examined ways and means of bringing idle Maori lands into production. Every idle acre of Maori land was a challenge to an eager purchaser, and the Liberal government was kept under continual pressure to reopen the remaining Maori lands for freehold purchase. Sir James Carroll succeeded in relieving the pressure but that was enough to give Sir Apirana Ngata the opportunity to introduce his policy of state-aided Maori land development through Maori land incorporations.

Maori land incorporations had their origin in chaotic conditions resulting from the enforced change of status of Maori land held under customary title to that of Crown title. The individualising of uneconomic shares was imposed by government decree. Many blocks of high potential had to be surrendered merely to meet the enforced costs of surveying, and unavailing litigation resulting from the tortuous decisions of the Land Court and the Validation Court. Incorporations allowed blocks to be amalgamated and placed under the care of a trust board by the East Coast Trust Lands Act. The board was charged with the responsibility of administration so that the debts might be paid off and eventually a profit made to the owners. These debts were eventually discharged and the success of these large-scale operations made possible the concept of the Maori land incorporations, which were promoted by Ngata in the late twenties.

In 1920 the Native Trustee was appointed to administer the estates of minors and persons under a disability. Between the years 1920 and 1926, a Royal Commission conducted an investigation into many of the long-standing Maori claims for compensation, mostly for confiscated lands. It provided a basis for settlement which was eventually accepted grudgingly by the Maori who decided that half a loaf was better than no bread. There are still innumerable outstanding claims which have lapsed because of costs and the refusal of successive governments to reopen them. The Crown claimed and insisted upon immunity from investigation for all of the land purchases conducted by it. 'Transactions with the natives for the cession of their title to the Crown are Acts of State and cannot be

examined by any Court.' (Judgement of Prendergast, C.J. and Richmond, J. in Wi
Parata v The Bishop of Wellington 1878).)

It will be apparent that the settlements negotiated were hopelessly inadequate
to provide reasonable compensation for the enormously valuable land claims.
The time is overdue to review the whole of these settlements in the light of modern knowledge of the culpability of the early perpetrators of so much malpractice
who abused the good name of the Crown and their personal responsibilities.
Every tribe in the country should possess adequate endowments of good land,
sufficient capital and tax incentives to ensure successful farming by tribal incorporations, which in themselves would restore the mana of the tribes in their own
districts and lay an economic base for continued socio-economic and cultural
progress.

The old avenues used by Maori elders of a past generation to pursue their
claims for redress of their many wrongs were full of blind alleys maintained by
successive governments to frustrate and eventually dishearten them. The Land
Courts, the Validation Courts, the Appeal Courts, the Supreme Court and peti-
tions to Parliament itself, all were the scene of so many costly failures that they
eventually fell into disuse.

Summary of Trust Boards Administering Monetary Settlements of Major Tribal Land and Lake Claims Settled in the 1940s

BOARD	CROWN SETTLEMENT	BASIS OF CLAIMS
Arawa Maori Trust Board, Rotorua	$12,000 annually in perpetuity.	In settlement of any claims which the Arawa people might have in respect of certain lakes in the Rotorua district.
Tuwharetoa Maori Trust Board, Tokaanu	$6,000 annually in perpetuity, also half of fishing licence fees above $6,000.	In settlement of any claims which the Tuwharetoa people might have in respect of Lake Taupo and the surrounding waters.
Taranaki Maori Trust Board, Hawera	$10,000 annually in perpetuity.	In settlement of any claims which might be made in respect of confiscation of lands in the Taranaki district.
Tainui Maori Trust Board, Ngaruawahia	$10,000 annually in perpetuity, plus an additional $2,000 per annum for 45 years (first payment 1947).	In settlement of any claims which might be made in respect of confiscation of lands in the Waikato district.

Ngai Tahu Maori Trust Board, Kaiapoi	$20,000 annually in perpetuity.	In settlement of any claims which might be made in respect of purchase of lands belonging to the Ngai Tahu tribe in the South Island.
Whakatohea Maori Trust Board, Opotiki	$40,000 lump sum.	In settlement of any claims arising out of confiscation of lands of the Whakatohea tribe.
Wairoa-Waikaremoana Trust Board, Wairoa	$40,000 lump sum.	In settlement of any claims arising out of the cession of the Kauhouroa Block to the Crown, and rent for the lease of Lake Waikaremoana.
Aorangi Maori Trust Board, Takapau	$100,000 lump sum.	In settlement of claims arising out of the acquisition by the Crown of Aorangi Block.
Aupouri Maori Trust Board, Te Kao		Set up to administer communally owned land at Te Kao, and the proceeds of the sale of other assets.
Taitokerau Maori Trust Board, Whangarei	$94,300	In respect of claims in surplus lands passed to the Crown on review of early private purchases.
Tuhoe-Waikaremoana Maori Trust Board, Rotorua	$200,000	In settlement of claims for lands allotted to the Crown and roads not constructed in the Urewera, and rent for the lease of Lake Waikaremoana.

Maori Land Today

The state of Maori land tenure and development has changed very little since the original period of consolidation, which started with Ngata in the early thirties and reached its zenith in the mid-forties under Fraser. The demands of the post-war period saw a rapid decline in funds allotted for new development and this situation has been maintained ever since. Added to this policy of deliberate run-down in the Maori land development programme has been the mass of legislation passed in 1953 and subsequently in 1967 designed to open up as much Maori land as possible for purchase by Europeans. Both policies have been successful to a point but, as had been stated, they have fallen short of their objectives. The reason has been difficulties built into multiple Maori land ownership.

Ngata had long recognised the importance of large-scale Maori land development as the effective catalyst to promote the socio-economic status of the Maori people. He moved inflexibly towards his objectives of consolidating scattered interests into economic dairy and sheep farming units. The people had little to say

95

(such was his mana) when they were relocated in various regions that offered best opportunities at that time. Those who did not seize their opportunities were left behind and suffered accordingly. The result was that the Maori people were at last enabled to enter into the new technology of the farming industry. The tribes gained in economic strength and solidarity as farms gained in productivity. Business skills were acquired through their associations with the new regional dairy companies, mechanical skills were given a great impetus as the men learned to handle machinery, and Maoritanga gained in stature as great canoes and handsome tribal meeting houses were erected in the major Maori centres.

The Second World War also added a new dimension to Maori leadership, as young Maori soldiers found a new outlet for the higher levels of education they had gained access to in the late thirties. The country itself just as suddenly discovered a hitherto untapped and apparently unheeded pool of Maori labour. Young men and women flocked to the towns, soon to be followed by their elders. The rural scene was kept stable by the Labour government's policy of expanding Maori land development until curtailment in 1941. The decreasing flow of money for land development soon cut down the need for fencers, stockmen and shearers on all the large schemes until, finally, the relocation policy accelerated another massive movement of the people into the cities.

The large-scale development policy of the first Labour government effected the consolidation of what had been scattered and uneconomic family and individual interests into viable large farming units which were called Maori land incorporations. During the mid-fifties large numbers of long-term Maori land leases to Europeans were resumed by their owners, and many a Maori rehabilitation farmer was set on his feet within three years by bonanza wool prices.

The post-war period brought about new demands for capital but, because of an adverse political climate, the Maori was unable to compete successfully for his share. The result was that land development and farming in general began to run down, the small farms of the Ngata era proved uneconomic and the subsistence-level Maori farmers gave up and followed young people to the cities which offered better pay, housing, working and education opportunities. The enforced rural stagnation was accelerating the new phenomenon of urbanisation.

The Labour government made signs in 1949 that it had finally recognised the effects of its loss of a positive policy, but it was too late. The 1949 election introduced the National government and with it a policy unsympathetic to the proposition that the state should undertake massive development of Maori land on behalf of Maori only. The new government's first move to alter the protective nature of legislation was made in the 1953 Maori Affairs Act which was a consolidation of the rambling mass of legislation affecting Maori affairs, land and legal matters. The radical and discriminatory application of the principle of conversion, or the compulsory purchase by the state of so-called uneconomic interests in Maori land (Maori land valued at less than $50) aroused very little interest among Maori leaders. I challenged the move as the preliminary nibble at the lands of the Maori: next would come the bite (the 1967 Acts) and finally the swallow, the loss of the incorporations by the introduction of free trading in incorporation shares. Maori leadership had reached its lowest ebb and that is the prime reason for the chaotic state of Maori affairs at the present time.

Labour's brief return to office in 1957 to 1960 saw it attempt to rationalise the situation in education and Maori affairs. The findings of the Currie Commission and the Hunn Report were, unfortunately for the country as a whole, left on the plate of an incoming National government with a different appreciation of their value.

The Hunn Report made excellent suggestions to promote trade training among young Maori and urged the provision of more hostel accommodation, the development of pre-school education, the formation of a Maori Education Foundation, and the stepping up of the Maori housing programme to 2000 houses a year. These recommendations were all adopted but in lesser degrees than those recommended. There were other suggestions which were less acceptable to the new government which resorted to the stratagem of setting up a mini-commission with a frame of reference that reflected its own different concept of progress in Maori affairs: the need for greater facilities for selling Maori land.

The Hunn Report stated that the activities of the Maori Affairs Department needed to be accelerated to keep pace with the needs of a rapidly increasing Maori population. It was in this spirit that the major recommendations were advanced.

The major one was that the ceiling of Maori land development should be raised from the then token acreage of 10,000 acres a year to 20,000 and thereafter should be stepped up to some 50,000 acres annually. The Lands and Survey Department was to assume the task of development, and measures were to be taken to induce adequate numbers of young Maori to enter suitable farm training schemes, and additional farming land was to be absorbed into a comprehensive Maori land settlement programme at individual and communal incorporation farming levels.

The Maori Trustee was to adopt the policy of resuming expired leases of valuable reserve lands as these fell due, and every opportunity was to be taken to gain effective control of the West Coast (Taranaki) Settlement Reserves in trust for the Maori owners. The functions of the Maori Trustee were to be clearly defined so that he should become the administrator of an expanding asset. It was envisaged that the adoption of sound business-like methods would bring a new growth of income, which would be available in a realistic quantity to meet the expanding needs, cultural, educational, and socio-economic, of the exploding Maori population. The great increase in export income would also be a welcome addition to the economic solidarity of the country.

Provision was to be made for a five-yearly review of Maori affairs by a broad-based committee upon which Maori would have adequate representation. By this means legislation and policy implementation would proceed harmoniously to the stage where the need for separate Maori institutions, political and administrative, would have disappeared spontaneously by the simple process of natural evolution.

These proposals were unpalatable to the National government, which had a different ownership objective for Maori land and sought legislative avenues which would weaken and eventually disintegrate the bonds retaining the few million acres of ancestral land in Maori ownership. The answers were sought and found. The unpopular Prichard Waetford Commission was set up to pose the requisite questions.

The government had no difficulty overriding the united objections of the Maori people to the proposals presented in the Prichard Waetford Report and proceeded to bring down more contentious legislation embedded in the 1967 Maori Affairs Amendment Act, the Town and Country Planning Act, the Rating Act, the Estate and Gift Duties Act and the Administration Act. All of these provisions are in unilateral violation of the Maori version of the Treaty of Waitangi which had already been seriously breached in the 1953 Maori Affairs Amendment Act by provisions for alienation by minority quorums, compulsory conversion, purchase of undivided interests by the Maori Trustee, and elsewhere in the legislation by the Soil Conservation and Rivers Control Act 1941, Town and Country Planning Act 1953, the Counties Amendment Act 1961, and the Petroleum Act 1937.

The 1967 Maori Affairs Amendment Act

The 1967 Maori Affairs Amendment Act enforced the transfer to European status of all Maori lands owned by not more than four persons and this fruitless task has occupied the Maori Land Court for years. The sweeping legislation had insufficient safeguards and has created more than its share of confusion about the exact status of many areas of land in the minds of Maori owners. The second part of the Act, according to a superimposed explanatory note, is intended to promote the effective and profitable use of Maori land in the interest of the owners. But the emphasis is on alienation and the Act makes no contract to assist with finance and technology, the prime needs for the promotion of the ideal of the better use and administration of the land.

Part Three brought the Maori Land Court under the jurisdiction of the Town and Country Planning Act and the Counties Amendment Act. This has been successful in denying many Maori rights entrenched in the Treaty of Waitangi. It impedes the ancient right of Maori to build their homes on their ancestral villages, destroying Maori communities and driving Maori landowners away from their land into the cities.

Part Four provides new machinery for the valuable Maori land incorporations, but the Act promised so much contentious and disruptive material that the incorporations were forced into costly and bitter legal representations to secure the barest concessions. How much better it would have been if the legislation had been brought down as the result of total cooperation between the government and the incorporations, producing measures sought by the incorporations to improve their administrative capacity as trustees for their numerous shareholders. The government's intention to open the shareholdings to free trading was grudgingly withdrawn, but the minister insisted on retention of the provision that made shares of bankrupts in the incorporations available to the official assignee.

Another illogical provision was the power of share transfer to the Maori Trustee, the Crown, or any other state loan department, but not to any Maori who was not a shareholder. The upshot of this has been that the Queen and the Maori Trustee now regularly appear as the largest single owners in many blocks and incorporations that are not strong enough (through inefficient management by the Maori Affairs Department over many years) to resume shares themselves. The presence of these alien owners has a disturbing and inhibiting effect on the management, and steps should be taken to finance their removal as soon as possible.

Part Five makes the estates of Maori people subject to the common law affecting wills made by Europeans. If a Maori dies intestate, the rights of succession are now determined in the same way as for Europeans. The traditional Maori rights of succession have been revoked.

New provisions struck yet another blow at the preservation of Maoritanga. The general public is apt to become a little impatient with this type of protectionism. But the Maori people have long revered their footing in ancestral land as their turangawaewae which had to be retained if they wished to preserve their right to speak on matters of local interest. They could never again speak freely without the real fear of being told to 'sit down and keep quiet – you are a nobody. You have no footing here. Your rights have been sold. Your fire has gone out.' If a Maori left his ancestral land to live elsewhere his fire on the ancestral hearth was considered to have gone out. The longer he stayed away the colder the ashes became. He lost his 'ahi ka roa' which became 'mataotao'. The same thing happened when a piece of land was sold.

Maori people say that most of their land is held only as a trust to be enjoyed in their lifetime, and then handed on to their children. Creditors have hitherto been forced to accept this custom and have always made due allowances in securing their debts. If a man lives in a fine house which is known to belong to his uncle, only a fool or a speculator would lend him money on the value of the house. This is the analogy that the Maori draw in pressing for the retention of the traditional protectionist policy until such time as the material progress of the people demands its abolition.

Part Six relates to increased facilities to enable Maori to sell their interests in undivided freehold land. The effect has been to enable larger owners to increase their holdings and rationalise their farming activities. But many have been acquiring land as cheaply as possible to the stage where the land can be sold freely to

Europeans, thereby decimating Maori land reserves instead of creating more economic holdings for use by Maori. The Maori Trustee has also been pushing the new facility for conversion to the point where the Maori owners are now in the minority, with further disruptions of direction and management of one-time purely Maori holdings.

Part Seven established a conversion fund which is financed by state monies allocated from the consolidated account. This fund is administered by the Maori Trustee, who has increased his purchases through it from $109,554 in 1967 to $771,565 in 1972. Some indication of the determination to provide adequate funds for the policy may be seen in the fact that during this same period $3,039,595 was voted while only $2,098,110 was actually spent. If this was not enough evidence of the destructive policy carried out by the Maori Trustee, there is also the fact that the Trustee annually handles over $5 million as the proceeds of Maori land sales.

The inevitable result of the escalated level of conversion has been that great inroads of foreign ownership have been accomplished in the hitherto sacrosanct vested reserves. These consist today of the West Coast Settlement Reserves, the various remnants of the old Maori Township Reserves, the Tenths Reserves left over from the old New Zealand Company days at Nelson, Palmerston North and Wellington, and the valuable Greymouth Reserve. These areas were regarded as trust reserves by the Maori and their function was to serve as endowment trusts for generations to come. The same principle was followed when the tribes requested that certain land should remain forever in the ownership of tribal or hapu and family groups, but the courts were ever subject to the political pressures of those clamouring for more and more cheap land, particularly Maori land. Perhaps it is not so strange in a world of double standards that there is one law for the Maori land trusts which were readily abused and broken, and another for the European trusts whose titles have remained relatively inviolate. The Maori Trustee has efficiently resumed his former character of Maori Land Purchase Officer, and he is back working for the old firm, the Pakeha farming community and their lackeys, the government and the county councils.

The most destructive feature of this part of the Act is the power that the Maori Trustee has so freely used, to advertise among the Maori owners for willing sellers at ridiculous prices that deny the owners the natural right to share in the value of the improvements to the lands. The Maori Trustee makes it known to the European lessees of such land that he is willing to grant freehold title to those lessees who wish to do so by completing the purchase of the title from the Maori Trustee.

The 1967 Amendment Act required that all Maori land that had not passed through the Land Court to receive a Crown Grant of Title would be taken by the Crown as from the first day of January 1972. This further assault on Maori land received a stay of execution until the first day of January 1975. But the point is that most of the records of these lands are held in government files and the delays were largely due to the government and other Europeans using the courts to frustrate Maori claimants with such effect that the original claimants have long gone. A special court of enquiry needs to be appointed to assist Maori to complete their research and assist them with their cases in an appropriate court. This court would require adequate funds and a ten-year life in order to do justice to the task and ultimately salvage much of the honour lost by the insanities of four generations of land-lusting speculators.[1]

Conclusion

A review of the role of the Minister of Maori Affairs, the Board of Maori Affairs, the Maori Land Court, the Maori Purposes Fund Board and the Maori Trustee, and the long history of poor management from the viewpoint of the Maori people as sufferers rather than beneficiaries, would indicate far more scope for improvement in future management of Maori land affairs than could be accomplished by simple reorganisation. The importance of the minister must not be underestimated. His complete identification with contemporary party policies has led to politics that had been almost completely 'stop' rather than 'go' since the mid-forties, and completely in tune with the land acquisition policies of farmer-business orientated parliamentarians sensitive to the vote that puts them in the House.

This means that ministerial direction must be reduced and with it the sensitivity to inimical changes in the policies of the parties currently in power and contesting for power. The Board of Maori Affairs is an established failure and needs to be abolished. The Department of Maori Affairs itself needs a lot of soul searching and reconstruction in a completely different mould.

The empire of welfare officers is redundant and greater scope should be given to the Maori genius for voluntary organisation on the lines of the old Maori tribal committees, which should be affiliated to regional Maori Trust Boards which administer lands and funds on their own account. They must be made independent of subsidies now reduced to ridiculously low levels. The Maori wardens would be affiliated to the same regional authorities. The development of independent urban maraes with their own sources of funding would further remove tribal committees from their present state of impotence in the face of the many demands for their assistance.

The Maori Council as at present constituted has many weaknesses. The principal problems centre around the lack of effective leadership, the lack of funds, the persistence of tribal and regional isolation, the lack of effective liaison with the grass roots of the Maori people, an inability to use the growing pool of Maori and

[1]The Waitangi Tribunal was established in 1975, after this essay was written, and in 1985 its powers were made retrospective to 1840. Views expressed here should be read in the light of these developments.

101

European expertise outside the limited resources of the council itself and the apathetic approach to challenges to crystallise the solid mass of Maori opinion and expectation into requisite legislation. Maori representation should be increased to eight and the Maori Affairs Amendment Act, the Rating Act and Town and Country Planning legislation of 1967 repealed.

The Labour government's 1972 White Paper was a weak, piecemeal attempt to rectify some of the unfortunate legislation of 1967. But in no way could it be said to have repealed all destructive aspects of the 1967 and 1953 legislation affecting Maori affairs in general and Maori land development in particular. This could only be accomplished by the immediate repeal of the whole of the 1967 amendments and the conversion features in the 1953 Act, passing temporary caretaker legislation and then bringing down a major Maori Affairs Act which would finally define a correct direction for the future development of Maori land, cultural and social assets for the benefit of New Zealand as a whole.

The major need is to set up a federation of all the Maori incorporations and Maori trust boards and to rationalise for the first time the exploitation of this country's most valuable single asset. The objective would be to build up large regional Maori land trust boards by the year 2000. A federation of these could undertake the management of all Maori lands administered by the Board of Maori Affairs; it would have government representation which would be reviewed every five years and the ultimate objective of complete translation of administrative capacity to the federation, which in turn would review its own activities in the lights of its final objective: translation back to the owners themselves in the form of strong regional and tribal trusts.

The federation would have the funds to employ the best administrative brains in the world and introduce a fully computerised service to keep in close contact with the smallest and the largest stations which would gain savings in administration costs. The greater overall efficiency would enable the federation to employ and train more Maori to participate at all levels such as fencing, stock management, maintenance, sales, management in New Zealand and overseas, and export-import experience.

It would also allow a greater diversification of investment in stock and station firms, export contracts and shares in the freezing works and carrying firms, and a greater interest in forestry where the present long-term leaseholds granted to the state forest and other private milling and processing companies would be re-negotiated so that the owners would lease only for a limited caretaker period until they were able to enter into partnership contracts and complete takeovers. The Tuwharetoa and Whanau-a-Apanui forest schemes would present admirable opportunities for such partnership schemes. The same principle would apply to the utilisation of iron sands and other minerals. Short-term caretaker leases only would be negotiated, and the owners, once fully competent, would assume full management responsibility.

102

Expansion into eel farming and fishing ventures would be the next step, and also deer farming at Rangitaiki, with hunting and skiing at suitable stations acquired in the South Island. The review of the West Coast and Southland sales could bring an interest in coal, gold and greenstone.

The management of the initial enterprise could be handled by a joint Government-Maori Commission for the first five years with councils contributing in an advisory role. There would be a development council whose task would be to lay down reasonable target projections and report to the country at large on all aspects of progress. A Maori Education Council would take over the Maori Education Foundation and the assets of various churches that have abdicated their responsibilities in Maori education. The council would also build and maintain a modern secondary school complex with every facility backed by considerable funds and land endowments and charged with responsibility for developing educational courses appropriate to the needs of Maori students. The idea would be to make the schools co-educational and available to those most in need and most likely to benefit from its special advantages. This would call for a handsome endowment of a productive source of revenue, but should not be beyond the scope of New Zealand.

Another possible project would be the maintenance of one or two tribal ohu-type collectives which would eventually become self-supporting by developing vineyards, cash crop farming and other avenues designed to fit needs for intensive farming with emphasis on the collective use of land, money and labour. The special nature of these 'kibbutzim' would be that they would possess state-supported experts in various forms of culture with an emphasis on Maoritanga. Tribal lore and the classical culture forms such as whakapapa, oratory, modern Maori, the etiquette of the marae, carving and weaving could be available for those who wished to study in a specialised environment over the space of several months.

The immediate plan would be to replace current legislation with a new act that would consolidate the best features of the old. At the same time it would give a clear approach to the ideals of a satisfying independence based on the ability to exploit and develop the best features in the inheritance of the modern Maori: his land, his Maoritanga, and the technological culture of the Pakeha.

REFERENCES

T. Lindsay Buick, *The Treaty of Waitangi*, 1914.
T. Lindsay Buick, *The French at Akaroa*, 1928.
W. Pember Reeves, *The Long White Cloud*, 1898.
Paul Blomfield, *Edward Gibbon Wakefield*, 1961.
Guy Lennard, *Sir William Martin*, 1961.
A.J. Harrop, *England and The Maori Wars*, 1937.
A.H. McLintock, *Crown Colony Government in New Zealand*, 1958.
James Cowan, *Sir Donald McLean*, 1940.
Ian Ward, *The Shadow of the Land*, 1968.

Harold Miller, *Race Conflict in New Zealand*, 1966.
Hight and Bamford, *The Constitutional History and Law of New Zealand*, 1914.
J. Hight, *The English as a Colonising Nation*.
J.G.A. Pollock, *The Maori and New Zealand Politics*, 1965.
G. Rusden, *Aureretanga*.
J.A. Mackay, *History of Poverty Bay*, 1949.
Compendium of Official Documents Relating to Native Affairs in the South Island, 1873.
Diaries of Edward Meurant, 1842-1847.
New Zealand Parliamentary Debates.
British Parliamentary Papers.
New Zealand Official Year Books.

A VIEW OF DEATH

HARRY DANSEY

Tahuri mai o mate te tihi ki 'Tirau
Mowai rokiroki, ko te huna i te moa;
I makere iho ai te tara o te marama e-i.

Turn your eyes to the peak of 'Tirau
Now desolate, utterly; all is lost,
Gone, vanished as the moa;
Oh, broken is the tip of the crescent moon.

(a lament for Te Momo in Apirana Ngata's *Nga Moteatea*, Part I)

Death is the only certainty, all come soon or late to Te Rerenga-Wairua, to Te Rarohenga, to Te Reinga, to that state – no matter what name or symbol diverse cultures choose to signify that last act of those who have lived.

Such knowledge as I have of the Maori attitude to death has not been gained in a planned and orderly fashion. I know some things in depth and detail, others only in sketchy outline. And there are many aspects about which I know nothing at all. I rather envy those who have listened to wise and learned people and been guided through the relevant texts. Such will be able to approach the subject with some objectivity.

My approach is quite subjective. While others can be impersonal I am emotional. While others can observe and record and have no call unless they choose to pass judgement, I am involved and I take part, praise, blame, use and sometimes even endeavour to change the customs of our people. This is part of me and part of my life and I can no more opt out of it than I could have chosen not to have been born into it.

I also have difficulty in separating one aspect of the life of our people from another. We cannot think of the dead without reference to the living, or speak of the forester without considering the forest, or the child without thought of the parent, or the warrior without consideration of warfare. Thus I know, try as I may not to do so, I tend to digress and to wander along subsidiary pathways before returning to my highway.

It is much more difficult to write of the Maori attitude to death today than it was a century ago because the impact of European civilisation has brought many changes. We can establish with some confidence what attitudes once were, even taking into account regional differences. But the present situation is much more complex. We could find people or groups of people whose basic attitudes were little changed, although the forms by which these attitudes are expressed may well be quite different. On the other hand we can find people who, perhaps because of adherence to a religious faith which has come into the country in the period since the first contact with Europeans, have attitudes which are the same as anyone else who subscribes to that faith. Thus it is likely that a Maori member of the Church of Jesus Christ of the Latter Day Saints will have much the same attitude to death as a Mormon anywhere else, provided he is well schooled in the principles of his faith.

Members of the larger denominations, Anglican, Roman Catholic, Methodist or Presbyterian, subscribe in greater or lesser degree to the Christian teachings of these churches. A difference in the first three, which have been so long established in New Zealand Maori society, is that they have to some extent built up attitudes which, while orthodox Christian at base, are not quite the same as those of Church members elsewhere and not quite the same as the attitude of the pre-Christian Maori. The Christian practice, for instance, has been adapted to fit easily into the tangihanga or mourning ceremony, without losing its essential message. Many of the ministers of the churches are Maori and services are conducted in the Maori language.

Among the old-time beliefs which may or may not remain (according to the circumstances of the individual) is the attitude to the cause of death. In the case of violent death, in battle or by accident (but not all accidents), cause and effect can be seen and understood. In the case of death through what we would now call illness, the old-time belief was that the cause was not physical but spiritual. Bad influences – spirits if you like – were the cause of death. These might be spirits which were there, waiting, ready to attack anyone whose defences were weakened by a breach of tapu. They might also be spirits or inflences which were controlled by tohunga of the sorcerer class. Thus in all the affairs of the daily life care was taken to preserve the personal tapu so that death would not be given an opportunity of moving through a breach in the person's spiritual defence. If this did happen it was often possible for 'treatment' to be given by another tohunga.

The influence of tapu remains to a greater or lesser degree with many people of Maori ancestry. My observation suggests that it is less strong now than when I was a boy. I base this on observation of people doing things that their parents and certainly their grandparents would not have done, such as mixing food objects with body objects (washing clothes and table linen in the same washing machine).

The old-time term for the sickness which was attributed to the presence of evil spirits was mate atua, but this term does not appear to be much used today, the more common use being mate Maori – Maori sickness. I have often heard it referred to, in English, as 'the Maori bullet'. Perhaps the use of this phrase began when it was realised that some illnesses could be diagnosed and cured by modern means and these were called mate Pakeha. The ones which could not be so conveniently diagnosed and cured were obviously those caused by the old-time spiritual influences. Maori people still on occasion seek the advice and treatment of Maori practitioners for such complaints. You will not find their names in any list of medical people, but they are there and known and respected by many Maori. There are times when a Maori, deciding that a complaint is a mate Maori and not a mate Pakeha, will seek spiritual healing, not from a Maori practitioner, but from a Christian minister of religion who is able to assist in many cases within the tenets of his faith or perhaps even by bending his European-based theology just a little.

One such case I know of was a family convinced that an evil influence remained on a place by a road where one of the family had died in a car accident. An Anglican minister conducted a service on the spot and the family was convinced that the influence then disappeared. Whether the action was taken to bring peace to the spirit of the accident victim or to lay to rest some other spirit which may have been the cause of the accident, I don't know. All I know is that peace descended upon the bereaved family.

The Maori practitioner – I suppose it is proper to call him or her a tohunga as was the custom in the past – still frequently searches for the cause of the illness. He may find that the sick person – or the dead person – committed some offence and he then directs what must be done to end the influence of such an offence. This breach is usually called 'hara'. Many of these hara concern matters upon which the people involved have no knowledge. 'Did you go to such-and-such a place? Did you do such-and-such a thing there? Yes? Well, that was your hara.'

Or else he might say, 'Have you some heirloom, a tiki or a greenstone pendant or writings of your grandfather in your place? Yes? Well, that is what is causing your trouble.'

Then he would tell them what to do about it. Often the offending article would have to be disposed of or purified. Water comes into this purification, the worldwide symbol of spiritual cleansing as it is the medium of physical cleansing.

When it comes to death, it is not infrequent for the bereaved family to search for the cause of their personal tragedy in some spiritual reason. This is far from being a Maori characteristic alone. Many times I have been in the company of people – not Maori – who have been involved in tragedy and it is far from uncommon to hear a grief-stricken mother ask, 'What have I done to deserve this?' when mourning the death of a child.

A difference is that in many cases in Maori society an answer will be found. With Pakeha, the orthodox answer may well be that God's ways cannot be understood by man or that God in His own time will reveal the reason. This may be of comfort to the believer.

Thus one of the aspects of the Maori attitude to death is still that many seek to find a cause of death other than the obvious one of physical illness.

Another attitude to death in which the Maori differs from other members of the total New Zealand society is that the dead are to be cared for, cherished, mourned, spoken to, honoured in a way which others might consider to be over-emotional and over-demonstrative. It does not seem so to me, but it does to many of my friends. The closer my life ties me into my Maori background, the more the difference becomes apparent. The Maori — and I am sure this still applies to most Maori — want to see their dead, to have them with them until that ultimate commital to the earth. And most still seem to choose burial rather than cremation. The Pakeha attitude seems more based on the belief, usually unstated, that the dead must be hurried away, hidden from sight.

Very few Maori families have their dead taken from the hospital mortuary to the undertaker's chapel until the funeral, away from sight in a closed casket. The dead in most cases go home to a house or meeting house or tent on a marae where, round the open casket, surrounded by pictures of others who have died before, the family gathers to mourn and to greet those who come to mourn with them.

For me this is still my way of farewelling the dead and comforting the living. It is proper, satisfying, comforting, leaving me when all is over with no more tears to shed and fit to take up the business of life once again. In a strange way I feel emotionally drained and at the same time emotionally refreshed.

Another old-time attitude to death is that it must be avenged.

This is particularly applied to death in battle, and revenge — called utu — might not be taken for many years after the death although it was well remembered and constantly referred to. Obviously this is not the case in the present day. But it is not without precedent in the recent past. Reinforcements going from New Zealand to join the Maori Battalion in the Middle East and later in Italy during the Second World War would be reminded before they sailed — the little groups in their homes on their final leave — that the death of a brother or cousin or uncle had not yet been avenged. I can recall in Italy, as a member of that unit, having the same fact pointed out by an officer before a battle.

In days of peace, however, often the only vengeance taken is that of tears. An old saying repeated at funerals and in speeches on the marae during a tangihanga is this:

Te roimata i heke,
Te hupe i whiua ki te marae,
Ka ea aitua.

The tears that fall,
The mucus that is cast upon the marae
Avenge death.

Vengeance applies to war-like action, but there was another way of enacting payment for death. This was the old custom known as muru, which was raiding to get payment for some offence. It would often take place where some person or family was blamed for causing a death by accident. I do not know of any recent instance of this, although it was not uncommon up until about 1900. Perhaps if the cause of the accident was such that some compensation seemed right and proper, Maori may now adopt the Pakeha system of muru by civil process through the law courts.

The Maori attitude to death is influenced by the depth of his feeling for his relations. The term 'the extended family' has recently come into general use and is a good one. The Maori relationship is very extended indeed and so are the rights and responsibilities of relationship. I do not propose to go into details of the relationship pattern but there are a number of excellent texts which should be studied because with such knowledge much becomes clear. Without it much remains obscure. The death of a relation, even one whom I know little, if at all, affects me deeply, just because of relationship. To many Maori, and certainly to me, it is enough that we were related, enough to give me reason to mourn. The comment 'why, I hardly knew him' does not have the same import as it has to Pakeha. My relation and I are part of the same tree, we share the same ancestry and the claims of that ancestry are very real.

The origins of this feeling for relationship are ancient. It was not only an emotional tie, it was a practical, even a political thing. On it was based the structure that tied the ancient society together. Every way of strengthening it was used and thus we have the custom of arranged marriages and adoptions. These were calculated to reinforce old alliances and to make new ones. It is not peculiar to Maori and other members of the Polynesian people but was a political device widely used in Europe. There were those who tried – some times successfully – to beat the system. And there are many stories of people like Hinemoa who chose to run off with the wrong man (as far as her family was concerned).

When the European sets out on some project, his system is to form some new organisation or make use of an existing one, organisations which are not based on family ties or relationships. This is a practical, workable, successful pattern and has extended with his civilisation right across the world. The Polynesian system of tackling some project is, on the other hand, based on family groups. It is the head of the group who links with other heads, related in greater or lesser degree. The people come into the enterprise as families, as sub-tribes, as major tribes. It too, in its time, was a practical, workable, successful pattern and extended across the Polynesian world and beyond.

Now in New Zealand the Polynesian pattern remains as a thread running through Maori life. The European pattern also exists in Maori society today and can be found in those Maori organisations which are new in concept like the New Zealand Maori Council and its subsidiaries or the Maori Women's Welfare League.

Nevertheless, when it comes to efficient operation of these bodies, especially at the local rather than the national level, the power of the old relationship pattern exerts its influence when it comes to work to be done, funds to be raised or causes to be espoused.

The ways of deliberately strengthening relationships by arranged marriages and adoptions are not so much in evidence today, although there are still many adoptions. I do not think that where these occur the people involved think of it as a political device to make alliances against future stress. I think the purpose is to ensure the continuance of emotional ties, the building of bridges or aroha, love, between relations who may with the passage of time be drifting apart. So what was political and emotional becomes mainly emotional, but nevertheless very real and very important, even in present-day Maori life. Aroha, then, is one of the elements to be considered in any study of Maori attitudes to death.

So I would suggest that factors important in understanding these attitudes are tapu, utu, muru and aroha. All these bear to a greater or lesser degree on death in a Maori community today. But the greatest of them all is aroha. That is so today and I suggest it was a power in ancient times too.

So in death, drawn by the ties of love and respect and sorrow, the people gather to mourn. This is the tangihanga.

The tangihanga is the major Maori ceremonial occasion. Within its orbit is drawn virtually every phase of Maori custom and belief that exists today. Its strength is such that in spite of Pakeha opposition, criticism and derision for more than a century, it has survived and continues, with many adaptations and changes in form, but with the same purpose and spirit as in the past.

There is a need for ceremonial so that the dead may be properly farewelled, his or her virtues extolled (and, quite often, faults and failings almost brutally enumerated), the bereaved comforted, the ties of relationship renewed and the deep well of Maoritanga tapped so that all who come may refresh and strengthen themselves.

The principles demonstrated when visitors arrive upon the marae hold true for other occasions. There is the arrival, sometimes the challenge, the recognition, the call to enter, the entry, the pause for mourning and the tribute of tears, the speeches to and fro, the physical meeting and the soul-satisfying greeting of the hongi. There too one can see the canoe symbolism that lies so deep within the Maori way of life, the greeting of the visitors as if they were the canoe upon which their distant ancestors came from far-off lands.

To me, as I write, come flooding in the memories of faces, memories of sad songs, of cries, of earth upon a hundred coffins – oh, dull thudding sound like no other sound! I did not know this in early childhood for I lived in Auckland. But later, when my family moved to Rotorua, I came to know and to learn. We lived close to Whakarewarewa, the home of the Tuhourangi people of Te Arawa with whom I am proud to claim relationship, although my main ancestral ties are with Ngati Tuwharetoa and Ngati Raukawa. I slept as a boy on the verandah of our home, so close to the geyser valley that I could hear Pohutu roar and the water splash on the silica terraces.

When someone died – or perhaps when tidings of a death arrived – a watcher by the bed would go to the door and raise her voice in a long, heart-crushing wail, that cry which is the quintessence of human sorrow. Then another door would open and the cry would be repeated, quivering, moaning across Te Roto-a-Tamaheke, echoing on the cliffs of Tuturu and dying away in the forest of Moerangi.

Then, perhaps, my father in his dressing gown, would come on to the verandah and look into the night and sigh, 'That will be poor old so-and-so. He was very low yesterday.' And then we would talk a while and he might say, 'He was very close to us really. His grandmother was from Taupo, one of ours. I remember her very well, fine old lady...'

I saw many tangihanga at Whakarewarewa and Ohinemutu and other places in the Rotorua district in the decade 1930 to 1939. At Whakarewarewa I sat on the edge of the marae and watched the ceremonial and listened to the speeches, understanding little of them, I am afraid, unless my father translated for me. But to me that was only part of the whole occasion. To me it was also the pig-killing, the cooking in the ngawha – the boiling springs – or on hot stones in special hangi, for not all guests liked the flavour that our water bubbling from the heart of Papatuanuku gives to food. It was the drinking, the fighting, the gambling, the singing, the lovemaking, all the bustle and passion of a bustling, passionate people.

So I remember the tremendous tangihanga when Mita Taupopoki died in 1934. I can still see Whetu Werohia leading his men of Tauranga on to Te Pakira, the marae of the Tuhourangi people at Whakarewarewa, across which Mita in his fine cloaks gazed with sightless eyes from the porch of the carved house Wahiao. I can see Whetu, stripped to the waist with his taiaha between his teeth, leaping, twisting, dancing ahead of his hundred men, brown torsos gleaming, advancing with a booming chant in a solid mass at a jog-trot, with the bridge over the Puarenga shaking under them.

So I remember that great orator Rangiteaorere, standing in Tamatekapua meeting house at Ohinemutu, praising the wreaths round a coffin and then turning to the children gathered there and saying that here were the true flowers that did honour to the dead.

So I learned too of the inter-family and inter-hapu and inter-tribal jealousies and differences, of the slights real and imagined that were detected, that grew like mushrooms overnight in the emotion-packed atmosphere. I learned too of the way that such were put aside and the way ranks closed when something intruded from outside tribal confines. For the tangihanga is the time when the careless, thoughtless remark becomes the spark for the notable incident, the happening to be remembered and recounted and embroidered upon as time goes on.

Marriage brought me into the closest association with my wife's people of

Taranaki. There, the spirit was the same in its depth of Maoriness. But its expression was different in a thousand ways. Here too I have wept on many a marae. With them I have gone to mortuaries, lifted our dead into their caskets, borne them to the meeting houses, carried them to the cemeteries, stood by the graves as the bitter southerly threw the sea-spray in our faces, heard the thud of earth on the coffins, helped when the press of people had departed to put the possessions of the dead in the graves.

So many occasions! I remember when Rangi Metekingi, taiaha in hand, challenged the party which had halted at Putiki, Whanganui as it was, bearing the ashes of Sir Peter Buck to Okoki for burial. In his mouth he carried a single leaf which he dropped on the casket. Custom dictated that this green tribute had to be wet with tears. It was.

Kaati tena! Enough of that. I turn now to another aspect of death which gives a key to attitudes. I speak of the death of warriors.

In olden days the bodies of the dead were sometimes brought home, sometimes just the heads. Sometimes bodies were burned on the field of battle, particularly the bodies of enemy dead when the dead were to be honoured. The Taranaki war leader Titokowaru did this with the bodies of the Pakeha soldiers who died in the attack on Te Ngutu-o-te-manu. As the fire blazed he bid farewell to his dead enemy, Gustavus von Tempsky:

'...Ka tae hoki koe ki au, moe ana o kanohi. Tae hokitia, nau i kimi mate mou. Naku, ka moe koe.'

'...You came to me, now you sleep. It cannot be helped, you looked for death from me. And so you sleep.'

Tonga Awhikau, who was well over a century old when he died, described that fire to me 30 years ago. He was a boy of six in Te Ngutu-o-te-manu in 1868.

The survivors of a battle were not always welcomed on their return home. When Paitini Te Tapeka and his wounded friends got home to Ruatahuna after the Orakau battle in 1864 they were greeted by the women with a song of derision, the gist of which was that it would have been better if they had been killed too.

Sometimes when an action was fought near home there would be a tangihanga over the dead, the women coming on to the battlefield searching for their own close relations. At Te Morere, known as Sentry Hill, in Taranaki where Te Ua's second action was fought, the result was disaster for the Maori attackers. In this case the women came on to the battlefield to help the wounded and weep over the dead.

I wrote this into my play *Te Raukura* but it was so poignant for some of the Maori cast that some changes had to be made to the script and to the time the mourners remained on the stage. One of the women said to me, 'I tangi for those dead *real* each night.'

We don't, sadly enough, have to rake through the history of a hundred years ago to find examples when the Second World War remains alive in the minds of many. I can't really say that we all set out lightly because the First World War was only 21 years behind us and we have been brought up in the chill which followed it and in the shadow of the approaching conflict. Seven of us who used to go to school together all served in the army. Two were badly wounded and one was killed. As I have not read any account of how people mourn their warrior dead, I will write of it, if for no more than a tribute to my old friend.

The news came for the next-of-kin by telegram specially delivered. My mother, with two sons away, heard that one of our group was reported killed in action and immediately went to see his mother. Close friends and relations gathered and I would suppose the scene, except for the place, its surroundings and people, was much the same as in many thousands of homes all over the world that day: immediate, poignant, personal grief. Later, so my mother told me, they took his mother across the bridge at Whakarewarewa, across Te Pakira to Wahiao house and there the tangihanga was held. A fine whariki (floor mat) was laid down and propped against a cushion was the photograph of the soldier who had died so far from home. Round it were placed the pictures of the others who had died. To sit by the mother, in addition to her own close friends and relations, came the mothers of other men who had died and those who had lost husbands and fathers and brothers and sweethearts.

People came as to the other tangihanga, came with tears and words to bid farewell to the boy from home buried on an Italian hill. There was a church service and that sad funeral hymn *Piko Nei Te Matenga* was sung at home as it had ben by his Maori comrades in Italy.

Sometimes a Maori soldier killed in battle would lie in state as if he were at home. Usually this was not possible. I have seen it only once and the picture of it is crystal clear in my mind.

This soldier's death was a particularly sad one because it was right at the end of the war. I came in the dawn with a senior officer to the Italian farmhouse, more than a little shaken because of a close escape from possible death on the way. We entered the house, coming into a large room empty of furniture except a bed. On it they had laid the soldier, a fine young man of the Ngati Tuwharetoa people, looking in death the young chieftain he was. A grey army blanket covered most of his body and beside him were his rifle and his steel helmet. Seated beside him was his platoon commander and close by were other officers of the company. The company commander sat with bowed head on the far side. Standing against the walls or seated on the floor were his comrades, their rifles or light machine guns in their hands, grim, silent. I think of how young we were. And yet that was the age at which many of the warriors of old laid out their dead and mourned for them on the field of battle.

It is an attitude to death held by a diminishing section of the Maori people. Those young men did what they thought was proper and they did it within the teachings of their own people.

The return home from the war differed in some notable respects with the return of other men to New Zealand. The joy of being home was equally deep I am sure. But with the Maori Battalion something extra was expected. On the wharf at Wellington there was mourning for the dead. It took precedence and was very real. My company, all men from Rotorua, Taupo and the Bay of Plenty, went back to Rotorua as a body. The march through Tutanekai Street was a joyous one but when we reached Ohinemutu it was tears again. In front of Tamatekapua meeting house the photographs of the dead were on display. Even the young girls who took part in the welcome were dressed in black.

That afternoon we went to Whakarewarewa and again were greeted with the wail for the dead and the tears and the speeches appropriate for a time of deep mourning.

I did not go further but my friends from the Bay of Plenty carried on, joining the people in mourning at Rotoiti, Whakatane, Ruatoki and Opotiki. How easy was the role of the Pakeha soldier, sailor or airman home from the wars compared to ours. It was back to his family, no doubt to a warm welcome home party and then the renewing of old ties and the first steps towards settling down again in a civilian world. From us our people demanded tears and grief first – and deep in our hearts I think we knew they were right.

Let me hasten to say that I do not suggest that the sight of men returning from the wars did not arouse exactly the same feelings among Pakeha, particularly among those whose sons would never return. The difference is that our culture demands the expression, the public expression of this. The New Zealand European culture so firmly sets its face against public, visible, emotional expression of grief. I respect that difference and do not say that one way is better than another. But my way is my way and I will keep it.

This mourning for the dead warrior has until the recent present been a most important part of Maori life. One might be forgiven for thinking the situation an unnatural one, this continual reference to death through the violence of war. Analysis will perhaps show that this is not so.

There were only two periods when the Maori was not engaged in war or when there was not a substantial proportion of the male population who had had experience of it. Those two periods were from the 1870s until 1914 – about 40 years – and 1945 until the present day. And even in this last period there were Maori serving in Korea, Malaysia and Vietnam. A study of custom extending from ancient times to the present shows that as far as death in battle is concerned there is a continuity of spirit with much change and adaptation in practice. Let's classify it.

First there is the mourning on the battlefield, usually brief and poignant, the burial according to military custom and with Christian ritual.

114

Secondly, in the battlefield situation, there is sometimes the vow to obtain utu for the fallen.

Thirdly, there is the mourning at home, the tangihanga in nearly all its parts, except that the body is not there.

Fourthly, at the end of the war – or at convenient times during the war – there are visits to battlefields and cemeteries where the soldiers take part in services and farewell their comrades before returning home. At the end of the Second World War a party of Maori Battalion men visited all the cemeteries, including those in Crete.

Fifthly, there is the return home and the tangihanga on many marae.

Sixthly, there is the erection of memorials, gates, stones, flagpoles, houses, in memory of the dead.

Lastly is the commemoration in song, this often being done during the war itself.

These songs go on and on and are a living, most important part of present-day Maori life. I do not think there is anything similar in New Zealand European culture. The Pakeha has no war songs telling of the exploits of his soldiers, songs known by everyone and sung frequently by young and old. The Pakeha here seems to fight his battles and then want to forget them and get on with the pursuits of peace – and of course that's an excellent attitude. The Maori – or many Maori – still savour the memory of the wars and the songs carry this on among people born long after the soldiers have handed in their arms and equipment and gone back to farm or factory. I have heard groups of people half my age singing such action songs as *Te Ope Tuatahi* telling of the Maori Pioneer Battalion of 1914–18 of which there is now no survivor under the age of 70; *E Te Hokowhitu* which is a tribute to Moananui-a-Kiwa Ngarimu V.C. who died in North Africa; *Hoki Mai, Hoki Mai* which is a welcome to men returning from the Second World War; and even the famed canoe poi which was composed during the First World War to inspire people at home to support the war effort – *Hoea Ra Te Waka Nei* it is called and the waka, the canoe, was the people at home working for the men overseas. The translation in English is now seldom sung and so Pakeha seeing this delightful poi dance can't be expected to know that it contains a lament for the dead. Here's the translation of one verse:

> Small may be this our canoe
> Floating on a sea of tears,
> Tribute to the brave who fell,
> Gone where duty calls.

Another is the action song *Pa Mai To Reo Aroha* which is a tribute of affection from the people at home to the men serving abroad in the Second World War.

In this respect at least the memory of the dead in battle is kept green and must have some influence on the Maori attitude to death.

Our dead are very close to us in Maoridom. They do not lie alone in that short space between death and burial. We stay with them every minute and talk to them and sing to them. When we have returned them to the earth we remember them in song and speech. Each time we meet one another after being apart we pause and weep again, no matter how happy the occasion for our meeting.

My own dear Arawa dead are with me always, especially those who lie with their people at Muruika, in the land of their father, by the lake they loved; my father, my uncles, my cousins, close on one hundred of them now, veterans who followed the trail of blood-eyed Tumatauenga and kept the warrior tradition handed down through the ages to them – and may it, with them, end forever in a world to come which needs the warrior no more.

And if there should come a day when with the soft rain falling and the drums beating and the bugles blowing and the men marching and the women wailing and the guns firing and the gulls screaming you take me there, you may know that I will rest very content as the least in the honoured company.

For we will be in the heart of our own land, in the midst of our own people, which is the only place for the dead to lie. North is Mokoia, grey-blue in the mist; east is Whakapoungakau, hill of the longing heart; south is Moerangi where the sky sleeps and Te Tihi-o-tonga, peak of the south; and west is Ngongotaha with the lightning flashing its salute to death on the mountain's gaunt flank. For this is the land of Arawa and we are her people.

Ma Te Atua koutou e manaaki.

REFERENCES:

Te Rangi Hiroa, *The Coming of the Maori,* Whitcombe and Tombs, Wellington, 1950.
R.S. Oppenheim, *Maori Death Customs,* A.H. and A.W. Reed Ltd, Wellington, 1973.

GOD, MAN AND UNIVERSE:
A MAORI VIEW

MAORI MARSDEN

THE ROUTE TO MAORITANGA through abstract interpretation is a dead end. The way can only lie through a passionate, subjective approach. That is more likely to lead to a goal.

As a person brought up within the culture, who has absorbed the values and attitudes of the Maori, my approach to Maori things is largely subjective. The charge of lacking objectivity does not concern me: the so-called objectivity some insist on is simply a form of arid abstraction, a model or a map. It is not the same thing as the taste of reality.

I like to use a descriptive method to explore the features of consciousness found in Maori cultural experiences. So I shall describe the religious, philosophical and metaphysical attitudes upon which Maoritanga is based. While I will also do a formal analysis of some of the basic concepts out of which these attitudes arise, it is important to remember that Maoritanga is a thing of the heart rather than the head. For that reason analysis is necessary only to make explicit what the Maori understands implicitly in his daily living, feeling, acting and deciding.

I am concerned, then, with viewing attitudes from within the culture. To do this, the writer must unmask himself for he can only interpret his culture to another in terms of what the institutions, customs, mores and traditions mean to him. From there I must ask, 'Is this a view held by my Maori people generally? Do their actions, their words, their oral traditions express the same general attitudes which I find in myself?'

So this study is presented from a point of view that begins from an analysis of the meaning that a particular cultural element holds for me, then goes on to consider whether the same meaning is true for other Maori. For what is Maoritanga? Briefly, it is the corporate view that Maori hold about ultimate reality and meaning.

Our point of departure is found in the words of the formal welcome:

Haere mai te ihi; haere mai te wehi; haere mai te mana; haere mai te tapu.

Draw near o excellent ones; draw near o awesome ones; draw near o charismatic ones; draw near o sacred ones.

117

This is a formal welcome used on special occasions to greet especially eminent guests on to a marae. It serves as a welcome and as a warning. As a welcome, it pays tribute to the dignity and status of the guests, acknowledging that they are the 'chosen' of the gods – charismatic people to whom the gods have delegated authority and power, to manifest the will and operation of gods in the natural world. As a warning, it serves notice on those assembled that since these are the chosen of the gods, they are tapu people, set apart and dedicated to the service of gods. As such, they cannot be treated with indignity and impunity without incurring the wrath and retribution of the gods.

It is this last consideration which makes the ritualistic observance of marae protocol (kawa) so formal and even rigid. For both guests (manuhiri) and hosts (tangata whenua), the formal observance of local kawa ensures the avoidance of transgression and the giving of offence.

An analysis of the concepts which underlie this formal welcome reveals the basic themes and approach of the Maori to questions of ultimate reality and the relationships among God, man and the universe.

Ihi

The ihi has a close affinity with the Greek word 'arete'. Arete was derived from Aries, son of Jupiter. He was the god of war. Arete denoted the spirit of strife. By natural association, it came to mean manliness or vigour in battle. It later came to mean excellence in battle, and developed to include the idea of excellence or virtue blended with the impression of force. In Maori, for example: 'Haere ake ana te ihi me te mana o nga toa.' (A sense of vital force and power preceded the advance of the warriors.)

Ihi may be defined as 'vital force or personal magnetism which, radiating from a person, elicits in the beholder a response of awe and respect'. The closest English equivalent is 'personal or animal magnetism'. It is a psychic and not a spiritual force. Psychic force is an intrinsic quality in human beings, a personal essence which can be developed more highly in some than in others; spiritual force (mana) is a gift endued by the gods.

Mana

Mana means spiritual authority and power as opposed to the purely psychic and natural force of ihi. In a theological sense, it may be translated as charisma. To understand the full implications and connotations, we can borrow two more Greek words, 'exousia' and 'dunamis'. Exousia is derived from the verb 'exesti' which means, 'lawful or permitted'. It is normally translated as 'authority'. In the Greek sense, authority means 'lawful permission delegated by the superior to the subordinate'.

In the Maori sense, since authority is derived from the gods, mana as authority means 'lawful permission delegated by the gods to their human agent to act on their behalf and in accordance with their revealed will'. Since authority is a spiritual gift delegated by the gods, man remains always the agent or channel – never the source of mana.

Dunamis is the other aspect of mana. From it we derive the words dynamic, dynamite, dynamo. It is derived from the Greek verb 'dunamai' which means 'to be capable or to have power'. It denotes the ability or power to perform. Thus dunamis meant 'power, might, strength; the power to perform'. It meant also (in the New Testament sense) 'power in action, power to perform miraculous works, and the power of the spoken word'. To the Maori, mana includes all these ideas, but essentially it means 'that which manifests the power of the gods'.

Mana in its double aspect of authority and power may be defined as 'lawful permission delegated by the gods to their human agents and accompanied by the endowment of spiritual power to act on their behalf and in accordance with their revealed will'. This delegation of authority is shown in dynamic signs or works of power.

Authority and power in this sense must be clearly distinguished since it is clear that to exercise spiritual power outside the limits delegated is to abuse the gift, and results either in its withdrawal or in that power running rampant and causing harm to the agent and others.

A simple analogy will make the distinction clearer. A person approaches a traffic crossing and the lights turn red. He has power to cross but no permission. The lights turn green but his car stalls at that moment. He has permission to cross, but no power. His car starts and the lights remain green. He has both authority and power to proceed.

Tapu

The Maori idea of tapu is close to the Jewish idea translated in the words, 'sacred' and 'holy', although it does not have the later ethical connotations of the New Testament of 'moral righteousness'.

It has both religious and legal connotations. A person, place or thing is dedicated to a deity and by that act it is set aside or reserved for the sole use of the deity. The person or object is thus removed from the sphere of the profane and put into the sphere of the sacred. It is untouchable, no longer to be put to common use. It is this untouchable quality that is the main element in the concept of tapu. In other words, the object is sacred and any profane use is sacrilege, breaking of the law of tapu.

From the purely legal aspect, it suggests a contractual relationship has been made between the individual and his deity whereby a person dedicates himself or an object to the service of a deity in return for protection against malevolent forces and the power to manipulate his environment to meet needs and demands.

The idea of manipulating environment is based on the Maori view that there are three orders of reality – the physical or natural, the psychic and the spiritual. Whilst the natural realm is normally subject to physical laws, these can be affected, modified and even changed by the application of the higher laws of the psychic and spiritual.

By applying psychical laws (intellectual and emotional consciousness) in a scientific manner, man now manipulates that environment to suit his own purposes. This principle is no less applicable in the spiritual realm. In the Maori view, the application of spiritual laws to this end is dependent upon man's cooperation with the gods. This is brought about by entering into the contractual relationship already mentioned.

The method of entering into this relationship was by the tohi or sacramental rite of initiation. This consisted of two complementary acts: the dedication and the consecration. The act of dedication (tapae) consisted of offering up a person, place or thing to the service of the deity, a declaration of the purpose intended and a definition of the future role of the object dedicated. It was henceforth sacred and untouchable, the object was now tapu. It could not be put to profane use. The profanation of tapu was regarded as a transgression (takatakahi) of the gods to whom the object had been dedicated, and such transgression incurred vengeance.

The act of dedication was followed by the act of consecration – an act of praise extolling the power and virtue of the gods who were then invoked by name and petitioned to endue the person or object with mana. The prayers were accompanied by a sacramental act (tohi). Whilst the tohunga might participate in the consecratory prayers, the consecration was the prerogative of the gods. It was they who completed the rite, provided man fulfilled the conditions. The dedication was man's part, the consecration the response of the gods. Since the dedication was sacrificial, in the sense that it was offering a person's life or possession to the service of the gods, the sacrifice was accepted and consecrated by the bestowal of mana.

The bestowing of mana on people differed from that on things or places. In the former case, the spirit of the gods fell upon the person and filled or possessed him. The spirit of the gods guided and directed him, subject to his continuing assent. This was a covenant relationship which could be dissolved by either party not fulfilling the terms of the agreement. In the latter case, the gods placed guardian spirits over places or things to watch over the property dedicated to them. These guardian spirits (kaitiaki) manifested themselves by appearing in the form (aria) of animals, birds or other natural objects as a warning against transgression, or to effect punishment for breach of tapu. The Pakeha idea of haunting is similar to the idea of this role played by guardians.

Two popular misconceptions should be cleared away. Early missionaries and anthropologists perpetuated the incorrect idea that mana was the positive and tapu the negative aspect of some vague psychic or spiritual force. As we have seen, tapu is the sacred state or condition of a person or thing placed under the patronage of the gods. Mana is the enduement of that object with spiritual power through the indwelling spirit over it. Humans thus became the channel through which the indwelling spirit of the deity was manifest.

Another error popularised by early anthropologists was that primitive man held an animistic view of nature, by which they meant that primitive man believed all natural objects to be animated by its own spirit. For the Maori, there was a clear distinction between the essence (mauri) of a person or object and the distinct realm of the spirit which stood over the realm of the natural order and was indwelt by spiritual beings. Since the natural order was not a closed system it could be infiltrated and interpenetrated by the higher order of the spirit. In fact, the Maori further distinguished between the essence of inanimate and animate objects. Whilst all the created order partook of mauri (life force, ethos) by which all things cohere in nature, in human beings this essence was of a higher order and was called mauriora (life principle). This essence (mauri) I am convinced, was originally regarded as elemental energy derived from the realm of Te Korekore, out of which the stuff of the universe was created.

In a secondary sense a tapu object may be classified as an accursed or unclean (poke) thing. The condition of tapu is transmitted by contact or association and a person can be contaminated and polluted by it.

Where contamination occurs through contact with sacred objects in the normal course of a tohunga's duties, he must cleanse himself before resuming his secular life if he is to avoid spreading this contamination or avoid offending the gods. But where contamination occurs through transgression, then a person must not only be cleansed from the pollution but the effects of the mana brought into action by it must be neutralised if the person is not to suffer its ill effects. It is in this contaminating and polluting sense that tapu is classified as accursed or unclean, a state in which the personality becomes wide open to either attack or invasion by demonic and other spiritual forces.

So, we may define tapu as the sacred state or condition in which a person, place or thing is set aside by dedication to the gods and thereby removed from profane use. This tapu is secured by the sanction of the gods and reinforced by endowment with mana.

Wehi

Wehi may be translated simply as awe or fear in the presence of the ihi of a person, or of the mana and tapu of the gods.

It is the emotion of fear generated by anxiety or apprehension in case one gives offence to the gods, or a response of awe at a manifestation of divine power (mana).

The Pure Rites

To counteract the effects of tapu, the Maori employed what they termed 'pure' rites (purification rites). They were designed to cleanse from tapu, neutralise tapu, or to propitiate the gods. Where the intention was to cleanse from the contamination of tapu, the sacramental element used was normally water. For neutralising tapu or for the propitiation of the gods, the sacramental means was cooked food.

After a person occupied with sacred duties wished to resume his secular activities or after a person had inadvertently transgressed the tapu of an object, he washed himself in water dedicated to the god Rehua. Thus water used for the purpose was called Te wai o Rehua (the water of Rehua). Its function was the same as that of 'holy water' used by the Christian Church and an element of all major religions.

There is no forgiveness for deliberate transgression (takatakahi) since such transgression is a direct challenge to the mana of the gods. Such challenges were a common occurrence in Maori life and aimed at subduing the powers of the god of an opposing tribe or person. Should the mana of the opposing god prove too powerful, then the pure rite took the form of the 'pure whakanoa' designed to neutralise (whakanoa) or ward off the malevolent and debilitating effects of such mana.

Different types of food, ferns and other herbs were cooked in the 'umu pure' and after it became cold, the food was placed upon the person's head, the most sacred part of the body, and exorcism prayers recited over him. Popular belief held that by cooking, the mauri of the plant was released and thereby made common (noa) or neutralised, a state of things abhorrent to the gods, thus ensuring their departure. As tapu could be transmitted by contact, so could its opposite profane state be transmitted by contact with objects made noa (neutral, common, profane, sterile).

This belief accounts for an ariki (high chief) or tohunga being fed by servants, especially if they were engaged in projects of a very sacred nature. Contact with cooked food would neutralise their tapu and mana. It also accounts for other precautions practised by modern Maori of not ironing their clothes on a meal table, not washing their clothes with other linen such as tablecloths and avoiding placing their hats on a meal-table or passing food over a person's head. All such prohibitions are designed to avoid the depletion of mana.

One other form of whakanoa was employed in the official opening of a new building. During construction, a building was placed under the mana and tapu of Tane, god of the forest, and of the various gods of construction and carving. Before the building could be put to common, secular and profane use it had to be freed from the mana and tapu of the gods. The ruahine or tapairu of the tribe (the senior woman by descent of the senior family) accompanied by the tohunga and other members of the tribe, entered to 'takahi' (trample underfoot) the tapu of the gods under whose mana the building had been placed during construction. This neutralised it and decontaminated it of tapu. It ensured that future users of the building would be unharmed.

The mana of the male differed from that of the female. Whilst the mana of the male was viewed as being positive, that of the female was regarded as negative. Hence the mana of a high-born female was regarded as particularly potent in negating or neutralising tapu. As a consequence, the act of a woman stepping over a man instead of going around him was highly improper and reprehensible since such an action depleted the male of his mana.

The pure as a propitiatory act, whilst remaining essentially the same in basic form, was applied on many different occasions. It proceeded on the principle that all created things were the property of the gods who, as the regents of Io the supreme god, were responsible for the departments of nature under which that object came. All animate things were regarded as children of the departmental gods.

The pure rakau was used to propitiate Tane, god of the forest, before a tree was felled for canoe-making or house-building. A fire was lit under the tree and the first chip together with mauku fern was burnt. The scent, representing the essence of the tree, was offered up to propitiate Tane for the slaying of this forest child of Tane.

The same principle was applied in the harvesting of food crops, fruit, birds or fish. The food was cooked and whilst it was still steaming hot, it was elevated in the hands and 'waved' to and fro before the gods so that the essence symbolised by the rising steam could return to the gods. They were then petitioned to accept the essence while man consumed the substance. Thanksgiving for the bounty of the gods was given, after which the tohunga ate a morsel and buried the remainder. Only when this rite was completed could the harvest proceed.

Other propitiatory rites were connected with the ritual of the dead. They were known as the pure tupapaku (funeral rites), pure hahu (exhumation or disinterment rites), and the pure koiwi (interment of human bones). All persons on death came under the jurisdiction (maru) of the gods of the Po (for example Whiro, Maru, or Hine-nui-te-po). The tapu of the dead was particularly virulent and a person contracting such tapu through contact had to be purified and neutralised. The practice continues in modern times.

In most tribes, it is still the custom to wash oneself after returning from a funeral. In modern times, the pure whakanoa at a tangi has largely been replaced by the hakari (feast) which follows the funeral. Amongst some tribes, it is still the practice to mihi (pay verbal tribute) to the gods of the Po and exhort them to accept the essence of the food as their portion whilst allowing men the substance. This mihi has been largely replaced by the Christian grace.

In some places sextons at a particular funeral eat apart from the main body of the people. Their meal is laid out in the place where the corpse has lain during the tangi. This is to neutralise the tapu, both on the place contaminated by the tapu of the corpse, and that on themselves.

Times and customs change. The ancient reason for certain ritual acts can fade with the passage of time, or considerations of convenience and practicality can force changes. A practice creeping into some areas of Ngapuhi is holding the hakari before the funeral service, to avoid the inordinate amount of time taken up by it and thereby facilitate the departure of guests who have to travel long distances on their return journey.

I wonder whether this is the original reason for the hakari fading with the passage of time, or a question of convenience, or both. Whatever the reason, the winds of change enforced by acculturation continue to blow and bury some institutions under the sands of time; or temper the regard and value of others.

The post-funeral hakari of modern times must be viewed within the tangi. Though the element of local pride enters into it, the elaborate preparations and prodigal amounts of food devoted to the tangi remain for the Maori part of their ritual and social obligations to the gods and to the manuhiri. Hence no efforts are spared to fulfil obligations, on the premise that only the best is good enough for the gods, and that tribal honour is at stake before visitors. These considerations encourage locals to exceed the conventional demands of hospitality.

It may seem that the modern tangi retains some of its pre-Christian associations. This is true. But it must be remembered that the significance of the various rites is only partially understood or totally forgotten. Again, the various rites, whilst to a large extent retaining their traditional form, have been so Christianised that offerings once made to the gods of the Po are now made to Ihowa (Jehovah) or to Jesus Christ as Lord of the dead and the living. Other elements adopted from Christianity (the totally Christian church and funeral services) have become an integral part of the tangi. However these changes may occur, the general traditional form and underlying principles remain.

Tohi Rites

A dedicatory act placed a person or thing under tapu. The consecratory act was the means by which the person or thing was endued with mana. Earlier, we saw that whilst persons were filled with the spirit of the gods themselves to endue them with power, places and things were not filled or possessed, but brought under the patronage of the gods who consigned guardian spirits to oversee the object or place. The consecration of a person was accompanied by a sacramental act and these acts were called 'tohi'. This word means literally 'to endue'.

It is not generally realised that prior to the advent of Christianity, the Maori possessed a sacramental system which included sacraments parallel to those of the Christian church. This probably explains why Christianity was so readily accepted by the Maori and further explains his strong allegiance to the sacramental churches. Because of the parallel between the systems, we can make comparisons between them to help us understand the principles underlying both.

According to the Augustinian definition of Western Christendom, a sacrament is 'an outward visible sign setting forth and pledging an inward spiritual grace'. To the Maori, a sacrament is simply 'the means by which mana (charisma, grace, spiritual power) is transmitted to humans'. The means used could be a specific element (water) from the created order; or another person by tactile transmission. The personal agent instrumental in this act must himself have been previously endued with the spirit of the gods since he can only impart what he himself already has.

Baptism with Water

Iriiri, rumaki and uhi are alternative names for the rite of baptism. Iriiri describes the purpose or function of the rite. It means literally, 'to place upon, to endow' and signifies that baptism was the rite of enduement with authority. Uhi (to sprinkle) and rumaki (to dip into) describe the method.

A child was held over flowing water or the sea, which symbolised living waters, and the gods ruling over the different departments of nature were petitioned to endow the child with the mental and physical qualities desired. As the names of the different gods were invoked, should the child sneeze, cough or yawn, it was taken as a sign that the spirit of that god had alighted (iri) on that child. The child was then dedicated to those particular gods by immersing it in the water or by sprinkling it with water from a branch dipped in the stream or sea.

In this way, the child was incorporated into those gods to whom he had been dedicated and this gave him authority to invoke the names of those particular gods in times of crisis. Since the name signifies the extension of the personality, the god must come to the aid of the suppliant.

Secondly, the child was placed under the tapu of those gods. In other words, he was now removed from the sphere of the profane into the sphere of the sacred. His life was to be lived in the service of those gods in return for their blessing. In the Christian sense, it signifies the 'dying of the old life, and its burial; and arising to a new life in Christ'.

Here is part of the dedication used, according to tradition, at Maui's birth:

Tihe Mauri ora! Ki te Wheiao, ki te Ao-marama.
Ka tu kei runga, ko wai koe?
Ko Tu, Ko Rongo koe, ko Tane koe.
Ko te manuhiri i ahu mai i Hawaiki, nau mai.

This sneeze is the sign of the new life, in this world.
And when you are mature, whose shall you be?

You shall be dedicated to Tu, (god of war),
To Rongo (god of vegetation), to Tane (god of man and forest).
To you who come from Hawaiki
We welcome your presence.

Here we see that the sign of the coming of Tu, Rongo and Tane was apparent when Maui sneezed during the invocation of each of the names of these particular gods. Other gods such as Tangaroa, god of the sea, did not adopt Maui and bring him under their patronage. The dedication of Maui to these three gods carried the implication in the second line that when Maui matured he would not only be under the tutelage, but would have authority to invoke them in times of crisis. There is also the consecration, in which these gods who have come from Hawaiki Tapu (abode of the gods), are exhorted to fill Maui with their presence (nau mai).

Tohi Whakahaa

Tohi whakahaa, or tohi mauri, is the enduement of mauri (life principle) by infusion (whakahaa) of the breath (manawa). It was used on two main occasions: after neutralisation of a person's mana and vitality through the use of cooked food (umu pure); or at the initiation of a novice into the order of tohunga. In the former case, after a person had transgressed the tapu of the gods he went through the 'pure whakanoa' in which cooked food was placed on his head and the spirits causing his sickness were exorcised. This not only neutralised the mana and tapu of the opposing gods, but also the mana and tapu of his own tutelary gods, as well as debilitating his vital force. Sickness and death resulted from the depletion of the natural vital force through the agency of the gods or evil spirits, and this mauri ora had to be replaced through the tohi mauri.

In the case of initiation, the tohi mauri was designed to give a novice learning the arts of tohunga extra mauri, since the work he would take up would require inner strength in the battle against alien spiritual power and for the task of bearing his people's burdens. For this role he needed a double function of vital life force (mauri ora) for his physical and psychic health.

The method was the same for both. The tohunga ahurewa (high priest) bit the hollow of the head, (regarded as the spiritual mouth of the body) in order to open it up symbolically and then infused his breath (manawa) as the vehicle for mauri into the person by breathing on him. He thereby imparted his own vital life force into the novice.

Te Tuha

Te tuha was the tohi of the 'sacred spittle' employed by the tohunga taura (as distinct from the tohunga ahurewa), to impart mana. The taura were the tohunga of the dark powers and in order to impart their mana to their disciples, they spat

126

upon the disciple's head and invoked the spirits of the dark powers to possess the disciple and empower him with the dark arts of makutu and whaiwhaia – the casting of spells to bring sickness and death on their enemies.

Te Whakapaa

Te whakapaa was a tohi employed by a father before his death to impart the family mana to his eldest son. The eldest son could be by-passed by the father however, and the family mana given to a younger son. It was also employed by some chiefs to institute the eldest son into the office and functions that he himself had held. In both cases, the intention was the same: to establish the son in the position of the father as head of the family or head of the tribe. The method was to assemble the family and elders as witnesses and then the father or chief laid his hands upon the son's head and pronounced over him both the office and functions he was to assume, and then pronounced his blessing. This laying on of hands was normally accompanied by the tohi mauri.

For the other members of the family, the whakapaa was also used as a means of blessing, although the tohi mauri was not employed in these cases. A similar method was employed by the ancient Israelites to impart the father's blessing to their children. The corresponding rite in the Christian church is the rite of confirmation.

Kairarawa

A means to replenish mana was the rite of kairarawa or cannibalism. The word 'rarawa' in this context means with violence or with force. It is a term used to denote the forces that underlie the whole range of divine powers implied in the terms 'mauri ihi', 'tapu' and 'mana'. Kairarawa denoted the consumption of the life force and the psychic and spiritual forces of the enemy which replenished one's own powers.

Like concepts such as tapu, which included an opposition of ideas within the same concept, (for example sacredness and uncleanness), so the concept of kairarawa had its contrast in the concept of kaitoa. All warriors going into battle were dedicated to the god of war and specially consecrated. When a warrior fell in battle, especially if he was of aristocratic lineage, he was regarded as a person who, because of his rank and the tohi rites he had been subjected to, was a person of great mana, as well as of ihi. So the conquerors cooked him and ate certain selected portions of his body where they believed his mana resided. By eating his flesh they consumed his mana and ihi, and thereby replenished their own.

Eating the enemy's mana not only depleted the mana of the opposing tribe, it also brought the gods of those tribes under the subjection of the conquering tribe. In one sense it seems as if the fickle gods deserted the weak and sided with the strong. This eating of the enemy thus degraded the conquered tribe who were now treated with contempt by their conquerors. Degradation of the conquered tribe was termed 'kaitoa'. It signified that the toa (courage, strength) of the conquered had been eaten. Kaitoa means literally 'to eat the strength and courage of another'.

So cannibalism served two functions: first to replenish one's own powers (kairarawa); and second to deplete the enemy of their mana and thereby degrade them (kaitoa). During Hongi Hika's last battle in the Houhora area in the far north against the Aupouri, one of the war leaders, Houtaewa, was finally slain. During Houtaewa's lifetime he was regarded as the greatest warrior of the Aupouri. He was famous for his speed and agility in battle and it was commonly said that his mana resided in his thighs and legs. After his death, Houtaewa's legs were severed and cooked and certain portions eaten by Hongi and his warriors to gain his mana. The rest of his body was untouched out of respect for his bravery and because he was related to Hongi himself. His body was returned to the Aupouri by Poroa, who had for some time been associated with Hongi in his battles, but who was also a close relative of Houtaewa. In this instance, the purpose was solely that of kairarawa, not kaitoa, as evidenced by the return of the body for burial.

As the ancient Maori ate their enemies in order to replenish their vital force and take in the mana of the gods, so the modern Maori Christian goes to communion to take in the vital life force and mana of Jesus Christ by means of the 'aria' of bread and wine.

An interesting sidelight to cannibalism is the incident by which the Ngapuhi tribe received its name. Several generations before the migration of the Ngatoki-mata-whaorua canoe to New Zealand, one of Nukutawhiti's ancestors, an ariki called Arikitapu, was betrothed (puhi) to Karereoa-aitu, the ahurewa of the tribe. She wanted a human heart to eat, so they chose her niece because of her high rank, and by magical arts slew her and removed her heart. The corpse was taken to the lagoon of Moanarua and by occult powers she was transformed into a tani-wha. When Arikitapu's son was born, he was named Puhi to commemorate the event, and was variously called Puhi taniwha-rau (Puhi of the many taniwha) and Puhi-moana-ariki (Puhi of the sea of the nobility) to denote his association with Moanarua, reputed to be the stronghold of the mana of the ancient Polynesians.

The Tohunga

The word tohunga is often translated as 'expert' (for example tohunga-ta-moko is rendered in English as 'expert carver'). Such use is wrong and stems from the mistaken idea that because the Maori used this term in association with recognised experts in a particular field the word must mean expert. The word tohunga is derived from the stem 'tohu' which as a verb means a sign or manifestation. Tohunga is the gerundive of tohu and means a 'chosen one' or 'appointed one'.

The tohunga was a person chosen or appointed by the gods to be their repre-

128

sentative and the agent by which they manifested their operations in the natural world by signs of power (tohu mana). The choice of the tohunga in an official capacity as either an ahurewa to the tribe or as a leader in a particular field, rested with the gods and with the tribe. As young men developed, the seers of the tribe watched for signs to manifest themselves in these youngsters, such as being constantly drawn towards a group occupied in a particular pursuit, an inordinate preoccupation with a particular facet of life, a keen student in a particular field. Signs such as these were considered as the attraction and drawing of the gods to a particular vocation. These indications were put to the test by use of certain spiritual or occult rituals, and the young man was accepted or rejected. If accepted, he was dedicated and consecrated to the gods who empowered him for that particular office and function.

The function of a tohunga was defined by the qualifying adjective. Those who fulfilled the office and function of priests to the tribe were known as 'tohunga ahurewa'. As the name indicates they were the chosen ones (tohunga) of the 'higher way' (ahurewa). Their function was to mediate between the gods and the tribe to ensure the welfare of the tribe. They gave advice on the best time to engage in certain activities: where the best fishing grounds were at certain seasons; what the best methods were for ensuring success in economic activities. On the spiritual level, they were experts in propitiating the gods in the various religious rites and also in the sacred lore, traditions and genealogies of the tribe.

The second class of tohunga were the taura. They operated in the related field of the occult and black arts. It was recognised that they were inferior in mana to the ahurewa and less learned because they were denied access to the sacred lore of the kauae runga. In fact, many of the taura were drop-outs from the wananga. They had failed the tests that each pia (novice) was required to undergo before being initiated into the lore of the upper wananga; being rejected, many of these resorted to black magic in their search for power. Thus they were also known as tohunga whaiwhaia, an adjective meaning 'pursuer'. By their black arts, they cast evil spells on others and set the demonic spirits to pursuing their victims. Another name for them is tohunga makutu, tohunga who cast evil spells.

Some tohunga of this class developed out of the spirit of strife and jealousy that existed between rival families. To exact vengeance they sold themselves to the dark gods and conducted their nefarious activities in secret. Hence the name taura (rope) signifying their ability to bring people into bondage under the dark powers.

Specialist tohunga were experts in various fields of artistic activity: carvers, tattooers, and so on. Here the concept was similar to the Greek idea of the spirit of muses coming upon a person to endow him with their artistic abilities. This is how the mistaken idea arose that a tohunga-ta-moko meant 'an expert tatooist'. It means a person chosen by the gods of tattooing and empowered with mana to suit him for this task.

The office and functions of the Christian priest are the same in principle for the welfare and benefit of the people. The choice and the consecration remain the prerogative of the divine one: 'You have not chosen me, but I have chosen you.'

We have ranged over the basic concepts of ihi, wehi, mana and tapu, studying their implications in the religious and cultural milieu. We have glanced at related concepts such as mauri, noa, kaitoa, and the basic religious and sacramental rites associated with these. A comparison between the Maori and Christian sacramental systems has been made to show that certain spiritual principles are universal in application. It remains for these concepts to be placed within the context of the metaphysical, philosophical and religious thinking out of which they originated.

The Gods and Creation

In considering the place and role of gods, we are on less firm ground as various tribes have different traditions. Those who hold a common tradition do not agree in detail. For this reason, it is necessary to balance tradition with the body of oral literature used on formal occasions to sanction customs or to justify a particular course of action. A semantic approach will also help. By analysing the root meaning of words, the relationships between words in stylised sentences, the symbolic and evocative value attributed to each, and by a study of grammatical constructions peculiar to Maori, the inner thought and psychological thinking responsible for such constructions and methods of expression become explicit and highlight cultural values.

For this study, I will be taking the tradition of the Ngapuhi wananga, modified by the tradition of my own tribal elders and my observations over the years of variations in detail in tribal custom and oral literature of other tribes expressed on the marae.

Io, Supreme God

In the beginning, Io existed alone in the realm of Te Korekore, in his passive state as Io-matamoe, Io-mata-ane, Io-kore-te-whiwhia (Io of the slumbering countenance, Io of the calm and tranquil countenance, Io the unchanging and unadulterated in whom there is no confusion and inconsistency). Nothing existed before Io, for he alone was pre-existent as Io-matua-kore the parentless, as Io-matua the first parent, as Io-mau the precursor, as Io-pukenga the first cause, as Io-taketake the foundation of all things.

He held intercourse within himself, between the ihomatua of his active and positive thought, and between the ihomariri of his passive and negative self. So Io alone had a double iho (essence). He was both Io-mata-ane of the passive countenance and Io-mata-kaakaa of the flashing active countenance.

He was truly supreme god for he was Io-moa the exalted one; Io-tikitiki-o-rangi, the supreme one of heaven; Io-te-toi-o-ngarangi, the pinnacle of heaven; Io-nui the infinite one; Io-roa, the eternal one; Io-uru, the omnipresent; Io-mata-kana, the all-seeing one; Io-wananga, the all-wise; Io-mata-aho of the glorious blinding countenance.

Io dwelt tranquilly in the void of Te Korekore. He roused himself and stirred up his activity and communed within himself, for apart from his passivity and negativity, nothing existed. His essence flowed forth to fertilise Te Korekore. Then he spoke his command and the iho of the night was increased. He spoke again and the iho of Hawaiki in the night regions blossomed, and on succeeding commands the iho of the heavens, of light, of the rock foundation of the earth, and of the waters were increased. Thus were the essential foundations of the universe laid.

At that time, only the seed of potential being was established and there was no form or substance for this seed of creation gestated in Te Korekore. Then Io activated himself once more and he recited (tapatapa) the names of the different foundations of things: of the night and of light, of the earth and sky and waters, of the depths and heights, of the expanse of the skies and borders of the seas. Thus things became differentiated and took form.

Io called into being the night realms, and divided them into various planes of the great night (Po Nui); the extensive night (Po Rou); the enveloping night (Po Uriuri); the intensive night (Po Kerekere); the night streaked with light (Po Tiwhatiwha); the night streaked with broad light (Po Haehaea); the night of unseeing (Te Po te Kitea); the night of hesitant exploration (Te Po Tango-tango); the night of groping (Te Po te Whawha); the night inclined towards day (Po Namunamu ki te Wheiao); the night that borders day (Po Tahuri Atu).

Then Io illumined the nights with soft light so that they glowed like twilight (kakarauri). He divided the Po Tahuri Atu from the dawnlight (wheiao) with a veil (te arai) and beyond the dawn light he placed Te Ao Marama – the broad daylight.

In the night regions of soft light, Io established the several Hawaiki: Hawaiki Nui, Hawaiki-Roa, Hawaiki-Pamamao, Hawaiki Tapu (great Hawaiki, extensive Hawaiki, far distance Hawaiki, and sacred Hawaiki) in which Io chose to dwell with his divine assistants. The Hawaiki became the abode of gods and heroes. But no one, other gods included, could enter Hawaiki Tapu for it was sacred to Io. The other Hawaiki were also sacred and in ancient times were not mentioned in common talk except by oblique reference as Tawhiti Nui, Tawhiti Roa, Tawhiti Pamamao.

Having created the nights and the Hawaiki, Io brought into being the first gods, Rangi-awatea and Papa-tua-nuku, the male and female principles out of which all things derived. Awatea was the god of 'space and light' (watea and awatea) and the first heaven was created by him on the foundations established by Io. It was known as the heaven of Watea (Te Rangi-a-Watea). But having completed the first heaven, he looked below him and saw the spirit of Papa-tua-nuku (Mother Earth) and descended to cohabit with her. Out of this union sprang their first-born, Tane and the other gods after him: Tangaroa, Rongo, Tumatauenga,

Haumia-tike-tike, Ru-ai-moko, and Tawhiri-ma-tea.

But Rangi continued to cling to Papa-tua-nuku and gave up his task of completing the heavens. By this act, he doomed his offspring to dwell in perpetual darkness. Io the omniscient stirred his activity and sent the spirit of rebellion to stir the children to revolt. After consultation among the brothers they decided, with the exception of Tawhiri-ma-tea, to separate their parents and allow light into their world. After several abortive attempts, Tane conceived the idea of standing on his hands on Papa and thrusting against Rangi with his feet. His manoeuvre succeeded and Rangi was flung into the skies.

Tane was summoned by Io and after elaborate pure rites, he descended to the borders of Hawaiki Tapu where the sacred winds, the mouth-piece of Io, commissioned him to continue with the task of completing the heavens. So the heavens were completed and became known as the great heavens of Tane (Rangi-nui-a-Tane). At the same time as Tane received the mana to complete the heavens, Io delegated through Tane various tasks for his brothers. So they became the regents of Io to continue creation in the departments of nature. Thus Tangaroa became the god of the sea, Rongo the god of vegetation, Ru-ai-moko divided the lands asunder, Tawhiri took over the meteorological department and Tu took over the war office. Tane reserved two departments for himself on earth, the forest and birds, and the creation of man. The first human created was Hine-ahu-one (the maid that emerged out of the dust). Tane took clay, moistened it with water and sculptured the form of a female. He then infused the breath of his nostrils (hongi) into her and she came alive. Meanwhile, Awatea had been summoned by Io (prior to Tane's commission), deprived of his mana and banished into the Night Realm. It was the mana from Awatea that was given to Tane.

It is said that Io, the omnipresent one, established temples at Hawaiki Tapu in the Po regions, at the pinnacle of the heavens, at Whitianga in the east, at Hikurangi in the west, at Tokerau in the north and at Rarotonga in the south. These places were beyond the horizon, and were sacred to Io.

Thus the nights and the heavens, the earth and the water, were created, and all things in them. But it was Io who laid the foundations and delegated continuous creation to the offspring of Rangi and Papa.

Io had his divine assistants in the heavens and the night regions. Those of the heavenly realm were called Te Whanau-a-Rangi, the company of heaven. These included the apa (spiritual beings) called the whatukura and marei-kura, the male and female. And with them the pou-tiri-ao, who were all male. These were the personal assistants of Io. In the night realms, Io's assistants were the mairihau. Their functions were similar to those of the whatukura in the heavens, in that they were the sacred wraiths who transmitted Io's commands.

Maru was Io's chief assistant in the realm of Po and seems to have been a beneficent overlord of that region, since he is invoked in some areas during the pure feast at funeral rites to receive the spirit of the departed into Hawaiki. Hine-nui-te-po, a female attendant, guarded the entrance to the night realm and directed spirits of the departed along the path of Tane (te ara whanui a Tane i te Muri-wai-hou ki te Po-Tiwha). Whiro was the other overlord of the night region and while her functions were not clear, she seems to have been connected with the mourning rites and ceremonies symbolised by the greenery of leaves worn as a garland by visitors. These were deposited at the feet of the corpse and later buried with him. This garland was called 'te rau wharawhara o te aroha' (the kawakawa garland of compassion), or 'te rau parekawakawa o te aroha' (the wharawhara leaves of compassion). The Waikato and Taranaki tribes favoured the kawakawa as the symbol of love and compassion for the departed, while the Ngapuhi tribes favoured the wharawhara. Today any greenery serves the purpose.

Besides these three, innumerable other spirits dwelt in the night realms. The departmental gods lived in Hawaiki, as did the spirits of departed heroes. Besides these there were a whole host of other spirits beneficent or malevolent. The malevolent spirits were called hautupu. Other demonic spirits were called maitu, but these were sometimes invoked as familiar spirits who became guardians for members of a whanau, and in this role were known as kaitiaki. Their counterparts in the natural world were taniwha. These dragon-like creatures dwelt in certain localities and could be independent and unattached from the local tribe. As such, they were devourers of men. But where they were attached to the local tribe, they acted as guardians and manifested themselves as animals, fish, birds or reptiles. Strictly speaking, these were not spirits but occult powers created by the psychic force of ancient tribal tohungas and by the mana of their creative word, given form and delegated as guardians for the tribe.

The other occupants of the night regions were the spirits of departed humans called wairua. They descended along the path of Tane to the different Hawaiki in the night realm where they continued life and followed occupations little different from those on earth. The spirits of the departed that lingered on earth after death were called kehua (wraiths, ghosts) who haunted the living. Other wraiths who haunted the living were not of human origin but demonic spirits known as taipo (inhabitants of the dark).

Not all wairua of departed humans went to the Po. There was also a belief that many of them went to the realms of Rangi and others dwelt amongst the stars. But whether it was in the Po, in Hawaiki or in the Rangi, all these were regions in the spirit world. A path from earth led to the Po (te ara whanui a Tane) and another led to the Rangi (te aratiatia a Tane). Beyond the horizons and the stars, surrounding the earth, the night realms and the sky realms joined together.

The Maori World View

As we have seen, the created universe is divided into Te Po and Te Rangi, which in themselves are divided into twelve planes. In between floats the earth sphere or sphere of day (Te Ao Marama). The Po and Rangi are in turn encompassed by the realm of Te Korekore.

How did the Maori view the origin of the universe? What is its basic element? Is it material, spiritual, or both? Is it static or dynamic? Is history cyclic or lineal? Some of the answers to these questions are obvious. For instance we have seen that Io is the first cause from which all things originated. It is also obvious that the Maori does not, and never has accepted the mechanistic view of the universe which regards it as a closed system into which nothing can impinge from without. The Maori conceives of it as at least a two-world system in which the material proceeds from the spiritual, and the spiritual (which is the higher order) interpenetrates the material physical world of Te Ao Marama.

We may also conclude from the concepts of mana and tapu, and the nature of the creative acts of Io and his regents, that while the Maori thought of the physical sphere as subject to natural laws, these could be affected, modified and even changed by the application of the higher laws of the spiritual order.

In some senses, I suspect the Maori had a three-world view, of potential being symbolised by Te Korekore, the world of becoming portrayed by Te Po, and the world of being, Te Ao Marama.

Te Korekore

One is tempted to translate Te Korekore as the 'void'. But the traditional religious and theological ideas associated with the concept have hardened into such a rigid framework that one hesitates to use the term. Whilst it does embrace ideas of emptiness and nothingness, this by no means exhausts its meaning.

The word 'kore' means 'not, negative, nothing'. When the root of a word is doubled in Maori, it intensifies its meaning. For example 'kai' is to eat, 'kaikai' is greedy. Again, kore is an absolute concept. How is it possible to intensify that which is already absolute? By means of a thorough-going negativity, that which is negative proceeds beyond its limits and assumes the characteristics of the positive. While it does not entirely emancipate itself from the negative, it does become relatively positive. This is one of the characteristics of Io. He contains within himself all that is negative and positive, all that is passive and active.

Thus Te Korekore is the realm between non-being and being: that is, the realm of potential being. This is the realm of primal, elemental energy or latent being. It is here that the seed-stuff of the universe and all created things gestate. It is the womb from which all things proceed. Thus the Maori is thinking of continuous creation employed in two allegorical figures: that of plant growth and that of gestation in the womb.

The allegory of plant growth is as follows: te pu, more, weu, aka, rea, wao nui, kune and whe meaning primary root, tap root, fibrous roots, trunk, tendrils, massed branches, buds and fronds. That for human birth proceeds: te apunga, aponga, kune roa, popoko nui, popoko nao, hine-awaawa, tamaku, rangi nui a tamaku. This is conception, the first signs of swelling, the distended womb, the distended vagina, contraction, membrane ruptured, first stage of delivery and final stage. Both allegories are made explicit in the recital of the different realms.

> Te Korekore i takea mai, ki te Po te kitea, te Po tangotango, Po whawha, Po namunamu ki te wheiao, ki Te Ao Marama.

> From the realm of Te Korekore the root cause, through the night of unseeing, the night of hesitant exploration, night of bold groping, night inclined towards the day and emergence into the broad light of day.

According to the Io tradition, at the border between Hawaiki Tapu in the Po regions is Te Waipuna Ariki (the divine fountain of Io the fountainhead). This is the fountain through which the primal energy of potential being proceeds from the infinite realms of Te Korekore through the realms of Te Po into the world of light (Te Ao Marama) to replenish the stuff of the universe as well as to create what is new. Thus it is a process of continuous creation and recreation. Te Korekore is the realm of potential being, Te Po is the realm of becoming and Te Ao Marama is the realm of being. Through the great path of Tane linking these three realms there is a two-way traffic: the spirits of the departed descending to Hawaiki and that which is in the process of becoming ascending to the world of being.

Two conclusions emerge from this: the idea of continuous creation and the idea of a dynamic universe. These ideas are inclusive. The universe is not static but is a stream of processes and events. This concept also includes the idea that history is not cyclical but lineal – it is an on-going process. But the Maori did not develop the idea of a goal of history. The only hint that he aspired towards a final goal is the story of Maui's final attempt to gain eternal life for man by conquering Hine-nui-te-po, guardian of the portals of night. Perhaps because of his concept of Io's utter sacredness, he could not aspire to full divinity in that sense (though the Maori regarded himself as a descendant of the gods and many of his ancestors were demigods; man today can, by fulfilling certain conditions, still wield the mana of the gods).

Each man is an event within the one ongoing procession of nature and so is each created object. Man withdraws from the mainstream of the universal process by returning to the spirit realm of Hawaiki, there to continue a spiritual existence after the pattern of the earthly one. The idea of rewards and punishment was not developed by the Maori except in the limited sense of the super-heroes and demi-gods dwelling with the gods in Hawaiki Nui. Further, since the universe is dynamic and the earth is not simply Papa (rock foundation) but Papa-tua-Nuku (rock foundation beyond expanse, the infinite), the universe itself is a process or event within the cosmic process by which Io orders creation. The ultimate reality, therefore, is Io, and the expression of this reality is the cosmic process in which all things are immersed and find their reality. So the temporal is subordinate to the eternal, the material to the spiritual, for the situation below is ordered by an ideal determination from above by Io as origin of the cosmic process.

Whether this orientation is articulated or not, it remains the subconscious attitude of the Maori and is reflected in his whole mode of thinking and the expression of it in his language and its structure. For instance, there is no verbal tense in Maori. Time is a continuous stream. The temporal is subordinated under the cosmic process and denotes not time but sequences in processes and events which occur in the cosmic process. Hence the particles 'ka', 'e . . . ana,' and 'kua' attached to simple verbs denote the initiation, continuation and termination of particular processes and events. Again, the prepositions 'i', 'kei', 'ki' and 'hei' when joined with verbs and participles denote either the static or dynamic state of an object in relation to other objects. This characteristic is applicable to other prepositions such as 'a', 'o', 'ma', 'mo', 'no', which, while to some extent retaining their normal functions of denoting relationships among objects, assume the predominant function of denoting the static or dynamic state of an object.

Conclusion

Sufficient has been said to show that a detailed analysis of the underlying themes of the Maori culture has never been attempted. The major task consists not in analysis of outward institutional forms, a task adequately covered by Te Rangi Hiroa (Sir Peter Buck) and others, but in penetrating into states of mind for some kind of evaluation and understanding.

Only an approach which sets out to explore and describe the main features of the consciousness in the experience of the Maori offers any hope of adequate coverage. For the reality we experience subjectively is incapable of rational synthesis.This is why so many Maori react against the seemingly facile approach of foreign anthropologists to their attitudes, mores and values, and the affective states of mind which produce them.

I believe only a Maori from within the culture can do this adequately. Abstract rational thought and empirical methods cannot grasp the concrete act of existing which is fragmentary, paradoxical and incomplete. The only way lies through a passionate, inward subjective approach. Only a few foreigners alien to a culture, men like James K. Baxter with the soul of a poet, can enter into the existential dimension of Maori life. This grasp of a culture proceeds not from superficial intellectualism but from an approach best articulated in poetry. Poetic imagery reveals to the Maori a depth of understanding in men which is absent from the empirical approach of the social anthropologist.

The integration of an individual into full membership of society takes place over a long period of time. Not in formal schooling, but in his living situation. The process of learning, by which the raw material of the young is transformed into full citizenship, is inherent in the workings of each institution so that the instilling of values, norms and attitudes is effected by the apprenticeship to tribal life, that is, by existence in the cultural milieu.

Remembering that the cultural milieu is rooted both in the temporal world and the transcendent world, this brings a person into intimate relationship with the gods and his universe.

A CHURCH CALLED RINGATU

WI TAREI

I WAS BORN IN 1924, the third son in a family of 14. We had a rough time. We lived in a tin shack with a dirt floor and boxes to sit on. Things were especially hard for my mother and my oldest brother, who was expected to act like a second mother looking after us. My father drank and he drank heavily. And he swore and used to beat my mother and my oldest brother. At one time, when I was about six, he broke two of my brother's ribs and he began to bleed internally.

Well, my father became afraid that my brother was going to die. There was a lot of talk at this time about a prophet from Wanganui who was visiting our district and my father went to see him. The prophet told my father to go home and that everything would be all right; but he was never again to touch beer, never again to lay hands on his fellows. And this was the beginning of a new life for us. We all noticed the difference in him. And on the twelfth of every month he used to go away on his pony from Mapou where we lived, to the Twelfth at this marae 17 miles away, on rough roads. He would be away for about three days.

The change in him was profound. Before he used to swear and curse all of us and the animals; now he was quiet and considerate and his attitude to our mother changed. And my brother recovered. We were not allowed to swear either. To tell you the truth, I did not know what swearing was until I was 16 and started work with Pakeha.

Of all his children, I was the one he picked out to go to a Twelfth with him. He would not take any of the others. He just put me on the back of his horse and said he wanted me to go with him. That was in about 1931. I can still remember the feeling of awe I felt as we went on to the marae. Once we got on the marae and the bell rang, nobody was allowed out; and nobody else was allowed in. That first welcoming service gave me a feeling that was partly fear, partly of something beautiful. Certainly, it was beyond my understanding. And the hymns were weird to listen to; they made me feel that the skin on my head was not big enough; it prickled. That was my first baptism into the Ringatu Church. In those days the services lasted from the night of the eleventh of the month until the morning of the thirteenth – and there was nothing but church from the time you arrived till the time you left, about twelve services.

After this I learnt all the prayers and hymns. My father used to wake up early in the morning, half-past four or five o'clock, and start to sing. Well, I was seven or eight years old and I used to listen and ask him questions. I learnt a lot of the

Ringatu hymns that way and used to sing them with him. In time he 'called' a Twelfth for our own marae and involved the whole family, including his brothers. They were reluctant at first – they could not see how they were going to feed the people. But somehow they did. We grew vegetables in the gardens, and got edible plants and wild pig from the bush. And from those days our whole family was Ringatu. I became more and more interested and involved. I used to have discussions and then arguments with the older ones; I wanted to understand why they said things, why they believed things. In time I was invited by them to be a tohunga or priest for the church.

It wasn't always easy to grow up Ringatu. We were not supposed to take time off school for the services and tangis. The Health Department used to try to stop us holding Twelfths because of the danger of epidemics. But they used to allow other gatherings in the district at the same time.

A great deal of what the practitioners of Ringatu believe conflicts with what Pakehas have written about its founder, Te Kooti, and about the Ringatu Church. When I was at school what I learnt about New Zealand history was contrary to what the church taught me. Just recently, my girls were at Edgecumbe College and they were both A-grade at their Maori. But they were in conflict with their teachers. Education still promotes the idea that Te Kooti was bloodthirsty and practised Hauhauism.

Now the church itself is not so concerned about the stigma of bloodthirstiness, but they are concerned about the accusation of Hauhauism, because it can be proved easily that the Ringatu Church has nothing to do with Hauhauism. Hauhauism is not Christian; whereas Ringatu is based on the Bible and is one of the most Christian churches in the world.

I believe that Te Kooti is the only man in the world who has established a religion that fulfilled the teaching of Jesus Christ that 'Your body is the tabernacle of God'. Now the majority of churches teach that the house of God is the Book – when they want prayers or knowledge they open a book. Not so with the Ringatus; they believe that the house of God is within man at all times. Everything that we know from the Bible is committed to memory and taken with the church member everywhere, day and night, eating, sleeping, drinking – it is with him at all times because it is inside the man and then is spoken from the heart, not just from the lips. A man has lost meaning, lost sincerity when he has to start reading something like a pretend-speech, especially when it is prepared by somebody else. The speech of the Ringatu is spontaneous and he speaks of the subject in hand at that time; if it is a tangi, then he speaks of what is appropriate to a tangi and death. Once a Ringatu is made to read from a book, you can see him start to lose heart and lose interest.

This is one of the things that, to me, makes Ringatu unique and makes the founder of the church unique because he has fulfilled this injunction of Christ.

Te Kooti Rikirangi was born at a village called Pohau, on the outskirts of

Gisborne. There's a lot of disagreement about the year – some say 1812, some say 1814, some even say 1830. His father was Hone Rangipatahi and his mother Turakau. Their tribe was the Ngati Maru hapu of Rongowhakaata. Even before he was born a prophecy was made about him by an old man named Toiroa Ikariki who lived at Tuahura Pa at Marahara, on the northern side of the Mahia Peninsula. He said to Turakau: 'My child is within you; lightning in hell, lightning in heaven; the Lord of heaven is the man.' That was how Te Kooti got the name Rikirangi – it was Arikirangi, 'the Lord of heaven'. But he never used it, only his followers.

When the boy was about six years old, Toiroa decided he wanted to see him before he died. So he sent word for Turakau to bring him. Turakau and Te Kooti paddled by canoe from Gisborne to Tuahura, a journey of more than a day. When they got there the boy, all cramped up, leapt from the boat and began to wade to the shore. The old man was waiting at the water's edge and he put his hand on the child's head and said: 'My son, I saw you drifting across the waters of Poverty Bay on a raupo raft. You were crying. Not long returned, you had a church with the upraised hand.' This prophecy was where the name Ringatu ('upraised hand') came from for his church. He remembered it in later years.

He was educated at the Mission School at Waerengaohika, and some people have said that this was where he got his knowledge of scripture. But I do not believe it. His breadth and depth of knowledge – his understanding of scripture – was far greater than any missionary could have given him. It was inspiration.

Later, in 1865, he fought with European troops against the Hauhaus at Waerengaohika. After this battle he was accused of being a Hauhau spy and was arrested. He asked for a tribal but was not given one. As they led him away to imprisonment on the Chatham Islands, he said to his uncle who had accused him: 'I shall come back and I shall exterminate you, and all the women, and everything that moves.' And this was what he did three years later at Matawhero – it was utu, and Ringatus believe he was directed by God to do this.

We know what happened to him in the Chathams because of his notebook that was seized at Makaretu in December 1868 after he had fled from there. It is now in the Turnbull Library. He described in it how he had been isolated from other prisoners in 1867, because he had severe tuberculosis. He wrote in it: 'And the spirit of God aroused me and about me said: "Arise, I am sent by God to heal you that you may preach his name to his people who are living as captives in this land, that they may understand that it was Jehova who drove you all here." ' Te Kooti reported this and later apparitions to his fellow prisoners, and signs that appeared to them, like the trembling of the building in which they were gathered and an outbreak of fire, appeared to confirm his powers. Te Kooti noted: 'And from that time began the strengthening of [God's] servant, and of my speech and of my body, my fearlessness towards great men. Indeed from that time began the doings of all those things that had been spoken of to his servant.'

He became the spiritual leader of the Maori prisoners, and he began to rewrite the scriptures, to reorganise them according to his inspiration. Now here is the paradox. He had kept calling for a trial and he had not been given one. Therefore he had suffered a grave injustice. Yet if he had not suffered the injustice, then the prophecies about him would never have been fulfilled. Either way, he comes out of it with credit.

In 1868 he led the prisoners in a break-out and they captured the ship *Rifleman* without loss of life and sailed it back to New Zealand. From the moment he landed he was treated as a rebel and pursued by government troops. The pursuit became even more intensive after the massacre at Matawhero. But, as I have said, the Ringatus believe he was directed by God. He was never captured in spite of many battles and many sieges. He took refuge in the King Country in 1872, and in 1883 he was pardoned by the government and was allowed to return to his followers in the Bay of Plenty. But he was never allowed to return again to Gisborne, his original home. He predicted that he would not die by the hand of man and he did not. He was run over by a cart at Ohiwa in 1893.

While he was being pursued he preached his faith and taught people about scripture and built up the ritual of the Ringatu Church. It is the same ritual we practise today, and the church is strongest around the districts where he spent the last years of his life, Bay of Plenty and Urewera.

This church observes the Sabbath, and holds special huis on New Year's Day and in June. But the most important part of Ringatu worship is the observation of the Kaumarua, the Twelfth, on the twelfth day of each month. This is a cycle of services – of prayers, chants and hymns – devised by Te Kooti and carried on at his instruction.

The marae chosen for the Twelfth is closed off from dusk on the evening of the eleventh of the month until dusk on the twelfth. The Kai Tiaki or policeman of the marae is responsible for ringing the bell at the side of the meeting house porch to summon people in to prayer. The bell is rung slowly at first to warn people, and then quickly to indicate that proceedings are about to begin. Once the service has started, nobody is supposed to move or speak other than for praying or singing. It is also the responsibility of the Kai Tiaki to see that rules are enforced. He has the power to fine people for breaking them.

Each Twelfth may have five services. They will be led by a tohunga or priest. The tohunga who opens and closes the proceedings is called the Turei, and he will belong to the marae where the Twelfth is being held that month.

The purpose of each service is announced by the tohunga who leads it. It may be greetings, thanksgiving, pleas for protection or healing, or calls for assistance with private problems. The duration of the service is the time it takes the cycle of hymns, panui (verses from the Bible), psalms and prayers to go right round the meeting house. They are led by different people one at a time, moving in a clockwise direction around the house. They end when they return to the tohunga who began.

The services always open with a call for honour and glory to God, peace on earth and goodwill to all men. All the words of the hymns and panui are taken from the Bible – Te Kooti took passages of scripture and rearranged them to give them consistent themes and a feeling of completion at the close. Here, for example, is a Ringatu panui (Panui 7):

> Come my people enter thou into thy chambers and shut thy doors about thee.
> And none shall go out the door of his house until the morning.
> And the Lord will pass over the door and will not suffer the destroyer to come into your houses to smite you.
> I laid me down and slept, I awakened for the Lord sustained me.
> Now the Lord is that Spirit and where the spirit of the Lord is there is liberty.

This panui was constructed by Te Kooti under inspiration from five separate Biblical verses: Isaiah 26.20; Exodus 12.22; Exodus 12.23; Psalms 3.5 and Corinthians II, 3.17. But the forms – the tunes and the chanting – are all those of the pre-European Maori. In former times all these things had to be committed to memory, word perfect – no books or notes were allowed into the Twelfths. Now, to make it easier for the younger ones, prayerbooks are allowed.

The language used by the Ringatu Church, sung and spoken in its services, is classic Maori. This too is an example of the wisdom and foresight of Te Kooti. In the days of our ancestors we learnt our culture from special whare wananga, houses of learning. Today these have been replaced by universities and it is a great loss for the Maori people; the Maori language spoken today is weakened and corrupted. Te Kooti foresaw that this would happen. Although he was hunted and persecuted, he realised there would be a need to protect and perpetuate the most precious part of the culture of the Maori, his language. And so he devised the practices of his church accordingly.

The hymns are the most sacred part of the service. They can only be led by a tohunga, and everyone must stand for them. They are sung in traditional Maori tunes with the words drawn from Biblical verses – some whole or consecutive verses, others from various ones blended by Te Kooti. After they are finished an inoi waahi or prayer of separation (to separate the very holy from the merely holy) is necessary, and the congregation remains standing for this.

The panui are all chanted to the same tune. They too are verses from the Bible. Anyone can lead them, including women and children, and only the person leading has to stand. The psalms too are sung to a single tune and anyone can lead them. There has to be at least one in the course of a service. Prayers can be said by anybody, for any particular cause. Very often those causes may concern the sick, the crippled or the unhappy who have been especially brought to the Twelfth to seek relief.

Prayers close with the words, 'We glorify your holy name', and as this is said hands are upraised, the gesture of the church's name, Ringatu. All Ringatu ritual, including the services, closes with the Lord's Prayer, re-written and shortened according to Te Kooti's inspiration, and ending with the words, 'We believe and glorify thy holy name. Amen.' Then the services finish with two final prayers for deliverance from confusion and a plea that the doors of truthfulness, life and strength shall be opened up.

During the Twelfth, between the services, members get to their feet and discuss the politics, organisation, theology and affairs of the church. These discussions became more lively as the result of church disagreements and the formation of different sects.

Other bodies, including public health ones, have criticised the Ringatu practice of gathering for prolonged periods for the purpose of worship (two nights and a day). But this practice too is an example of Te Kooti's foresight. The time is not used for worship alone; it serves the function of blooding young speakers, for in Ringatu services seniority does not count; it also allows the Maori concept of hospitality to be lived fully. Maori hospitality demands that guests stay with their host; and his guests are the friends and foes who gather together in his name and forget all their differences for that period – a rare sight to behold indeed.

On the morning of the Twelfth, after a night of prayer and fasting, the hakari or communal feast is held. Everybody attending the Twelfth comes together in the dining room and eats and drinks in fellowship. Before the end of one Twelfth, a person will stand and 'call' the next Twelfth at another marae. In this way they circulate around different marae in the course of a year.

Tohungas are selected for training and for the ministry by other tohungas. They are people who display a special interest and aptitude, a distinctive spirituality. They must also have good memories to learn all the ritual by heart. They may become tohungas entitled to lead services, tohunga ture, also allowed to perform marriages, or tohunga takuta, who specialise in healing people. Many of them are identifiable because they wear the church symbol – the upraised hand – as a crest on the pockets of their jackets.

Ringatu is a registered church, it is a Christian church. As I have suggested, the thing that has hurt us most is the uninformed belief that we are Hauhau or non-Christian. Anyone who attends our services can see how wrong this is. And in our eyes Te Kooti, far from being a bloodthirsty renegade, was one of the greatest men that God sent to teach the people. In all the years of his mission – from 1867 to 1893 – he acquired more for the Maori spiritually and taught the Maori more about the word of God and Christianity, than all the other churches had managed to do in twice as many years.

THE ORIGINS OF THE
RATANA MOVEMENT

MOANA RAURETI

IN THE EARLY 1920s, Ratanaism swept Maoridom like wild fire. Its impact was nation-wide and extended beyond the shores of New Zealand – to Europe, Asia and the United States of America.

Within New Zealand, the name 'Ratana' became a household word – 'Ratana the Prophet', 'Ratana the Faith Healer' and 'Ratana the Miracle Man', became bywords. Ratana Pa near Wanganui became the Mecca of thousands of Maori. The demands of the travellers were such that the government was compelled to construct a special railway station to accommodate the traffic.

The Ratana movement began as a faith-healing cult and year by year from 1920 it gathered new hosts of believers. Its sphere of influence grew and the basis upon which its teachings rested became more obvious.

This movement was by no means the first of its kind in Maoridom – other movements, the Hauhau, the Ringatu, Te Whiti and Tohu movements and the King Movement of Waikato had preceded it, all coming before the turn of the century. And to a certain degree the Young Maori Party of 1900 which anticipated the Maori renaissance must also be considered.

Viewed in the light of its forerunners and considered in regard to the deterioration in the circumstances of the Maori people and their still unrequited land claims, emergence of such a personality as Tahupotiki Wiremu Ratana is not surprising. What is revealing and surprising is that, in a Maori generation presumed by the Pakeha to have superseded its past almost to the point of extinction, a leader such as Ratana could still appeal to Maori sentiment, superstition and loyalty, and weave around his teaching – and the religious observances associated with it – so many elements of the traditional past.

With the Ratana movement there was an outward manifestation of the inward desire of the Maori race to retain their pride and dignity as a people and to be given the opportunity for self expression. If, as some assert, the movement did not achieve the high ideals to which it strove, then it can be said that it was only in the material workings and ramifications of the movement that faults could be found. What is important is the fact that aspirations to greater heights and ideals were provided.

As with its predecessors, the movement represented a protest against the encroachment and growing dominance of Pakeha power. Its inspiration, initially faith-healing, and the magnetic personality of its leader, gradually succumbed to the more basic motives of a concerted drive for the satisfaction of old land grievances, political complaints of the past, and a very keen apprehension of the future.

Also as with preceding movements, there was distrust of European ideas and methods, understandable in the light of the land confiscation of the 1860s. For example, the influence of the confiscations was felt considerably when the policy of development and settlement of Maori lands was first launched in 1929 under Sir Apirana Ngata. Many of the Ratana adherents stood aloof, partly from fear of losing their lands and partly from general distrust of government motives. It was not until they saw the material benefits that the gradual surrender of their former isolation became noticeable.

Tahupotiki Wiremu Ratana was born on 25 January 1876. His fourth standard primary education, although extremely limited in the light of present-day education, was extensive for the average Maori of that time. Throughout his early life he lived on the family estate at Orakei-nui, a small Maori settlement 12 miles east of Wanganui. This was later to become Ratana Pa. The estate consisted of some 800 acres and the family engaged in sheep farming and carried out extensive wheat-growing. As a young man he was said to have been quite 'wild and woolly' but on marriage he settled down to the routine of home and farm life.

A Methodist from birth, religion did not play any really significant part in his life until he was about 40. About 1916 he started to take considerable interest in church matters and inklings of his later calling made their first appearances. His behaviour was considered to be eccentric and consideration was given at times to having him institutionalised in a mental hospital because of these outbreaks.

At that time, Mere Rikiriki, the Maori prophetess who lived up the Wanganui River, held considerable sway over the western Maori people and it is believed Ratana came under her influence (along with hundreds of other Maori). It is said that Ratana received the first elements of his power from her.

On 8 November 1918, the turning point in Ratana's life came in the form of a divine revelation. It is said that a cloud appeared from the east and struck Ratana unconscious on the veranda of the family home. On his recovery he immediately proclaimed a vision which had bidden him go forth and do good among his people.

The miraculous healing of his own son Omeka is recounted below. His influence and mana as a faith-healer spread until by 1920 hundreds of Maori were flocking to him at Ratana Pa, bent on the alleviation of their troubles and cures of their ills and sickness.

Ratana had by this time developed – naturally, perhaps, considering the mission he had taken upon himself – an intense love and interest in his fellow man. As they came to him, they were encouraged to stay at the pa to be near him.

Adherents sold up or heavily mortgaged their farms and built homes and meeting houses at Ratana Pa. Those who were not so financial – the vast majority – merely moved in with their scanty belongings and somehow managed to exist on the frugal means at their disposal. Ratana took all these under his wing and their way of life became that of the traditional communal pattern. In order to feed and maintain his 'morehu' or 'hosts', Ratana was forced to utilise his own family's lands to provide cropping facilities for their bare sustenance. In early 1921 there were only four houses at Ratana Pa and the population, totalling some 400, was all housed in tents. There was no work to be had and the onus to provide for the people fell on Ratana himself. It is stated that some days there was little or nothing to eat, but so great was the faith of the people in their leader that they persevered and stayed on with him.

The mana of the prophet had now become so great that because of the incessant demands of people from all over the country he undertook a tour of New Zealand. He made triumphal progress throughout both islands, travelling with a huge retinue to practically every accessible village. The sick were brought to him in their hundreds and he effected cures on the spot, so it is said. In certain areas he was cold-shouldered, but on the whole the tour had the effect of expanding his influence and increasing his mana and prestige. This was followed by a world tour in 1924 and a tour to the United States of America in the following year.

The movement had now become a complete entity and on the repeated pressure of his adherents a separate church was set up and proclaimed as such in 1925. Following this development, it was only natural that some form of permanent church building be instituted. Building of the Temple started in 1926 and it was opened in 1927 on Ratana's birthday. It was designed and built by the local Maori and is a fine and imposing building. It is a fitting centre of worship for such a movement. Symbolism is prominently featured in its layout and construction.

By this time Ratana was well launched into the political field. It was from here on to the early thirties that the movement reached its zenith. The village itself had reached proportions where it was no longer a little isolated settlement, but a township with something over a hundred private houses, and a number of meeting houses constructed on tribal bases. The population, too, had risen steeply and generally the appearance was one of a firm and progressive settlement. Some of the early residents had returned to their former localities, but for this steady exodus there was a correspondingly greater influx. Work as a means of sustenance became imperative.

By 1928 Ratana had embarked on extensive wheat-growing activities on the lands adjacent to the settlement, providing basic occupation and employment for the residents. As the land available was restricted and did not permit sufficient areas to be fallowed, these cropping operations became unprofitable after a period. Work therefore had to be found outside the pa. Today the Ratana Pa labour force plays an integral part in the economic situation of the Wanganui district.

With the building of the township, and the operation of the intricate organisation of the church now fully established throughout New Zealand, the transference of emphasis from the spiritual sphere to the more material ones of economics, town planning (what little there was) and housing construction became apparent. The fervour of discipleship tended to wane considerably. Indications of decline were at hand. Ratana himself became a nonentity in the movement and its direction fell to the network organisation of apostles, bishops, preachers and counsellors, whose vision and capacity for leadership did not seem adequate. Further, the quiescence – quite apparent – of Ratana's power of faith-healing and such incidents as convictions in a court of the leader himself for driving under the influence of liquor, together with the lavish expenditure of money by the movement's leaders, questionable operations and financial position of the movement's bank – all these combined factors tended to put the movement in disrepute.

Then, too, officialdom, in the form of the health authorities, became very vociferous in the matter of health and sanitary conditions in the pa. With very little attempt at town planning, the township had simply grown, with few provisions to safeguard health by the proper installation of facilities. Bad as the conditions were under normal circumstances, these were aggravated a thousand-fold whenever the Ratana hui were held. Generally there were Christmas and Easter hui, but the biggest was on 25 January, which commemorated Ratana's birthday. At the height of his power, estimates of attendance have been placed at up to 12,000. Bad sanitary and health conditions were intensified by the prolonged nature of these meetings; the people were held from two to three weeks at a time by their leader, and sometimes longer than this. It was fortunate in one respect that Ratana's birthday fell on 25 January. Apart from their own contributions to the hui (the visitors brought most of their own food and provisions), they were required to assist in the harvesting of the wheat crops. One contemporary has observed that there was no more inspiring sight than to see the wheat fields at Ratana literally covered with hundreds of people reaping the golden harvest.

With the emphasis on meetings and the consequent gathering of young and old there tended to be less importance placed on the spiritual aspect of the movement and an increasing stress on festivities. Sport, in itself a fine thing, became part of the meetings. Drink, as would be expected, made its entry and the name of the movement became distastefully associated with it. Unfortunately, the leader himself set no good example in this respect and indulged in drinking bouts. Well-informed sources verify the fact that at these meetings casks upon casks of beer would be brought into the pa for consumption by the gathering. They go so far as to state too that bags and bags of wheat were merely traded over the counter of the Whangaehu Hotel, for gallons of whisky and beer.

If these assertions are correct then it can be seen that the movement had degenerated in no small degree from a deeply spiritual one to a commonplace secular organisation engaging at times in discreditable actions.

By the time of his death in 1939 Ratana had to all intents and purposes lost his power over the people. The double tomb of him and his wife lies immediately in front of the temple, a constant reminder to the adherents from near and far of their once great leader and Mangai.

The following figures provide evidence of the rapid growth of the movement up to the mid-thirties and its subsequent gradual decline.

Ratana is thought to have commenced his faith-healing in 1919. Taking this as the base, in the short space of seven years the movement gathered 11,567 adherents representing 18.2 percent of the total Maori population. By the mid-thirties it had grown to 16,337, or 19.8 percent of the total population. It has generally been conceded that although the new adherents came from all denominations, in the main they came from the Anglican faith. The census figures of 1936 relating to Anglican membership seem to confirm this, as there is a decided drop from 34.2 percent to 30.2 percent. Thereafter there is a rise in Anglican figures and a correspondingly gradual decline in the Ratana figures.

However, in assessing these figures it must be borne in mind that they are the only official figures available and they are to be treated with a certain amount of reserve. At the time when the census figures show the movement's membership to be in the vicinity of 12,000 the Ratana records claim some 40,000 adherents.

Faith-healing

The cure or attempted cure of illness by means other than the application of physical remedies, has come down through the generations. It is associated culturally with the practice of makutu or witchcraft and communication with atua or supernatural beings, through the medium of the tohunga. It is quite probable that the beliefs and superstitions centering in what was known as 'Maori tohungaism' survived from that period when the Maori world was peopled with gods and atuas and personified spiritual forces.

Healing by the laying on of hands, featuring prominently in the Scriptures, gave confirmation to Maori beliefs in these matters – certain passages in the Scriptures made a tremendous impression on the Maori mind. Ratana's ability as a faith-healer therefore had both native antecedents and biblical precedent to draw on. Because of this dual tradition, faith-healing found ready acceptance whenever medical authorities failed. The patient or relative would immediately declare that the affliction was a 'mate Maori' – a Maori sickness – curable only by Maori means. The doctor who declared the case hopeless resigned the patient to the charge of the relations, and the patient in time found himself in the hands of a tohunga, who would normally use a combination of religious prayer and magic to restore the sick person to health.

It was under these conditions that Ratana found prominence with the alleged cure of his own son. At the age of six, Omeka, Ratana's son, suffered a serious illness which necessitated a long stay in hospital. Medical authorities were baffled by the sickness and were unable to diagnose the trouble. In time, the child was allowed to return home, medical opinion being that nothing more could be done for him. Deeply concerned and at desperation point, Ratana sought solace in prayer and fasting. After many days, a needle which had been embedded in the child's knee forced its way out and the boy immediately started to recover.

This indeed was an event to be classified in the Maori mind as a miracle. Thus were born the faith-healing powers of Ratana – powers which he was to exercise in the curing of his own immediate circle of friends initially, but later to extend to thousands of others throughout the country.

To what extent the sick and ailing shunned orthodox medical treatment and relied on Ratana's faith-healing is difficult to assess. There is ample evidence to justify the assertion that this did become the case, but in fairness to Ratana it must be stated that he was never anti-medical in attitude, despite the failing of medical authority in the case of his own son. This is firmly supported by Health Department officers who worked amongst the people at Ratana Pa. The writer has been informed by one such district nurse that Ratana offered no opposition to medical authority in the matter of sickness. His adherents may have, but he offered every cooperation. Where a case was felt to be within the province of medical authority, that patient was directed by Ratana himself to go for attention. The officers could always appeal to him in the event of any trouble with his adherents.

His attitude to healing the sick was based on the two issues of the spiritual and the material. Medicine catered for the material and physical. He catered, at divine instigation, for the spiritual side of man. Whenever the sick and infirm were brought before him, all he did was to pray and enjoin them to believe in God for their own cures. Ratana effected cures by medium of letters. Because of this easy means of contact, ailing people from all over the world wrote to him for help. These letters are still retained in the Ratana museum. Money enclosed in the letters was carefully returned because, at that time, nothing material was allowed to interfere with the spiritual nature of his work.

Ratana's powers as a faith-healer were fervently believed in by thousands of Maori and some Pakeha. The vast collection of crutches, walking sticks, invalid chairs, spectacles, medicine bottles, earphones and trumpets, bandages and various other articles, deposited as evidence by those cured, is still to be seen in the museum or 'Ghost House' as it is called today. Many attempts have been made to explain scientifically the remarkable cures attributed to Ratana. It is within the field of psychology that solutions to these problems lie. Phenomena of mass hysteria, suggestion, auto-suggestion and even some form of hypnotism must be taken into account in the explanation of Ratana's cures. It will readily be realised that Maori, with their background and traditions of makutu, tapu and tohungaism, were comparatively easy subjects for mental suggestion and were highly susceptible to it.

It has been stated by critics, scrutinising the validity of the cures claimed, that the reports of the wonderful cures ascribed to Ratana were mostly furnished to the press – and consequently the public – by the adherents of the movement. It is not a reflection on the Maori race to say that the Maori is no more inclined to coolness of judgment and accuracy of statement than the Pakeha has shown himself to be in the case of similar faith-healing movements.

Only one of Ratana's cures, as far as is known, has come under the direct attention of the medical profession. It was the case of Fanny Lomas, a European woman of Nelson who had been bedridden for 20 years with spinal trouble. In her own published account she claims to have been cured merely by receiving a letter written by Ratana himself. From the account it would seem that Fanny Lomas was a highly neurotic person, and the cure could quite well be related to mental suggestion.

It would seem that by the mid-twenties, once Ratana had embarked on politics and things temporal, his faith-healing power waned until he finally lost it altogether. His adherents recognised and realised this and often besought him to remain fast in his faith-healing activities. Having turned to politics and worldly things, it was a foregone conclusion to the Maori mind that the power given to him from divine sources would be taken away. And so it was.

Formation of the Church

In the dynamic exposition of his creed, Ratana drew to himself all manner of people, irrespective of creed and race. Yearbooks show that there were Pakeha adherents – for instance in 1926 there were listed 193. Ten years later, the 1936 census shows a membership of 461.

Amongst the adherents the 'morehu' or the masses came from the orthodox churches, mainly the Anglican Church, which in the early twenties accounted for some 30 percent of the Maori people. The Anglican Church has always reigned supreme as the mother church in Maoridom followed by the Ratana, Roman Catholic, Methodist, Latter Day Saints, Ringatu and others. Amongst the newcomers were lay readers of other denominations and in certain instances practising clergy. Paraire Paikea, later to become M.P. for the Northern seat, was a Methodist minister of 10 years' standing. It became the practice up to the time that the movement was formally constituted as a church that whenever religious services were held all denominations participated. As a result of this the services were long, cumbersome and wearying.

One of the features of the Maori is his fine tolerance of religious taste. He is no zealot or bigot denying to others the religions that please and satisfy them. The traditional Maori view is that all pray to the same God in the final analysis – how and in what form is of little importance. Of primary importance, is the fact that there is a service to God.

Under circumstances outlined, the movement continued its existence – a group of several denominations but with unifying influence. It was to be a matter of time before the 'morehu' would become a more compact and integrated body, and, becoming conscious of its unity, would one day demand the formation of a separate church.

That demand came in 1925 and on 31 May (The Feast of Pentecost) the Ratana Church was formally proclaimed. It had now joined the ranks of the orthodox churches with the power of administering all the usual rites of passage. The newly formed church busied itself with the internal organisation required and on 8 July 1925, 78 elders were proclaimed 'Apostles of the Church' by the General Council of the church and various other bearers of church office were appointed.

The all-important form of service was determined. Ratana himself was a Methodist, as indeed were practically the whole of the western Maori people at the time. The bulk of the 'morehu' came from the Anglican Church – therefore it was only natural that the newly constituted church should have a decided Wesleyan-Anglican bias.

Amongst Maori thinkers there was and still is divergence of opinion on the church's stability and capacity to guide Maori religious life. However, one thing is certain – Ratana touched the deepest springs of religious enthusiasm not only amongst the Maori but amongst others. It is said that the secret of his power lay in his knowledge of the Maori mind. The Maori wished to express his religious life in his own way – to interpret divine truth according to his own conception of it and build up a theology of his own. The constant bickering amongst the early European churches ever since 1840 had not helped in any way to stabilise the Maori conception of a church.

Ratana patterned his church on simple Wesleyan lines, adding Polynesian flair, ritual, ceremony, colour, and symbolism and presenting to the world a church at once authoritative and yet appealing. There is much that is poetical and inspiring in the survival and revivals of the older Maori faith and the conservative Maori finds in it a link with his fathers and a mode of expression for the spiritual fervour which is a very strong characteristic of the race. Designed as it was, the new Ratana Church was to stir the heart of many a Maori who saw in it links with his past and his future.

Some mention must be made of the composition of the movement. Unlike the preceding Maori movements, which were mainly of a local nature and restricted to certain districts, the Ratana movement knew no territorial or tribal bounds. Where the Te Whiti and Tohu movement and Hauhauism were confined largely to the Taranaki district, Ringatuism to the Taranaki and East Coast areas, and the King Movement to Waikato, the Ratana movement on the other hand had a New Zealand-wide influence and as such affected all the tribes in the country. Those who followed the movement to the extent that they were prepared to forego all, giving up their homes, families and tribal affiliation, and moving to live in Ratana, were those who within their own areas and tribes did not have deep and stable roots. The effect of Ratanaism was to create a detribalised unit, devoid of tribal affiliations. This was a strange and completely new departure for a people steeped in tribal tradition. The pervading influence of the leader and movement therefore can be judged in this light.

Tribal differences and affiliations became submerged by purely religious and spiritual considerations and this exists within the Ratana Pa community to the present time. The community is purely the Ratana 'morehu', having no tribal status. It is only under extreme pressure that they will make reference to their tribes at all. If one thinks of the Ratana community in terms of a division, then that division is not on a tribal basis, but rather on the territorial basis of the 'four winds', Tai Tokerau, Tairawhiti, Waipounamu and Taihauauru.

This aspect is possibly maintained and accentuated by the fact that permanent meeting houses have been built to cater for visitors from the four areas. Each area is responsible for the maintenance and upkeep of its own block of meeting houses. In this way the idea of a territorial division within the community is kept ever before it.

Liturgy and Symbolism

From the very outset, the movement had a decidedly religious character. New and distinctive features are an integral part of any cult. Thus Ratana proclaimed himself as the 'Mangai' or 'Mouthpiece of God'. The movement went further. To the Christian trinity was added, in invocation and exhortation, a hierarchy of angels termed 'Nga Anahera Pono', or the 'True or Faithful Angels'.

The addition of the 'True or Faithful Angels' to the doctrine of the Holy Trinity caused quite a furore within contemporary ecclesiastical circles, many churchmen condemning the action as near heresy. However, this doctrine has been maintained within the church and still exists despite many recriminations.

It is reasonable to explore the factor which activated Ratana to introduce the new concept of the ministry of angels. It has been stated previously that Ratana owed his success as a leader amongst the Maori people to his deep appreciation and understanding of the Maori mind. He realised at the time that the Maori was still steeped in fears and superstitions of tohungaism, sorcery and black magic. The air was still peopled with evil spirits ever watchful for opportunities to do harm where and when they could. Based on this knowledge and drawing freely from biblical sources, Ratana introduced this doctrine which to him was a powerful lever in freeing the Maori people from the fears of black magic and tapu.

Dr Ellison, another Maori who could appreciate the workings of the Maori mind, stated in 1930 in his capacity as Director of Maori Hygiene:

There appears to be no reason to doubt that the founder of a movement which was to absorb many adherents of other churches, had set out with the resolve to eradicate tohungaism and witchcraft.

A close examination of the ministry of angels with relation to the Holy Trinity shows that there was no attempt to place the angels on the same footing as the Holy Trinity. In the same way that Ratana himself was purely a 'mangai' or 'a mouthpiece' and was an intermediary between God and man, so too the angels formed a further and higher link between God and man. His conception of the channel of communication was that all prayers and supplications passed through him as the mouthpiece, thence to the angels, thence to God. Here was an easy chain of communication allowing free and uninhibited two-way contact between God and man, with intermediaries enhancing the people's prayers.

A possible explanation of this aspect is rooted in the traditional Maori worship of Io – the supreme God. Io was so sacred that the ordinary mortal being did not have access to him. That right was reserved only for the tohunga and the highest-ranking chiefs. By the institution of the ministry of angels, Ratana catered for the old Maori concept of sacredness and indirect contact with God, at the same time conceding the European concept of the approachability of God. The intermediaries in the form of the Mangai and the 'Anahera Pono' were compromises between the two modes of thought and worship.

Nowhere is there a clearer indication of this concept of a chain of communication than in the Temple itself at Ratana Pa. Half-way up the walls, starting from the main entrance, is a broad band consisting of three chains painted blue, white and red, representing the Father, Son and Holy Ghost. This band runs the length of both sides of the Temple, ending above and to right and left of the altar, in three separate circles representing the Trinity. From here the band takes a downward slope to a level representing the Anahera Pono. There is a further downward step to the Mangai level and a further step down again to the altar. As with other churches, this is the level of the clergy and people. The chain of communication with the respective positions of the Mangai and Anahera Pono is clearly defined. Symbolism, so dear to the Polynesian heart, has been given full effect in this and other spheres of the church and portrays vividly and effectively to the relatively simple mind of the Ratana adherent, his dynamic relations with his God.

A very controversial issue is whether or not Ratana by his own actions attempted to deify himself. Having set himself up as a Mangai he became a figure apart. In the chain of communication he became, it is claimed, more God than man. As the leader of a vast religious movement where he had achieved his mana through faith-healing, it is only natural that he would become a figure out of the ordinary. If he did not unconsciously ascribe that status to himself it is only reasonable to expect that his following would. And they did. It was claimed by members of other churches that the disciples of Ratana perverted the idea of true religion by allowing this veneration of Ratana the man to stand between them and their worship of God.

Whatever the situation, even if the adherents in their own zealousness did tend to think of him in terms of God at times, evidence points to the conclusive fact that Ratana did not at any stage in his career attempt to set himself up as God, nor did he ever expect to be treated as God.

It has been stated that lavish use of symbolism was made by Ratana within his movement. Once the movement had become firm, the well-known Ratana badge of faith was evolved. This 'star and moon' badge – emblem of the movement – consisted of a five-pointed star partially enclosed in a quarter moon. The stress here was on the celestial – this recognition and constant reminder of Ratana's heavenly association and divine appointment. The five points of the star were coloured blue, white, red, purple and pink, representing the Father, Son, Holy Ghost, Anahera Pono and the Mangai respectively. On either side of the badge was an A and an O, these representing Alpha and Omega – the beginning and end of Ratana's work.

It can be seen in this, as with other forms of symbolism used, that Ratana drew heavily upon biblical sources and Maori tradition, combined with not a little of his own native ingenuity.

The badge of faith became prominently displayed before the New Zealand eye. It appeared in the form of coat lapel badges, motor-car radiator caps, on letter-heads, and at one stage was painted on the front doors of all Ratana adherents' houses. The very colourful and imposing array of garments in the form of cassocks, robes, surplices and head veils worn by the officiating clergy and supporting sisters of the faith were lavishly emblazoned with the Ratana badge. The public was thus kept fully aware of the existence of the Ratana movement.

It is relevant here, perhaps, to mention the actual service itself. Ratana always encouraged music to be incorporated in the service, so much so that at central headquarters the Ratana band was formed and became widely known throughout the country. Smaller bands were formed in other districts. It is thus not difficult to visualise the impressive services that were conducted at the height of Ratana's power, with the use of band music, the colourful procession of clergy and supporting sisters of the faith, the singing of the beautiful Maori hymns, and the essentially simple but inspiring form of service.

I remember such services as a boy and I have a full and ready appreciation as to why the movement appealed so much as a church to thousands of Maori, who could appreciate beauty in colourful pageantry, music, and the simplicity and deep reverence of the Ratana service and faith.

The Tours Abroad

One of the highlights of the Ratana movement was the world tour conducted by Ratana in 1924, followed in the next year by a similar one to America. The tours, particularly the first, caught popular fancy and gave the movement a truly international interest.

Imbued with the idea of recovering lands wrongfully taken by the Pakeha, the leaders of the King Movement saw salvation for the Maori only in the proper application and execution of the terms of the Treaty of Waitangi. If the terms of the Treaty that had been signed in 1840 could only become effective then all would be well. In the proper ratification of the Treaty of Waitangi lay the secret of success in the long-waged battle to reclaim Maori lands.

A crusade was conducted throughout the land amongst the Maori people, Ratana and otherwise, and a petition was drawn up imploring the King to give effect to Queen Victoria's pledge that Maori lands would be protected. This crusade lasted four years, at the end of which the covenant had been signed by some 40,000 people. In its zeal to further the cause the Ratana movement decreed that its Mangai and accompanying party should go direct to England and interview King George V and lay before him the grievances of the Maori people. Accordingly, a party of 40, including 16 elders and 24 young people comprising the concert party, sailed in April 1924 by the *Maheno* to Sydney. There they transshipped to the S.S. *Barrabool* and sailed to England via Capetown, arriving in May. An audience was sought with the King, but this was refused and the expedition proved fruitless. However, the party toured through England, Scotland, Wales and Ireland, and its concert party received wide acclaim throughout. Undaunted by the refusal from the King, the leaders decided to call on the League of Nations in Geneva – to present their troubles. The party travelled to Geneva through France and Switzerland but were refused a hearing by the League of Nations. Whether Sir James Allen, High Commissioner in England, acting under instructions from New Zealand, was to blame for this is difficult to say.

The party then sailed from Marseilles for Japan to present their case to the Japanese emperor and government. It was claimed that they were sympathetically received. The party returned to New Zealand by way of Manila and Sydney, arriving on 23 December. The tour had taken nine months, in which the party had travelled thousands of miles in quest of what they believed to be justice for the wrongs of the Maori. When the party returned from Japan it was with the glorious news that their objective had been achieved. What exactly this constituted was not known, but a rumour began that a treaty had been made with Japan wherein it was pledged that Japan with its 50 million people would support Ratanaism and would see the wrongs of Maoridom righted.

Some credence could be given to this as during the Second World War, when Japanese forces were sweeping southward over the Pacific, some ugly rumours were current that the Ratana adherents were preparing to welcome the Japanese. The Japanese had allegedly guaranteed protection to the Ratana people in the event of landing in this country. It is interesting to note that the symbol of the rising sun on the Ratana flag commemorates this so-called treaty. Disturbed by the rumours, the British government, at the instance of the New Zealand government, made an official inquiry and received a reply from the Japanese government as follows:

> There is no truth whatever in the statement that Ratana was received by the government of Japan during his recent visit to this country. No promise of support of any claim advanced by Ratana was either given or implied officially or privately by the Japanese government nor was any communication made to Ratana by a minister or by any responsible official of that government concerning the administration of affairs in New Zealand.

Within the first few weeks of 1925, strong resolutions against the reported treaty were passed by representative gatherings of Maori at Wanganui, Dannevirke, Rotorua, Tuahiwi, Waitara, and Hastings. Such was the reaction of the rest of Maoridom to the treaty proposals.

In September 1925, Ratana, with a much smaller entourage, travelled to America and did an extensive tour for three or four months. It is reported that he was very warmly received and to commemorate that tour there appeared on his flag the symbol of the olive leaf. It is reasonable to assume that this tour was purely in the interests of mission work, although there is some suggestion that public appearances, and lectures involving monetary benefits, were also a factor.

A point which caused considerable speculation was the question of how these tours were financed. It is authoritatively stated that the initial contribution, and by far the greater portion, was made by Ratana himself. A large block of his mother's lands in Taranaki were disposed of to defray the costs of the tour. The concert party also made its contribution to the travel funds by charging for its performances. Finally, the adherents supported the venture not only morally but also financially, and much money passed to the touring party in the spirit of the traditional Maori 'he whakaaro' and 'hei tautoko i te take' – 'a gesture or thought in support of the cause'.

Any impression that the funds came from the so-called Ratana Bank is completely erroneous as this bank was not formed until after the departure of the touring party. Ratana himself only became aware of its existence when at Marseilles. He expressed complete disapproval and took the founders of the bank to task on his return to New Zealand. Be that as it may, the bank continued to flourish.

Because of the continued allegations that the tour had been financed by the 'morehu', through the Ratana Bank, Ratana produced a written statement signed by the officials of the bank verifying that no finances whatsoever had gone towards the tour. This was made public and, in part, satisfied the critics.

The Political Field

Ratana prophesied that he would control 'nga hau e wha' – 'the four winds'. At other times he would say his power would extend to the 'four corners' or 'nga koata e wha' of New Zealand, or yet again that he would cover the 'four seas' – 'nga tai e wha'. Speaking figuratively and in language appealing and comprehensible to the Maori people, he meant that his influence would be felt throughout the length and breadth of New Zealand. But in this he was not referring to his religious influence so much as the political influence which his movement was to have upon New Zealand as a whole.

The prophecies made in the mid-twenties were to remain unanswered until 1932 when the first seat was captured for the movement. It was not till 1943 that the prophecy was realised completely when all four of the Maori constituencies were represented by members of the Ratana movement. This was indeed a remarkable achievement for a movement which on its first entry into the political field was derided by critics and cynics as being doomed to early failure. Within the succeeding years the political movement became established with the parliamentary Labour movement. It grew in stature and reached its political zenith when the four Ratana members actually held the 'balance of power' in the Parliament of 1946-1949 – both Labour and National parties holding 38 of the Pakeha seats each. The four Maori seats, allied with the Labour party, gave that party power of government. The term 'balance of power' implies pressure groups or dictatorial attitudes, but it must be made clear that even though the opportunity may have existed for the Ratana members to have adopted these attitudes, at no stage did they exert undue pressure on the government of the day, nor extract in their own interests for their movement or the Maori people any more than would normally have been given by a sympathetic and understanding government. It is reasonable to question why the Maori members did not take this opportunity to exert pressure on the government. The writer can only advance his twofold assumption, that the Labour government had already shown a very real and sympathetic understanding of Maori problems and was giving effect to measures for their alleviation; and secondly that the members elected were not of the calibre and quality to make unwarranted demands of a government, nor did they have sufficient political acumen to capitalise upon the opportunity. It will be remembered that the Prime Ministers Savage and Fraser had taken to themselves the additional portfolios of Minister of Maori Affairs. The Maori race held both in the highest esteem.

How did all this start? What were the factors which finally influenced Ratana to subordinate the purely religious and faith-healing concept of his movement to his political aspirations?

Reference has been made elsewhere to the real basis for the formation and development of Maori movements. Accepting these assumptions, it will be seen that the religious and faith-healing aspects had drawn the race together in as near a unified form as possible. It was only a matter of time before a subconscious group desire for rectification of the ever-present land troubles would appear. And so it was with the Ratana movement.

During the early twenties when Ratana's influence was at its highest, he was approached by Tupu Tai-Ngakawa and Rewiti Te Whena, leaders of the King Movement in Waikato. They did not seek bodily cure and health as did the thousands of others, but they came for the express purpose of seeking a cure for the long-standing land troubles: 'Kahore mo te mauiui tinana, engari te mauiui o te papa whenua' (Not the ills of the body but the ills of the land). Ratana's reply was 'Kei te pai! Whakakotahi ki te Atua i te tuatahi – ana tatou ki te whakakotahi ki te whenua' (First unite in the Lord, then we will unite in the land) – thus the genesis of the political swing. It was realised that the only effective method of having the land matters aired and settled was through Parliament. Parliamentary representation became imperative. It is as well to remember at this stage that the four Maori seats had been established in 1868 and up to that time nothing had been done by any government to satisfy the incessant demands of the Maori people for settlement of their confiscated land claims. It was not until 1926 that a Commission on Native Lands was set up to hear the grievances of the people by a government that had become uneasy and was suffering from rather belated pangs of conscience.

Initially, Ratana himself had no strong political views, but as the political impetus in the movement grew, mainly through the demands of his followers, he then took an active interest in the parties of the day. He adopted the practice of inviting various members of the current political parties to address his people at Ratana Pa. Of the political exponents, the movement seemed to favour Harry Holland and Michael Joseph Savage, because in the Labour policies the Ratana people saw something of a likeness to their own philosophy. Clearly the Labour party was a friend of the ordinary working man. Also the words of King Tawhiao rang strongly in their ears – 'Ne oku hoa, ko te humeka, te parakimete, te watimeka, nga kamura, nga pani, nga pouwaru' (These are my friends, the shoemaker, the blacksmith, the watchmaker, the carpenters, the orphans, the widows). As Harry Holland and Joseph Savage expounded their political beliefs of working for the common man, the Ratana people saw a kindred group towards which they could lean. The fiery and eloquent presentations by Bob Semple also appealed greatly to a race which appreciated all the effects of forceful oratory. But Ratana was not content to rush headlong into an alliance with any party and his first candidate of political office, his own son Tokoura Hami Ratana, entered the field in 1922 as an independent candidate and remained as an independent until after 1935 when he accepted Labour Party endorsement. From that date, the movement allied itself with the Labour Party and continues to do so. One of the principal planks in the Ratana political platform was the recovery of the lands so doubtfully acquired by the Pakeha.

The following short political biographies give an idea of the extent of the movement's political activities. They are in chronological order.

Tokoura Hami Ratana: Western Maori
Stood as an independent in 1922, 1928, and 1930, against Sir Maui Pomare and in 1931 against Taite Te Tomo. Defeated Te Tomo in 1935 then contested the seat in 1938 for Labour. He held the seat until his death in 1944. He was Ratana's eldest son.

Eruera Tihema Tirikatene: Southern Maori
First attempt in 1923 was lost by a casting vote. Second attempt, 1931, lost by 15 votes. Was successful in 1932 on the death of T. Makitanara and held the seat until his death in 1967. In 1943 he succeeded P.K. Paikea in the Labour ministry, representing the Maori race (without portfolio).

Paraire Karaka Paikea: Northern Maori
A Methodist minister 1915-25. Executive member of Ratana movement 1925. Private secretary to Ratana and chief executive officer 1926. Contested Northern seat unsuccessfully against Tau Henare in 1928, 1931 and 1935. Became Secretary of the Maori Advisory Council, New Zealand Labour Party 1936. Defeated Tau Henare in 1938 and held the seat until his death in 1943. Became Minister representing Maori race (without portfolio) 1941-43. Member of the War Administration 1942.

Tiaki Omana: Eastern Maori
Contested against Sir Apirana Ngata in 1935, and 1938. Defeated Ngata in 1943 and 1946. Held the seat until his death.

Tapihana Paraire Paikea: Northern Maori
Elected on the death of his father (see above). Held seat from 1943 until his death in 1963.

Matiu Ratana: Western Maori
Son of Ratana. Elected to Parliament in 1945 on the death of his brother Tokoura (see above). Died as result of a car accident in 1949.

Mrs Iriaka Ratana: Western Maori
Widow of Matiu Ratana. First Maori woman elected to Parliament. Held the seat from 1949 until her retirement in 1969.

Matiu Rata: Northern Maori[1]
Elected on death of T.P. Paikea. Was a railways worker and vice-president of the

Ratana youth organisation. Became Minister of Maori Affairs and Lands 1972 to 1975.

Paraone (Brown) Rewiti: Eastern Maori[2]
Elected in 1967 on the death of Steve Watene, a Mormon, who was the only member to break the Ratana hold on Maori seats since 1943.

Mrs Tini Whetu Marama Tirikatene-Sullivan: Southern Maori
Elected after her father's death in 1967 (Eruera Tirikatene), when she had been studying for a doctorate in Canberra. Appointed Minister of Tourism and Associate Minister of Social Welfare in 1972, and Minister for the Environment in 1974.

Koro Tainui Wetere: Western Maori
A farmer and formerly electorate secretary for Mrs Iriaka Ratana. Succeeded her in 1969.

An examination of these biographies shows that the Ratana Movement under the influence of Labour had by 1977 dominated the Maori electorates as follows: Southern since 1932: 45 years; Western since 1935: 42 years; Northern since 1938: 39 years; Eastern since 1967: 10 years.

In addition, in the Parliamentary succession to these seats, there had been one case of son following father, one of daughter following father, one of brother following brother, and one of wife following husband.

The dominance by the movement is truly impressive and refutes the cynical claims of the early days when the political canoe was first launched. Ratana did not live to see the complete fulfilment of his political prophecies, but at least by the time of his death in 1939 his prophecy was practically accounted for with Ratana members holding three of the four Maori seats. The only outstanding seat was that of the Eastern Maori electorate held by the very able and formidable Sir Apirana Ngata. Apart from Steve Watene's brief tenure of that Eastern Maori seat, Ratana members have held the 'four corners' since 1943.[3]

What have been the results of the movement's expedition into politics? It has been said that the movement has not produced anyone of outstanding ability during its long term of political ascendancy. This may be true. At the same time one has to bear in mind that comparisons are usually drawn with the exceptionally high standard of Maori representation in the persons of Sir Apirana Ngata, Sir Maui Pomare, Sir Peter Buck, and Sir James Carroll. Their service to Parliament, comparable with only the best in European representation, tends to set any other service in sharp relief and relegate the average to mediocrity. It is unfortunate perhaps that the Ratana members followed such a dazzling period of Maori representation.

There is no question that the movement as a political force is something to be contended with. It is fair to state that its political success within the Labour Party in the past has been due to the block vote system promised by Ratana people in favour of the Labour candidates. Members of the Church have tended to vote in

160

block for the candidate as a church member rather than to have any political allegiance to a party. It is only incidental that through an alliance between the movement and the Labour Party the Maori vote has now tended to be expressed in terms of the Labour Party.

Ratana Members of Parliament were fortunate in that they were able to share the credit for the spectacular advances in Maori welfare that followed the election of the first Labour government: Social Security (especially the family benefit, medical benefits and higher payments for the unemployed) ensured that the Maori would never again be at a serious material disadvantage in relation to the Pakeha; and the settlement of the Ngai Tahu and Waikato claims[4] for compensation for lands taken illegally removed one of the major grievances that had brought Ratana politicians into prominence. It was inevitable that Ratana MPs should present these developments as, to some extent, a delivery of their election promises. The giants of the past – Carroll, Ngata, Buck, Pomare – all had spoken eloquent words in Parliament; but none had been able to improve the lot of their people to the same extent.

Because these benefits persisted, the Ratana claim to have substantially lifted the Maori standard of living has been self-perpetuating and self-justifying.

FOOTNOTES

1. Matiu Rata resigned from Parliament and from the Labour Party in 1979, and the Northern Maori seat was won by Dr Bruce Gregory, who is not Ratana.
2. Paraone Rewiti retired in 1981 and was replaced by Dr Peter Tapsell, another non-Ratana.
3. But see Notes 1 and 2.
4. In the late 1980s these claims were raised again for renegotiation, and at the time of republication had not been settled, although the Waitangi Tribunal found largely in favour of the Ngai Tahu claim in 1991.

THE KINGITANGA

ROBERT MAHUTA

NEARLY 120 YEARS AFTER ITS FOUNDATION in 1858, the Kingitanga (Maori King Movement) survives as a major source and organ of Maori activity. The current leader is the sixth to hold that position by hereditary descent. And not only does participation show no sign of decreasing numerically, it is increasing. This survival has occurred in spite of the fact that the government threats to land and chiefly authority that provided the original reasons for the movement's formation have long since disappeared.

A Kingitanga Chronology

This chronology lists key stages in the history of the Maori King movement including events leading up to the setting up of Potatau as the first Maori King, the land wars, religious and political movements, tribal leaders, internal happenings and contemporary issues. Relevant publications are listed where appropriate.

1840   Treaty of Waitangi, conflict over interpretation.

Buick, T. Lindsay, *The Treaty of Waitangi*, 1914.
Ngata, Sir Apirana, *The Treaty of Waitangi*, and explanation, 1922.
Ross, R.M., 'Te Tiriti o Waitangi', texts and translations, *New Zealand Journal of History*, Vol. 6, No. 2, 1972.

1845   Pirikawau visits England and upon his return relates Grey's statement to Queen Victoria that Te Wherowhero was the most powerful chief of the time. Te Whiwhi and later Wiremu Tamehana take up the cause for a Maori King.

1856   Te Heuheu Iwakau stages a large inter-tribal meeting at Pukawa, Lake Taupo, to discuss the reasons for setting up a King.

Grace, John Te H., *Tuwharetoa*, A.H. & A.W. Reed, pp 442-457, 1959.

1858   Potatau (Te Wherowhero) installed as first King.

Tamehana, Wiremu, *Account of Native Meetings at Ngaruawahia and Rangiaohia*, letter published in *Southern Cross* newspaper, 9 July, 1858, describing events surrounding the election of the first Maori King.
Winiata, Maharaia, *Founding of the Maori King Movement*, centennial celebrations booklet compiled from oral sources, 1958.
Jones, Pei Te Hurinui, *King Potatau*, an account of the life of Potatau Te Wherowhero, the first Maori King, 1961.

1860   'Te Riri Pakeha' – land wars in Taranaki and Waikato.
        Tawhiao installed as second King.

        Gorst, Sir John, *The Maori King*, background of events leading up to the Waikato War, 1864.
        Sinclair, Keith, *The Origins of the Maori Wars*, second edition, Auckland University Press, 1961.
        Sorrenson, M.P.K., 'The Maori King Movement 1858-1885' in Chapman, R. and Sinclair, K.,
        (Eds), *Studies of a Small Democracy*, Auckland University Press, 1963.

1863   N.Z. Settlements Act confiscates over a million acres of Waikato tribal
        lands in retribution for rebellion against the Crown.

        Sorrenson, M.P.K., Land Purchase Methods and their Effect on Maori Population 1865-1901,
        J.P.S., 65: pp 183-199, 1956.

1867   Tawhiao meets other Maori religious leaders – Te Ua Haumeene, Te Whiti
        and Tohu, Te Kooti, Aperehama Taonui.
        Appointment of first Te Kaumarua (Council of Advisers) at Taharoa.

        Winiata Maharaia, *The Changing Role of the Leader in Maori Society*: pp 57-79, 1967, dis-
        cusses factors leading to the rise of protest leaders.

1875   Donald McLean makes peace overtures. Maniapoto chiefs refuse.

1876   Grey offers compensation terms to Tawhiao. King's advisers refuse Grey's
        terms.

1881   Peace formally declared between Tawhiao and Major William Gilbert
        Mair on behalf of the government.

1882   Members of Tawhiao's Te Kaumarua take part in Maori Land Court pro-
        ceedings.

1884   Tawhiao leads deputation to England to seek redress for the confiscation
        of Waikato lands.

1885   Ngati Maniapoto chiefs agree to construction of main trunk railway line
        through the King Country.

1894   Mahuta becomes third Maori King. Sponsors Henare Kaihau for Western
        Maori parliamentary seat.

1902   Richard Seddon and Mahuta discuss Treaty of Waitangi and confisca-
        tion issues.

        Govt. Printer, *Notes of Meetings between the Governor (Land Ranfurly), Rt. Hon. R.J.
        Seddon, Hon. James Carroll and Native Chiefs and People concerning Native Land
        Legislation and Native Affairs Generally during 1898 and 1899*, 1900.

1903   Mahuta appointed to Legislative Council 1903 to 1910. Transfer of king-
        ship to younger brother Te Wherowhero.

        Parliamentary Debates, Vol. 126: 580 for discussion over Mahuta's appointment.

1911   Maui Pomare seeks Kingitanga support for Western Maori seat.
        Confiscation of Taranaki and Waikato (muru raupatu) as his platform.
        Reminds Mahuta of traditional debt as repayment.

Cody, J.F., *Man of Two Worlds*, a biography of Sir Maui Pomare, 1953.

1912   Te Rata becomes fourth Maori King.
        Carroll and Tupu Taingakawa argue over title of 'King'.

1914   Te Rata leads second deputation to England.
        Moves to conscript Waikato tribesmen forcibly during World War I.
        Conscription issue sees rise of Princess Te Puea as effective
        Kingitanga leader.

1920   Te Puea moves on to site of Turangawaewae Marae, Ngaruawahia.

1921   Te Puea taxes river tribes to assist in construction of Turangawaewae.

1922   Conflict with Ratana Movement.

Henderson, J., Ratana, *The Origins and the Story of the Movement*, p15, A.H. & A.W. Reed, 1963.

1929   Opening of Mahinarangi meeting house.

1930   Death of Pomare. Taite Te Tomo gains Te Rata's support for Western
        Maori seat. Te Puea sponsors Te Hurinui.

1933   Koroki becomes fifth King.
        Harry Holland collapses at Te Rata's graveside. Tangi at Waahi.
        Kahui Ariki accompany Holland's casket to Wellington.
        Tumate Mahuta begins negotiations to settle confiscation issue.

1938   Death of Tumate, body conveyed by canoe to Taupiri.
        Confiscation negotiations prolonged because of World War Two.

1942   Mahuta's remains taken by canoe from Hukanui to Taupiri.

1946   Peter Fraser concludes confiscation negotiations with Waikato tribal
        leaders. Waikato-Maniapoto Maori Claims Settlement Act passed fixing
        compensation amount.

1947   Establishment of Tainui Maori Trust Board.

Jones, Pei Te Hurinui, *First Annual Report of Tainui Maori Trust Board*, 1947.

1948   Koroki leads deputation to Parliament concerning the King Country Pact.

1950   Commemorative celebrations for migration canoes held at Turanga-
        waewae.

1952   Death of Princess Te Puea.
        Tribal discussions over memorial to Te Puea.

1953   First visit of British Royalty to Turangawaewae.

Jones, Pei Te Hurinui, 'Maori Kings' in Erik Schwimmer (ed.), *The Maori People in The Nineteen Sixties*, Longman, Paul, 1968. pp159-165 for a background of events leading up to this visit.

1965   Opening of the Mangere marae.

1966   Death of Koroki. Te Atairangikaahu succeeds as first Maori Queen.

1968   Te Atairangikaahu invested Dame Commander of the British Empire.

1974   Opening of Kimiora. Second visit of Elizabeth II to Turangawaewae.

1975   Te Atairangikaahu visits United Kingdom and Europe.
        Return of Taupiri mountain to Waikato tribes.
        Waikato tribes agree to file application for investigation of title to the
        Waikato river.

This in brief is a condensed history of the movement. It is by no means exhaustive, but in talking to leaders and elders of the movement, these are the events they feel are important and are constantly recounted in marae oratory.

Structure of the Kingitanga

At the head of the Kingitanga today stands Queen Te Atairangikaahu whose main supports are the Kahui Ariki and the Te Kaumarua. The Te Kaumarua (Council of Twelve) is the traditional body of kaumatua who act as advisers to the head of the movement in regard to matters of kawa (etiquette and procedure) and policy-making in general. The Kahui Ariki (paramount family) are generally defined as the descendants of Tawhiao, although in real political decision-making terms this tends towards the more senior lines of the aho ariki.

Whilst individual members of the Kahui Ariki are associated with different Christian churches, the official religion of the movement is Paimarire (Hauhau) which has been described by some observers as a mixture of ancestor worship, Christian doctrine, Maori mythology and belief in the millenium.

Perhaps the most dynamic and politically oriented institution within the movement is the Runanganui (tribal council) made up of delegates from local marae committees. The council meets sporadically and is most effective in resolving issues affecting the movement as a whole. Three recent examples of its activities were the organisation of fund-raising for the Kimiora building, the staging of the annual Coronation celebrations and mobilising support and fund-raising for the Queen's 1975 trip to the United Kingdom and Europe.

Three other groups help to give the movement shape and form. The first is the Tainui Trust Board, a body set up to administer compensation monies from government for land confiscations. The second are the Poukai committees (28 in number) which stage regular loyalty gatherings throughout the Kingitanga area and play an important role in financing activities of the movement. The third is the Te Pou o Mangatawhiri group based on Turangawaewae Marae, which is concerned with day-to-day activities and provides much-needed finance towards the maintenance of facilities and the payment of costs of functions held at

Turangawaewae in the name of the movement.

This description differs somewhat from earlier accounts in that the position of Kingmaker (Tumuaki) does not seem apparent. Theoretically, the Tumuaki has had his own council of advisers and tribal council (Kauhanganui) whose activities were focused mainly on political factors external to the movement, such as government legislation, or the relationship of other tribes, organisations or people to the movement as a whole. The Tumuaki himself stands in a paternal relationship to the head of the movement and the groups which function around him tend to derive their effectiveness from the personality and following of the office-holder.

Surrounding and intertwining themselves around the position of the Queen are semi-protest forces who tend to see her position as a means for expressing past grievances or injustices. This, of course, needs to be understood in terms of past conflicts with Europeans and also by the fact that the Queen symbolises Maori values and institutions which are being continually threatened by Pakeha domination. Winiata (1958: 85-86) cites the following examples.

> Some years ago Maori rights in the King Country were threatened by the drive from liquor and other interests to break up the Maori-Pakeha pact which prohibited the establishment of licensed hotels in that area. Koroki led the deputation of some six hundred people to Parliament, but he uttered not a word. Tita Wetere and the writer presented the Maori case on his behalf. There have been similar instances in other ariki positions. For example, Te Heuheu was responsible for the movement in the late 1940s that dispatched a lawyer to Britain to appeal for a consideration of the Treaty of Waitangi before the Privy Council. In each case, Koroki and Te Heuheu were symbolic leaders, acting as the mouthpiece of the Maori people as a whole, in protest against encroachment on their rights.
>
> It is the embodiment of values, the focusing of Maori sentiment, the fixing and preserving of Maori culture, that summarises the principal function of the sponsored type of leader, a logical conservative: 'hei pupuri i te mana' – 'to hold on to Maori prestige'. The method, paradoxically enough, is to refrain from active participation in movements, but rather to exercise a silent and passive, symbolic leadership. The strength of the ariki is in his isolation from the mundane affairs of the tribe. On the other hand, his presence is necessary to add dignity to the proceedings, although he need not speak. He may be the figurehead in diplomatic negotiations with the European or with other Maori groups, but he is usually hedged about by other leaders such as the kaumatua, the educated leader and the tohunga, who share

166

among them those duties whose sanction comes from the ariki. Thus when Queen Elizabeth visited Turangawaewae marae, Koroki received her, though it was a kaumatua who recited the welcome ritual, and it was an educated person who translated his speech into English.

More recent examples can be found in approaches for support from various Maori organisations such as the Kotahitanga, Te Roopu Matakite and Nga Tamatoa.

The Kingitanga Today

Today when people talk about the King Movement, the connotations generally evolve around the terms Maori Queen, Turangawaewae, Waikato and the Tainui canoe. The issues for protest from its past such as land, mana, chieftainship and Maori rights tend to be under-played in a way that is almost paradoxical. The question of how long the movement will continue to survive in its present or a modified form places its followers in a dilemma. The reasons for its establishment in the past have virtually all disappeared. There is no land to preserve, inter-tribal wars ended over a century ago and the old tribal law (or lore) has long been superseded by Pakeha law. Why has it continued to persist up to the present day?

To its adherents, the philosophy and activities of the movement provide them with an alternative set of symbols and values and indeed an alternative life-style to that of the forty-hour week, quarter-acre section and mortgage and all the other necessary commitments for survival in the modern age. The Poukai (loyalty) gatherings, Coronation celebrations, life crisis rituals and many other hui staged by the movement provide a network of occasions within which people can come together to laugh, sing, play, work and talk about those things they deem important. It is at these hui that dreams are recounted, Tawhiao's promise of the millenium is retold and people's hopes for the future are revitalised.

To the casual onlooker it all seems a waste of time and money. There seems to be little discussion of topical issues. Most of the speech-making seems confined to the past, the dead and local traditions. Topics of a controversial or sensitive nature tend to be discouraged and whaikorero is restricted preferably to the kaumatua. Yet it is within these very symptoms of apparent indifference and ignorance of events around them, that some of the basic problems facing the movement can be found.

With an annual cycle of approximately 50 tribal gatherings in one form or another, the Waikato is one of the most active areas for hui in New Zealand today. This in turn places a severe strain on marae communities in providing workers and foodstuffs. In some areas hui tend to be infrequent and consequently more time and preparation can be devoted to organisation and staging. Within the Waikato, however, the sheer volume of gatherings is placing an unbearable strain on tribal resources, especially on the central Kingitanga base at Turangawaewae Marae.

Urbanisation has seen the movement of young people and families from the rural marae to towns and cities in search of work. This rural depletion has meant the loss of a virile young workforce to handle the many tasks on the marae during the staging of hui, such as cooking, cleaning, fund-raising and even whaikorero.

For the kaumatua, migration has resulted in a constriction and weakening of his sphere of influence within his community, the transmission of knowledge process is disrupted and there is difficulty in ensuring that kinship rights and obligations are upheld.

For the Poukai marae who are expected to provide large quantities of Maori foods at their annual gatherings, the loss of food cultivation areas and the depletion of freshwater and sea food resources inhibits their ability to extend traditional hospitality and places an added financial burden on the organising committee.

Marae development within many smaller communities suffers from lack of capital, a draining-off of resources for major marae, the conservatism of marae trustees and finally the present inadequacies of governmental subsidy assistance.

The relationship of the Kingitanga to other Maori groups is also a matter of concern. Since the conflict with the Ratana movement in the 1920s, conscious efforts have been made to heal the breach and there have been several exchanges of visits. The Queen is patroness of the New Zealand Maori Women's Welfare League and appears to have maintained contact and communication with the league and its local branches in the Waikato relatively well. Communications with the New Zealand Maori Council, however, have not been as effective and this can probably be attributed to the basis upon which their respective boundaries of influence have been defined. The council was set up by statute, whereas the movement came into being because of settler pressures on the land and attempts by tribal chiefs to preserve their authority over the land and their tribes. At the community level there has always been conflict between the marae committees (based on kinship) and the Maori communities who derive their authority from the council and ultimately government. Since its inception, the New Zealand Maori Council structure has not functioned effectively in the Waikato, whilst at the same time the King Movement has not seized some of the obvious advantages deriving from the council's administrative structure. Because of the similarity of doctrines between the Kingitanga and the Ringatu Church – and the hospitality and refuge offered to Te Kooti by Tawhiao – relationships between these two groups have endured. Given these observations, there have been moves within Maoridom over the past few years to try to bring the various groups together, if not in unity, then certainly on those issues which affect Maori people nationally.

Turning to relationships and attitudes between the Kingitanga and Pakeha organisations including government, the situation seems less clearly defined. Contacts have fluctuated over the years, with some leaders encouraging closer ties with the dominant power group and others preferring to remain aloof. It is nevertheless significant that today political leaders and vice-regal representatives, as well as heads of state from other countries, as a matter of course visit the Kingitanga headquarters at Turangawaewae and pay their respects to the head of the movement. They in turn are accorded the rituals and hospitality befitting their rank, and they experience at first hand some of the reasons why Maori people wish to retain their identity.

This perhaps explains the confusion which invariably arises over the relative status of the Maori Queen within society at large and her position vis-a-vis the government. To some extent the hospitality extended at Turangawaewae reflects on our international reputation abroad. Yet the movement has been careful not to become too closely identified with government policy or administration and reserves the right to accept visitors and to stage gatherings for their benefit. It is somewhat ironical today that the head of a protest movement whose tribe lost nearly all of their lands in the early stages of contact is now accepted as a hostess for visiting stage dignitaries.

The aura of legitimacy exemplified by the conferment in 1968 of the title 'Dame' on Queen Te Atairangikaahu and the invitation in 1975 by the British government to tour the United Kingdom marked a new era in the development of the movement. Whatever motives have been involved, the movement has now arrived at the crossroads. To some observers the movement is and has always been a separatist brown power group whose continued existence poses a threat to the goal of assimilation. To others it reflects a conservative Maori viewpoint, too amenable to compromise and out of touch with the feelings and aspirations of the young. Could the actions of patronage referred to above be interpreted in the same light as the earlier offers made to Tawhiao, Mahuta and others? At this stage it is difficult to predict what course the movement will take. Will it become enveloped in the complexities of modern life or will it continue to maintain its independent and somewhat aloof stance outside the mainstream? Current indications are that the movement is in good health and one can only presume that so long as it has meaning and relevance for its adherents then so long will it continue.

THE RELEVANCE OF MAORI MYTH AND TRADITION

RANGINUI WALKER

IN A CULTURE THAT LIVES AND GROWS, there need be nothing outmoded or discredited about mythology. Properly understood, Maori mythology and traditions provide myth-messages to which the Maori people can and will respond today. All that is needed is that these myth-messages be more clearly signposted.

The stories of Maori myths are set in the remote past associated with the mythical homeland of Hawaiki. They deal with the origins of the gods from the primaeval pair Ranginui and Papatuanuku, the creation of the world and the origins of man and his institutions.

The actors in the myths are often endowed with supernatural powers as they act out their dramas in an age of miracles and supra-normal events. In doing so, the actors, whether they are demi-gods or legendary heroes, provide lesser mortals with larger-than-life models for human behaviour. The actors are heroes or villains. They love, hate, fight and pursue revenge just as their human counterparts do. They also dramatise the age-old conflict between good and evil. Occasionally they provide prescriptions for practical behaviour in given situations. These are the myth-messages of a culture.

In a closed system, myths are self-validating. The story-teller, by reciting his genealogy to the canoe ancestors and back to the Hawaiki homeland, can ultimately link himself to the legendary heroes and the gods.

The validity of his myths was not questioned by the Maori until the post-Christian era when they were displaced by the mythology of the new culture. Today, 'korero purakau' has the same negative connotation of untruth as 'it's only a myth'. This is unfortunate, since an analysis of Maori myths will show that even today Maori will respond to the myth-messages and cultural imperatives embedded in their mythology. It is possible to follow a recurrence of themes in a continuum across mythological, traditional and historic times. But the erosion of Maori culture by that of the European has made the thread binding it to its mythology more tenuous. The myth-messages now need to be spelled out to be understood by the modern Maori.

One way of looking at mythology is to read it as the mirror-image of a culture. Myths reflect the philosophy, ideals and norms of the people who adhere to them as legitimating charters. Sometimes a myth is the outward projection of an ideal against which human performance can be measured and perfected. Alternatively, a myth might provide a reflection of current social practice, in which case it has an instructional and validating function.

Maori myths are arranged in a progressive sequence of three story complexes. From the cosmogonic myths to the Maui myths and the Tawhaki myth there is a progression from the creative activities of gods and demi-gods to the activities of real men.

The Creation Myth

The creation myth begins logically with the procreative act of the primaeval pair Ranginui the sky father and Papatuanuku the earth mother. But the procreation took place in a world of darkness that inhibited growth, progress and an increase in knowledge[1]. To this end, the separation of the earth and sky was accomplished by Tane-Mahuta. This separation let light and hence knowledge into the world. Although this was a necessary precondition for the growth and development of man, the act of separation is seen as the first sin. It was an act of kohuru (cruelty) against the first parents.

Tawhirimatea, the brother who opposed the separation, introduced the theme of utu (revenge) so basic to Maori society. He sought satisfaction from his brothers for their part in the crime against his parents by attacking their creative efforts with winds and mighty storms. Thus he started the wars of the gods. First he vanquished the children of Tane by smashing down the trees as food for insects, rottenness and decay. Then he attacked the seas, causing a separation of the species. The descendants of Tangaroa hid in the oceans to become the progenitor of fishes while Tumawerewere fled inland to establish the family of reptiles. The helpless Rongomatane and Haumiatiketike were hidden by their mother in the bosom of the earth. As the undistinguished brothers in the family, their dependence on maternal protection condemned them to a lowly estate. Rongo became the god of the kumara and cultivated plants while Haumiatiketike became the god of the fern-root and uncultivated plants.

Tumatauenga was the only brother who withstood the wrath of Tawhirimatea. As the personification of the fierce and warlike nature of man he won an exalted place in the cosmogony as the god of war. The revenge of Tumatauenga on his brothers for their desertion during Tawhirimatea's attack justifies man's superordinate position in nature. Tumatauenga debased his brothers by turning them into food and common use. He made canoes, lines, spears, hooks and spades out of the children of Tane. He fished up the children of Tangaroa and dug up the descendants of Rongo and Haumiatiketike. Although the myth does not explicitly say so, it is possible to argue that Tumatauenga's actions introduce a basic dichotomy in Maori life between the sacred and the profane. Tapu in the sacred sense emanates from the gods. By the act of eating his brothers or turning them into artifacts, Tumatauenga profaned them. Herein lies the ritual and cultural significance of cannibalism. It is the ultimate debasement of a defeated enemy.

Although Tumatauenga emerged superior, he was a god made in man's image and likeness. He was neither vanquished by nor victorious over Tawhirimatea. The elements wage continuous war against man, who in his turn has to maintain constant vigilance.

Hineahuone

The gods searched for the ira tangata (the human element) in nature. Tane's procreative efforts brought forth the different species of trees, birds and insects. Eventually he came to the conclusion that a separate act of creation was necessary. Tane fashioned Hineahuone, the earth-formed maid, and gave her the breath of life.

He cohabited with his own creation and produced Hinetitama, the dawn maid. He then cohabited with Hinetitama until the day she asked who her father was. Hinetitama guessed the awful truth of her incestuous relationship with Tane, from his evasive reply to 'ask the posts of their house'. She fled from him to the world of darkness where she was transformed into Hine-nui-te-po, the goddess of death.

Alpers[2] sees Tane's offence against his daughter as the first sin in Maori mythology. But in Grey's account of Maui's fishing up the land and the desecration of the fish by his brothers, the narrator states quite unequivocally that this was the second evil which took place after the separation of Ranginui and Papatuanuku[3]. The main inference to be drawn from the myth is the clear indication of the incest taboo. Although incest in the creation myth was necessary to bring about an increase in the human line, Hinetitama's flight from Tane indicates that as a practice it was socially unacceptable.

The Maui Complex of Myths

The importance of Maui as a culture hero derives from the circumstances of his birth. He was the potiki, the last-born of five brothers. In a society where succession was based on primogeniture, his rank was low in the family pecking order. In addition he was an aborted child cast away on the ocean by his mother in the top-knot of her hair, from which circumstance he derived his name Maui-tikitiki-a Taranga. The potiki in Maori society is the indulged child; as such, it tends to be precocious. So it was with Maui. He was quick, intelligent and resourceful. He was bold, yet cunning and deceitful. From his penchant for deceiving his elders he was called Maui-nukurau-tangata, the trickster of men. Maui is the epitome of the idealised character in Maori society. He is the model for all men and more particularly for teina, junior children. Provided they had the traits so admired by society, they too could aspire to leadership, to a place of honour. Maui is the hero who rises above circumstances to prove that the principle of primogeniture was not incontrovertible.

When Maui was rescued from the sea by his ancestor the myth relates how he was revived by being suspended over a smoky fire. This was the method used by Maori to revive a drowned person. This incident in the myth was both a reflection of current social practice in dealing with a particular crisis and also a directive, an instruction as to how to proceed. Myth-messages of this kind illustrate that myths are more than just-so stories.

On his return to his family, Maui was given a favoured place in his mother's affections by being allowed to sleep in her bed. The favouritism of Maui intro-duced the theme of brotherly rivalry hinted at in the wars of the gods. The disap-pearance of his mother in the daytime and her reappearance at night caused Maui to wonder over the whereabouts of his parents. The myth introduces a basic theme in Maori society, a child's search for his parents. In a society where visiting chiefs were accorded sexual favours by local women, illegitimate births were common. Maui in searching out his parents was acting out a recurrent theme in centuries of tradition. Rangiteaorere of the Arawa people and Tamainupo of the Waikato are two examples of famous fighting chiefs in traditional times recon-ciled with their fathers after they had reached manhood.

The way Maui tricked his mother by hiding her clothes and spying on her is an indication that deceit and trickery are acceptable if socially desired ends are to be achieved. These were the means that enabled Maui to follow his mother to the land of his father.

Maui's encounter with his parents illustrates an important social convention concerning the identification and introduction of strangers in Maori society. Maui's mother was not certain of his identity and it would have been a breach of etiquette to ask directly who he was. The impasse was resolved by the classic ploy of locating the direction of the stranger's origins. It is socially acceptable to ask 'Are you from the North? The South? The East? The West?' but not 'What is your name?' Once territorial and hence tribal origins have been established, it is rela-tively easy to identify the person. This convention is one of the powerful myth-messages of Maori society, because it persists to the present day. In an urban situa-tion where young Maori from different tribes meet each other for the first time, they respond to the social imperative embedded in the Maui myth. They begin to fraternise not by asking each other's names, but by the question, 'Hey boy, where you from?' Once tribal origins are established they then search for mutual rela-tives. This done, the bond is formed.

The social recognition of Maui was completed by his father performing the tohi (purification) ritual. The tohi legitimated Maui and reconciled him to his father. The mistake in the ritual is the Maori rationale for the loss of immortality. Maui's father knew his son would be the first man to die. But the incident is more

173

than this. It is a myth-message that emphasises the correct performance of ritual. Waiata (songs) and karakia (prayers) must be recited word-perfect. The penalty for failure is misfortune and death.

In encounters with his other ancestors, Maui acts out the role of both arch-trickster and benefactor to mankind. He deceived his ancestress Muriranga-whenua with the shabby trick of concealing food from her. Yet despite this, she favoured him by giving into his keeping the enchanted jawbone. His use of this as a weapon to beat the sun and slow its passage across the sky and as a fish-hook to fish up the land is the prototype of all bone artifacts. It was Maui who benefited man by proving the special properties of bone weapons and fish hooks.

In a parallel episode, Maui obtained the secret of fire from another ancestress called Mahuika. Although Maui tricked her into giving away all her fire fingers he almost lost his life for being too presumptuous. The encounters with Muriranga-whenua and Mahuika illustrate an important principle in Maori life. Elders are indulgent towards precocious grandchildren. They are the repositories of wisdom, knowledge and tribal lore. The young must obtain this knowledge, but the elders are ambivalent and even reluctant to give it up. Maui had to wrest their secrets from them by persistence and deceit. It is the wisdom of the elders that gives them the advantage over the young. The surrender of their knowledge is a diminution of their mana, therefore it is not obtained easily. Only a child with the requisite qualities able to get the better of elders will prevail.

The myth of Maui's fishing up of the land is a good example of Maui's resourcefulness and ingenuity. He outwitted his brothers' attempt to leave him out of the fishing expedition by rising earlier than they did. Undeterred by their refusal to give him bait, Maui demonstrated his resourcefulness by beating his nose and smearing blood on the hook. This action of beating the nose to draw blood was reduplicated in the semi-mythical tradition of Ngatoroirangi's encounter with his arch-enemy Manaia. Ngatoroirangi effected a surprise attack on his enemies by instructing his men to beat their noses, smear themselves with blood and to feign death. The victory was called Ihumotomotokia, the 'beaten noses'. Either Maui provided the original inspiration or the later story is a reiteration of the strategy. Cunning and resourcefulness are what counted in the Maori mind. It is a consistent theme throughout the mythology.

The crime perpetrated by the greed of Maui's brothers in cutting up the fish before the appropriate ritual had been conducted has already been alluded to. That it was condemned as the second sin emphasises the need to conduct appropriate thanksgiving rituals for the gifts of nature. The myth-message teaches that failure to respect nature brings its own evil consequences.

The episode where Maui turned his brother-in-law Irawaru into a dog is more than just an origin myth for the dog as suggested by Alpers[4]. It introduces the theme of strained relationships between brothers-in-law. The *bête noire* in Pakeha society is the mother-in-law, but in Maori society it was the brother-in-law.

174

The relationship stands for treachery and murder. The theme is reiterated in subsequent myths and traditions. The legendary hero Tawhaki was almost murdered by his brothers-in-law. Tuwhakararo was killed by his wife's relatives. Even Kupe the navigator drowned his brother-in-law Hoturapa when he sailed away in his canoe while the latter was engaged in freeing their anchor stuck on the bottom of the seabed. The strained relationship between brothers-in-law is a good example of the continuity between myth and tradition. The mythological precedent provided by Maui and Irawaru is reiterated time and again in the stories of both eras. Because the theme bears constant repetition, the conclusion is drawn that it was a myth-message and social imperative of the first order.

Maui's final encounter with the goddess of death Hine-nui-te-po as foretold by the ill-omen of his purification rite ended in death for Maui. The episode justifies the Maori belief in the predictive power of omens, as well as providing a rationale for death. Despite his prowess, Maui was in the end defeated by death. The conclusion arrived at is that death for mankind is inescapable, so man should resign himself to its inevitability. Not even the greatest hero of the Maori could conquer death.

Rupe and Hinauri

After Maui's death the myth sequence is continued by his brother Rupe, who went in search of his sister Hinauri. Hinauri had been so bereft at having her husband turned into a dog that she attempted suicide by throwing herself into the sea. Maui had searched for his parents while Rupe searched for his sister. The theme that there is an obligation on a hero figure to search for parents or siblings indicates that Maori society held these primary relationships as particularly binding.

Rupe extended his search even to the tenth heaven, where he visited Rehua. The incident of Rehua offering as food for his guest the birds which lived in his hair and fed on lice, has two implications. First, myth systems are not perfect. Often in minor matters of detail they are astray. The birds in Rehua's hair werre bellbirds and tuis. These are not carnivorous but nectar feeders. Secondly, the myth deliberately arouses disgust and revulsion. The head is the most tapu (sacred) part of the body. The notion of eating food which had been in contact with the head is so repulsive to the Maori that it hardly bears contemplation. This is the precedent for the social taboo that anything which has been in contact with the head, such as combs, hats, or articles of toilet, should not be placed on a table where food is prepared or consumed. Rehua's repast is an effective dramatisation of an important myth-message.

On Rupe's second visit to Rehua's courtyard he found the place filthy with childish excrement. Rupe's action of fashioning wooden scoops to tidy the courtyard and the building of a heketua (privy) provides a model for the proper disposal of human waste. The horrible fate of Kaitangata, who was killed when the unfastened handrail of the privy pitched him over the cliff, carries the additional message to ensure that it is properly constructed.

Kae and Tinirau

The theft of Tinirau's pet whale by Kae introduces a basic theme in Maori life. Utu (revenge) is correct when there is a 'take' (just cause). Kae is cast in the role of a villain who exhibits the negative characteristics of cunning, greed and treachery. Tinirau entrusted his pet to carry Kae to his own village. Kae broke Tinirau's trust by sitting fast on the whale when it reached the shoals, thus stranding and killing it. As previously indicated, myth systems are not perfect. Occasionally they exhibit curious errors in minor detail. The myth relates that sand entered the fish's gills, whereupon it suffocated and was dragged ashore to be cooked and eaten. This is another indication that peripheral details are unimportant in myths. It is the myth-message that counts.

Kae deceived Tinirau. The latter would have been fully justified to storm into Kae's village to demand compensation. Indeed, he would have been justified in going to war. But Tinirau set about his revenge with subtlety and cunning more than equal to that of his adversary. Instead of sending a war party to Kae's village, Tinirau sent a party of women. Kae's people were put completely off guard by this subterfuge. With the aid of their charms and enchantments the women were able to abduct Kae and deliver him to Tinirau. Kae was executed for his crime and became the first mortal killed in revenge. The myth-message is quite clear. Revenge is a social duty. Villains deserve to die. Ideally, the mission should be executed with subtlety, cunning, and an appropriate strategy designed to achieve its purpose.

As the mirror-image of society, mythology reflects social practice. The death of Kae does not close the account. It engenders a continuing vendetta in subsequent generations. The Popohorokewa retaliated by killing Tinirau's son Tuhuruhuru.

Whakatau Potiki

In the next generation Whakatau Potiki repeats the theme of a junior brother becoming the heroic figure. He had the task of avenging the death of his brother Tuwhakararo, killed by the descendants of Kae. Tuwhakararo went to visit his sister, who had married into the Ati-Hapai tribe. The treacherous way he was murdered re-emphasised the dangerous nature of relatives by marriage, a theme introduced in the Maui myth. Tuwhakararo was the first human victim of cannibalism and also the first to have his bones hung up as a trophy in the meeting house.

The exploits of Whakatau in achieving revenge for the death of his brother read like a military manual. The myth sets out a model of military behaviour, how to review warriors, practise order of battle and to arrange for their disposition in assault columns, support columns and reserve columns.

176

The myth contains sound military advice on the selection of the hard core of well-drilled capable warriors for a dangerous mission. These are the hoko-whitu-a-Tu, the hundred and forty warriors of Tumatauenga, the fighting unit favoured by the Maori.

In his conduct of the campaign, we see Whakatau acting out his role as a heroic figure in a classic manner according to the dictates of war. His every act was a model of precise military behaviour. Reconnaissance of the enemy village, the lone exploit, disguise, capturing and interrogating a prisoner to gain intelligence of the enemy while at the same time denying the enemy information, are all there. Cutting the prisoner's tongue out might seem a harsh and capricious act, but the myth-message is clear, keep your enemy ignorant of your presence and your intentions. In carrying out a daring lone exploit into the house of the enemy we see Whakatau behaving in a heroic manner. Whakatau becomes a model, somewhat idealised perhaps, by which subsequent human generations can measure the performance of their heroes. It is the bold, intelligent and resourceful hero, like Whakatau, who gains victories.

Whakatau's revenge for the death of Tuhuruhuru reinforces the myth-messages of knowing your enemy and devising the appropriate strategy to defeat him. He defeated the local champion in single combat by asking him what was his special skill. On learning he was a skilled diver Whakatau invited him to dive to the canoe. But Whakatau had taken the advance precaution of having with him a calabash of oil. This he poured on the water to still it so he was able to see the diver and kill him as he surfaced. The second adversary, who was a skilled jumper, was invited to leap into the canoe. But unbeknown to the enemy he had a noose waiting in the bottom of the canoe. As soon as the warrior landed, the noose was pulled tight and he was easily despatched with a club. In this way, Whakatau defeated ten opponents. The myth-message for the owners of the myth is that it is possible to defeat an enemy with superior forces by strategy and subterfuge. That way victory is made more certain.

Tawhaki

The Tawhaki myths begin by reiterating the theme of the dangerous nature of the brother-in-law relationship. The treacherous attack by his brothers-in-law would have ended in Tawhaki's death had not his wife found his shallow grave and with great fortitude dragged him home. When Tawhaki was revived by his wife he instructed her to warm him by building up the fire. The myth-message in the story was attached to his instruction to build up the fire with an uncut long length of wood. Hinepiripiri was pregnant at the time. When her son was born he was named Wahieroa, Long-length-of-wood. This is the prototype of using personal names to mark important events. In a preliterate society, personal names were used to commemorate significant incidents in the history of a people. Names are more than just names, they are the signposts of tradition and history. At a deeper level the name not only recorded the wrong done by Tawhaki's brothers-in-law, but acted as a constant reminder to avenge the incident. When a person so named reaches manhood his name acts on him and his kin as a social imperative. If revenge has not yet been achieved, then for him, it is a social duty.

The use of personal names to mark important events is a theme found as a continuum through myth and tradition into historic times. Names like Tutamure (pricked by a snapper), Te Waharoa (suspended the gate of a pa) and Horonuku (landslide) come to mind. The practice continued into modern times with names such as Tunisia, Alamein and Egypt to commemorate relatives killed in World War II[5].

The story of Tawhaki's revenge against the Ponaturi, the goblin-like people who lived underwater and came ashore to sleep in their house at night, carries a number of myth-messages. The story establishes that a son has a sacred duty to recover the bones of his father hanging as a trophy of war in the enemy house. It also reinforces earlier myth-messages about gaining information, knowing the enemy and identifying his weakness. Tawhaki learned from his mother, the captive doorkeeper of the enemy house, that the Ponaturi were vulnerable to the sun's rays. Accordingly the appropriate strategy was devised of blocking up the opening in the house to induce the Ponaturi to oversleep until the sun was well above the horizon. Tawhaki also used incantations to reassure himself and to ensure the success of the mission.

Tawhaki's victories against his enemies spread his fame far and wide, even to the heavens. The myth of the celestial maiden Tangotango's nightly visitations to the hero's bed is an indication of the sexual mores of Maori society. Women had equal liberty with men to initiate love affairs. Tangotango provided both a social precedent and legitimation of actual social practice. It was no aberration in sexual behaviour when in traditional times Hinemoa eloped to join Tutanekai on Mokoia Island or Wairaka crept into a lover's bed, only to discover next day that she had slept with the wrong man.

When Tangotango's child was born, Tawhaki's remark that the child smelt offended his wife so much she parted from him. But before she disappeared into the sky he asked for a 'koha', some consideration out of compassion whereby he could win back her favour and resume normal relations. Her advice was to beware of the loose vine and to grasp only the vine that was firmly rooted in the ground.

Eventually Tawhaki went in search of his wife. In previous myths Maui and Rupe searched for parents and a sister. Tawhaki's search for his wife indicates that this is a pivotal relationship of equal importance to those of parents and siblings. It is a socially important bond that should not be lightly given up.

On the journey to the vines by which entry would be gained to the heavens Tawhaki and his brother Karihi warned their two slaves not to look at the sacred citadel of Tongameha. The pa was too tapu for the eyes of slaves. Predictably, one slave could not contain his curiosity. He looked. His eyes were torn out and he perished. The myth-message establishes that the commands of superiors must be obeyed. Any such command backed by the force of tapu carries with it the sanction of death. The incident validates the awesome power of tapu, and one can imagine the effect the story had in socialisation of the young.

The incident in which Karihi nearly lost his life when he grasped the loose vine reminded Tawhaki of obligations to his family at home. He sent Karihi back to care for their family while he continued the expedition alone. Tawhaki climbed up the vines to the tenth heaven, where he adopted the disguise of an old man as he watched his brothers-in-law fashion a canoe. At the end of the day Tawhaki went through two trials that were a test of his sincerity. First his brothers-in-law adopted him as their slave and made him carry home their axes. As he followed them he was accosted by women who added insult to injury by making him carry firewood as well. This was Tawhaki's expiation for the insult to his wife. After revealing himself Tawhaki was reunited with his wife. He then fulfilled his parental duty of conducting the purification rite for his child. The incident of breaking open the end wall of the house to carry the child out set the social precedent for this practice as a mark of the mana of high-born aristocrats. The story of Tawhaki is one of the few with a happy ending, as he was semi-deified to dwell in the heavens.

Rata

In the next generation Wahieroa was killed by the demon-like Matukutakotako who emerged from a hole in the ground during the phase of the new moon to roam the earth and devour men. It was the duty of Wahieroa's son to avenge his father's death.

In the pursuit of his revenge we see Rata repeating and reinforcing the messages of previous myths. Rata travelled to the enemy's dwelling place where he learned about his enemy. From the keeper of the portal to the underground lair he gained intelligence about the habits of Matukutakotako. He learned it would be dangerous to attack his enemy at the pool he used as a mirror to dress his hair. So he attacked and killed him at the first pool where he bathed himself. The story reinforces the meessage that knowledge of the enemy is basic in devising tactics to defeat him. The attack should always be concentrated on the point of weakness.

With the death of his most formidable adversary, Rata then turned his attention to the recovery of Wahieroa's bones from the Ponaturi. For this expedition he needed a canoe. In felling the tree and shaping his canoe, Rata neglected the propitiatory rites to Tane. On his return to the site the next day a supra-normal event had occurred. The canoe was nowhere in sight, but the tree was standing back in its position. After repeating the performance Rata secreted himself at the end of the day to keep watch on the canoe. It was then that he saw the 'haku-turi', the denizens of the forest, fairy folk, birds and insects swarm round the desecrated child of Tane to re-erect it. When he leapt out of his hiding place to remonstrate with them, they turned on him and scolded him instead for his misdeed against nature.

The incident of Rata's canoe is a myth-message of conservation. Before natural resources are appropriated for man's use, propitiatory rites to the appropriate deity must be observed. Their observance ensures that nature is not treated wantonly, but with due care and respect.

The Link With Tradition

Maori traditions begin with the migratory period from the Hawaiki homeland in the fourteenth century. Unlike myths, the heroes in the traditions are human ancestors with whom direct genealogical links can be demonstrated. Although the stories recounted in the traditions were not recorded in writing, the owners treat them as historic events.

While myth events were located in a remote past, traditions have a depth of 26 generations, or six and a half centuries. Yet despite this difference, the distinction between myth and tradition is not sharply demarcated. Undoubtedly the actors in the traditions were real men, but their activities have much in common with their mythological predecessors. That is to say, they were remote enough in time to be endowed with supra-normal powers. They also exhibited personality traits reminiscent of the heroes of mythology. The early traditions also transmitted myth-messages.

The traditions of the Tuwharetoa as recorded by Grace[6] provide a good example of the transition between myth and tradition.

Tamatekapua

Tamatekapua, captain of the Arawa canoe, is an heroic figure who bears a remarkable similarity to Maui, the model hero of mythology. Like Maui he was daring, resourceful and a trickster. The only difference is that he did not have supra-normal powers and he exhibited a human failing in his predilection for women.

Tamatekapua displayed his penchant for trickery in the episode where he and his brother Whakaturia used stilts to steal breadfruit from the tree growing over Uenuku's house. The pursuers caught up with the thieves on the beach and captured Whakaturia by chopping him down from his stilts. But Tamatekapua escaped by persuading his enemies to chop his stilts so that he fell into the sea instead of on the land. Then in a daring lone exploit he displayed heroic qualities in the rescue of his brother. He saved Whakaturia, who was suspended in the rafters of the enemy house, from being asphyxiated, by the ruse of getting Whakaturia to persuade his captors to let him demonstrate his dancing skills to them. At the climax of the dance, which called for a mighty leap, Tamatekapua threw the door open to allow his brother out, then slammed it shut while they made their escape.

The Arawa canoe then made a hasty departure to escape the forces of Uenuku. But before he left, Tamatekapua tricked Ruao into going ashore so that he could steal his wife. This incident, together with Tama's abduction of the high priest Ngatoroirangi and the seduction of Kearoa his wife, on the journey to Aotearoa, all serve to enhance the mana of Tamatekapua.

When the canoe made its landfall at Whangaparaoa, Tamatekapua overturned the prior claim of the Tainui canoe to a stranded whale by attaching an old rope, as a sign of ownership, under the rope of the Tainui claimants. Whether or not the episode actually occurred is immaterial, because in effect it is a myth-message indicating that the end justifies the means. The same ruse was used in the building of shrines to establish prior claim to land. In their exploration of the interior Ngatoroirangi made his house and post, as signs of ownership, look older than those of Tia who had preceded him. Clearly, a man of mana will stop at nothing. It is expected of him that he will use cunning and deceit to get the better of a rival.

Ngatoroirangi

As the canoe ancestor of the Tuwharetoa, Ngatoroirangi is a hero figure who fits easily into the realm of mythology as well as the era of traditional times. The episode where he created a whirlpool that threatened to engulf the Arawa canoe as punishment for Tamatekapua's seduction of his wife demonstrated his supranormal prowess. In his exploration of the interior of Aotearoa, Ngatoroirangi was credited with the creation of the fresh water whitebait. This episode is the mythical basis for the origin of an important food resource to the tribes of the interior, which serves to further enhance the mana of Ngatoroirangi as an ancestor hero. He gave further demonstrations of his supra-normal powers at Tongariro, when he killed Hapeketuarangi, the rival claimant, by bringing down dense black clouds, snow and sleet on the mountain. He is also credited with calling forth the volcanic fires in the thermal region of the island.

Ngatoroirangi is a hero figure at the half-way house between myth and tradition. It is interesting to speculate what would have happened had Maori society remained undisturbed for another six hundred years. It is probable he would have been exalted entirely to the realm of mythology and semi-deified along with the legendary Tawhaki.

Tia

Tia, who explored the interior at the same time as Ngatoroirangi, is notable for the place names he bestowed on the land to mark his passing or to commemorate an event. At a place where he noticed clouds of dust in a river he realised someone was ahead of him claiming the land. That place he named Atiamuri (Tia who follows behind). At Mamaku he inadvertently touched a dead body, thereby becoming tapu. Because he had to perform a decontamination ritual involving the swallowing of food he named that place Te-horohoroinga-nui-a-Tia (The great swallowing place of Tia). At Lake Taupo he noticed an unusual formation on a cliff resembling a cloak. He named the lake Taupo-nui-a-Tia (The great lake of Tia).

As he proceeded along the Waikato River he encountered rapids. These he named Aratiatia (The stairway of Tia). Tia's use of place-names to mark the discoveries in his journey and to commemorate events is a direct reflection of mythological precedent. Personal and place-names are the signposts of the history and traditions of the Maori people. 'They were the immutable, tangible markers of tradition'.[7]

Conclusion

Myths and traditions possess the same dynamism as the culture that bears them. Although the moral truths which are the myth-messages are relatively stable, points of detail may be altered to suit local circumstance. It is this reworking of a myth that sometimes creates an incongruity, such as lice-eating tuis and bellbirds in the episode of Rupe's encounter with Rehua. The dynamism of a culture's myth-system is also reflected in the elevation of an ancestor hero such as Ngatoroirangi to the realm of mythology. Not only are myths reworked, but they are continuously being added to from the expanding fund of stories from tradition.

Maori myths and traditions are logically arranged and related systems that fulfilled explanatory, integrating, validating, historic and socialisation functions for the people who owned them. Although possessing supra-normal powers in an age of miracles, the heroes of myths and traditions behave basically in human ways. They love, hate, fight and die just as their living counterparts do. Embedded in the stories are themes and myth-messages that provide precedents, models and social prescriptions for human behaviour. In some cases the myth-messages are so close to the existing reality of human behaviour that it is difficult to resolve whether myth is the prototype or the mirror image of reality.

FOOTNOTES:

1. Sir Peter Buck, *The Coming of the Maori*, Whitcombe & Tombs, Wellington, 1958, p. 434.
2. A. Alpers, *Maori Myths and Tribal Legends*, Longman & Paul, Auckland, 1964, p. 237.
3. Sir George Grey, *Polynesian Mythology*, Whitcombe & Tombs, Wellington, 1956, p. 34.
4. A. Alpers, op. cit., p. 238.
5. R.J. Walker, 'Proper Names in Maori Myth and Tradition', *Journal of the Polynesian Society*, Vol. 78, No. 3, 1969, p. 405.
6. J. Te H. Grace, *Tuwharetoa*, p.405, A.H. & A.W. Reed, Wellington, 1959.
7. Walker, op. cit.

BEING MAORI

JOHN RANGIHAU

MY FEELING OF IDENTITY and commitment to Maori things is the result of history and traditions, and the fact that I grew up in a Maori community. In this community there was always a sense of the value of land and the emotional ties Maori have to it. As a result of these things I am strongly of the feeling that I am totally a New Zealander and cannot be regarded as anything else.

My education as a Maori was a matter of observation while I grew up in this complete community. It was a community where children were allowed to do their thing, where there was a place for the aged, and a place for the middle-aged. These places were within the structure of tribal organisation. I had to move through this as an apprenticeship for group living. We had to learn the dynamics of group living. We had to learn how to live together because we were in one another's pockets. If we didn't problems would have arisen. From the time we were children we had to learn what it meant to be part of an extended family. We were warned not to do some things and we learned by others' experience.

Th essence of community apprenticeship was young people learning by participating, by becoming carriers of wood, by chopping the wood and by setting up the hangi. As you grew older you moved on to being in charge of the butchers, the hangi men and the people who gathered food. You went through all these processes. Then you were allowed to go and listen to elders speaking on the marae and in the meeting houses. So you progressed by observing and becoming involved in all the activities of the marae. That traditionally was the way a young man fitted into place as the elders died off.

Kinship bound us together in this situation. To me, kinship is the warmth of being together as a family group: what you can draw from being together and the strength of using all the resources of a family. And a strong feeling of kinship or whanaua tanga reaches out to others in hospitality. I am reminded of a book written by Eric Linklater about his travels in New Zealand, where he talks of the New Zealand morning and afternoon tea and how he dreaded functions where they served morning tea because of the large quantity of cakes and pastries. It seemed to him this was a particular New Zealand way of showing hospitality. Now I like to think that some of this has come from the Maori. I believe New Zealanders have been influenced by Maori hospitality laws. The whole basis of them is the business of showing concern for your neighbour, concern for him as a person, and therefore sharing his daily life and sharing the things of the community. And caring.

Whanaua tanga to me also means that whenever a person feels lonely he will go round and visit some of his kin and it is just as enjoyable for the kin to receive a visit as it is for the person to go. In other words there is as much joy – or perhaps greater joy – in giving as in receiving. And so we give of one another to one another – we give the talents we have so everybody can share in these sorts of experiences.

It may be a little idealised but it has worked in our home areas over the years. It seems to me it could overcome some of the neuroses that urban dwellers are suffering because they are shut in. We should be harnessing our communities so they can become sharing, caring and loving for Pakeha and Maori. But particularly for Pakeha: to overcome physical and mental breakdowns in the suburbs. I would hope to see the future planning of our cities and towns with more awareness of the need for people to socialise, to be able to come together as a group with common interests. Polynesian life should influence our whole thinking towards enjoying these sorts of things. We have difficulties, of course, with our young people going into cities and not finding the kind of community they knew at home. We tell them there are many aspects of Pakehatanga they have to learn.

The broadest number of people in the Pakeha society fall into a middle-class category and these are the people responsible for the standards that are set. Coming from a fairly permissive society, our young people are part of the community at home and participate in the activities of the community. They know how far they can go in their behaviour there. But the values placed on their behaviour and actions in rural Maori areas are totally different from those they will meet in the urban situation. One of the biggest things we try to talk to the young ones about is the absolute loneliness they will find in a crowd of people and how they will tend to congregate in areas where there will be a number of Maori people. Unfortunately the areas where Maori congregate are places like the local pubs or the racecourses. That, to me, is an indictment of our total society; these are the only places where Maori feel they are on the eyeball-to-eyeball level with the rest of New Zealand society.

There's no doubt about it. Young people find it very difficult to move to areas where the dominant culture is practised in so many ways to which they are unaccustomed. They don't feel welcome; they feel it's a cold-as-steel world and one which they are not geared to live in because they have come from a community where everybody knows what everybody else is doing, where there's a warmth, which is the community embracing them as part of the community. For this reason I think it's much harder for them than it is for the Pakeha who is new to the city.

My own tribe, Tuhoe, moved to the city later than most. They had managed to retain a little more of their Maoriness than others. We believed that these young Moari kids who were so lonely in the cities needed to know that their own people were concerned about their plight, not by mere words and by their elders saying 'we know how you feel', but by the elders acting in a way that was seen by the

184

young as real interest. And so the formation of our own tribal societies in the city was an attempt to bring them together and allow them to see their people from home moving into their situation in towns.

A good deal of movement has occurred from the cities back to the country as people go home to recharge their batteries. But this wasn't good enough because sooner or later the third or fourth generation people will not have the same sense of going back home because they won't have lived through experiences in the country as their parents have. So it seemed to us that we should try to take into the urban situation aspects of tribal living; aspects that would be real to them but which would also stand the test of urban pressures exerted on the members of the tribe. So we had to do something about teaching Maori things.

One of the things that has struck us over the last ten years is the clamour raised by young Maori folk in thecities to learn more about their culture. And they're saying the elders are not teaching them enough. To a certain extent I agree. I agree that the way we teach our culture has completely changed from the traditional one and we have to find new ways of being able to pass information down. This is why we developed a method of calling back all the young people into the home area. We can only teach them culture according to our tribe. So we only call in those folk that come from our tribe.

I also believe young folk can live with a greater amount of assurance if they know who they are. Then they can move into the Pakeha world full of self-confidence because they have no difficulty about the question of identity. They recognise themselves fully because they know their history. And this was why we established our whare wananga, or school of learning, which will be an annual event. We will take in forty to fifty young people of both sexes and teach them things they would not be able to get through traditional methods of learning in the city.

You can't do this sort of thing in an urban situation and you can't afford it because of the pressure on you; for work, and for economic security. It seemed the only way we could do it was to get young people who had settled down and were interested in learning about their culture and to take them back into their home areas to go through a course for three weeks in which we could deal with Maori things in depth. But only in sufficient depth to whet the appetites. So that if they became interested, they had to pursue it. There was enough in it for them to have a look and decide.

The main thing about having the whare wananga was the opportunity to learn about their Maoritanga and at the same time carry on with their ordinary living and working. For us it was a two-fold thing. One, they learnt their kawa and their customs and their traditions; two, it allowed them to stand up tall in their new society because there was no question about who they were and where they had come from and where they were going. In other words they wouldn't fall into the international category of dislocated people.

185

The only place we can teach these things properly is the marae. You get a whole feeling that descends on you there. Maori people have a saying that you walk into a meeting house and you feel the warmth of it because you know that meeting house is named after an ancestor. And you are amidst people who have passed on. All the things they have said over the years are echoing through the meeting house and you immediately feel a warmth. Beyond that, you're living in a valley where the young people have a history and where their ancestors have come from. And so you have a very different climate from that of a classroom.

How good you become learning this way depends on how well you can say your thing on the marae without having recourse to notes. So you have to be able to learn things and absorb them and recall them at will to fit different occasions.

One of the important things we are passing on this way is that Tuhoe will make no concessions whatsoever in things that happen on their marae because we have given way in every other area of Maoriness. The marae is the repository of all the historical things, of all the traditions, all the mythology and other things which make up the intangibles of Maoriness and which for me are a very important part of being Tuhoe. From now on we will see that everything is carried out according to the Tuhoe protocol. We welcome all people to use our marae. But we ask that they fit in with the etiquette which is part and parcel of me and every other Tuhoe person. Only in this way can I foresee that we will be able to keep our culture alive. Not the sort of culture that asks us to go out and entertain tourists and profane our sacred things. But it will be that type of culture that asks us to do things because they have meaning for me and the rest of Tuhoe. And if we keep this place absolutely sacrosanct then it will never lose its aura, it will never lose its ethos. And those are the things that make me what I am.

Another thing that has concerned us over the years is people who come in without being told what they should do and just trample all over the marae. When there's a tangi on, they move in using cameras. This has been one of the things I have disliked about allowing the public generally to come in on some Maori occasions. Instead of being discreet and asking questions about how they should move, they just trample over things which are dear to our hearts. Sometimes to excuse them I say this is ignorance. But they have been fairly blatant about it and almost say, 'Well, it doesn't matter what your customs and traditions are. We are the more dominant group, therefore you must give way to us.' Sometimes I feel anger rising in me and I excuse them by saying, 'Oh well. You have to make excuses for those ignorant Pakeha because they don't know better.'

The climate is changing. But there always will be some people who, in the face of anything of this sort, have tendencies to break down traditions for breaking-down's sake. If there's any future strain between ourselves and the public it will be in these areas: Maori are careful not to trample over etiquette, and others move in like bulls in so many china shops and break so many cups. Pakeha and tourists do this badly. I was living in Rotorua for a time and I could see this happening where there was a tangi on. They came gawking at the doors. It's all very well to say that they're tourists. This conjures up images of people coming from overseas. But of course there are a number of New Zealanders who are tourists here too, particularly in areas like Rotorua. And they are just as guilty of doing that sort of thing as tourists from overseas.

If you're going to church and you know there's a funeral on, you would not go into that sort of place, because you realise it's private. Now it seems to me that there's no difference between a funeral service in church and one on the marae. People should observe the same sort of respect for both occasions. They do in church because it is part of the Pakeha culture. But Maori buildings and things are open to public inspection and it doesn't matter that it is a very private, intimate occasion.

This wouldn't happen in the Maori world because you would be aware of the spirit of the land you are going to, and of the mauri or life force of this land. You are aware of this through a number of ways. When I take strangers into Ruatahuna I stop and we get out of the car and I say to them, 'This is an old Maori custom'. These days, what I ask people to do is stand in silence for a little while and pray in their own way. It doesn't matter what sort of person I take into the area, I do it. There was a young Australian boy who came in from Rotorua and became very sick so they had to rush him back. He had come in with my wife and as soon as he became sick she said, 'Oh that was my fault, I didn't do the right thing by him.' And I knew exactly what she meant.

All this stems from the fact that down through the centuries the Maori has been very close to nature. People who live in this way apply to nature and to things around them this feeling of aura. In the case of the Maori, they give everything a mauri and this takes them into the world of conservation and being very much aware of the environment and how much they owe to their environment. So they do not create an imbalance. For Maori generally I believe there is this emotional tie to the land because of their mythology and because of the way they have been taught where they have come from – the whole mythology of creation.

In addition to the land ties, I have become aware of my identity in other ways. In modern terms, I am an ex-member of the Maori Battalion. At the time that was just a question of doing one's bit. But there was also a lot of pressure brought to bear on us by elders in Tuhoe. You didn't really think of this as part of your commitment to New Zealand until after the war. And then we came back into a situation which had not changed in any way, where we were still treated as second-class citizens, where we were still not allowed to purchase alcohol and where we had to get Polynesians or Indians to do this for us. Suddenly there was an annoying thing at the pit of our stomach about having gone away to free this beautiful land and yet still being treated like aliens in our own country. This whole question of commitment was brought up before my eyes when I thought about the boys who made the supreme sacrifice, about the times the battalion had to go in, and the comradeship that grew out of fire between ourselves and other units of the New Zealand division; the way we teamed together when we were on leave; the way the Pakeha soldiers had a very good relationship with us. I was struck by the fact that this was the price for total citizenship in New Zealand. I felt I was totally committed to the land of my forebears and this meant for me another commitment to be accepted by the dominant group. I was to be accepted as part of the New Zealand scene, not as a noble savage or a descendant of noble savages, but as a person with rights and privileges I had fought for and bought.

In the immediate post-war years I had the hope that the relationship forged through fire overseas would be carried on. But one always had the feeling that sooner or later things would slip back into the old ways and you'd really not have made a great impact. In 1957 I suddenly came face to face with the whole problem by realising that I couldn't get accommodation in a number of towns in New Zealand simply and purely because I was Maori. Travelling around at that time I became more and more convinced that nothing had happened in terms of social relations as a result of the war and that things had slipped back. I was travelling as part of my training that year, and in three different towns it was very hard for me to get accommodation in hotels, let alone flats.

And I remember having to do a particular piece of work in one town. I had to get rooms in a hotel ten miles away in an area where there was a large population of Maori. This stuck in my craw a bit. Perhaps we were to blame in that we didn't live up to the standards that were set by hotel keepers. But I was always struck by the fact that I was in the type of job that not too many Maori were in and I was moving around in circles where I was accepted by Pakeha people. Yet in this basic thing of getting accommodation in a hotel I just wasn't able to break through. One of the funny things I remember was having been turned down by three different hotels. I went to the nearest telephone box and rang one up, saying that my name was Turner. I was immediately accepted for a room. When I went around I was told, 'Oh, Mr Turner, we're sorry. We didn't realise you were a Maori.' In other words Mr Turner appeared to be Pakeha and appeared to be acceptable. But as soon as Mr Turner turned up and was Maori, the crunch came.

I would like to believe the climate has changed considerably; I would like to believe we are making advances in beginning to understand one another better. Perhaps people's attitudes are changing simply because at the moment the Maori bandwagon is rolling for so many people. But one of the things we are always aware of is that you cannot legislate against attitudes. These are things you really can't touch.

Some people have reacted to unequal treatment by advocating separatism. I can see separatism as a legitimate defence mechanism for Maori. I should qualify this. I feel that separatism is a very murky sort of area – there is so much mixed thinking about it. But I know exactly how *I* feel about it. There are two schools: one is where you are separated out by legislation; and the other where you separate yourselves out by choice so you can retain your identity. I want to be able to establish my own identity so I can stand up tall and be counted as part of the New Zealand scene and not be regarded as someone beneath others. Because I know who I am and because I know my background, I can do this in a much better way than if I were a mixed-up Maori-Pakeha who looks Maori and has Pakeha values.

You see, when Pakeha say we are all one people, they seem to mean that you're brown and a unique feature of the indigenous scene. But they want you to act as a European provided you can still retain the ability to poke out your tongue, gesticulate and do your Maori dances. That is Maori culture. The other part says to me, we want you to become part of us and lose all your institutions and all those things which are peculiarly Maori like the Department of Maori Affairs and Maori representation in Parliament. We want to give the world the image of all of us being absorbed into European culture or New Zealand culture. I can't go along with this because I can't feel I can be a Pakeha. What's more, I don't want to be a Pakeha. There are a lot of things which I do not like, compared with the things I do like in the Maori world. But I'm being asked to become a Pakeha so that I can then be counted as a New Zealander. Cor blimey, I am a New Zealander and you can't take that away from me. I am a New Zealander, a Maori New Zealander and I can't see that it should create such a fuss every time I talk about retention of my culture and setting up Maori institutions like marae and everything else.

You get people who scoff and say what is it these Maoris want? But separatism to me isn't separatism. It's just me trying to live out my life against the pressures exerted on me by the more dominant group. If they want me to be an honorary white, as has happened in other parts of the world, then I'm afraid I cannot go along with it.

Separatism has become a dirty word in New Zealand because we are so mixed up in our thinking – we are mixed up as a group of people on how we should act in a multiracial society. It will take us some time before we can clarify our own thoughts on this. The Maori have already clarified their thoughts. They want to be able to enjoy those good things which have been given them by the Pakeha culture. But they also want to retain the values that have been part of their culture and which they believe are good in present circumstances. It's not just a question of wanting to be militant or wanting to set up separate things in order to live our lives in a vacuum of separateness.

You know the number of people, Pakeha people, who know better than I do how I am to be Maori just amazes me. I could never be so audacious to suggest to Pakeha that I know better than they do how they are to live as Pakeha. But I am constantly reminded of the number of Pakeha people who know better than I do what is good for me. It is about time we were allowed to think for ourselves and to say things for our reasons and not for the reasons set down by Pakeha experts. The Maori is content to stand right where he is, retain his culture and retain his identity, and be himself, not a foreigner, in his own country.

Although these feelings are Maori, for me they are my Tuhoetanga rather than my Maoritanga. My being Maori is absolutely dependent on my history as a Tuhoe person as against being a Maori person. It seems to me there is no such thing as Maoritanga because Maoritanga is an all-inclusive term which embraces all Maori. And there are so many different aspects about every tribal person. Each tribe has its own history. And it's not a history that can be shared among others. How can I share with the history of Ngati Porou, of Te Arawa, of Waikato? Because I am not of those people. I am a Tuhoe person and all I can share in is Tuhoe history.

To me, Tuhoetanga means that I do the things that are meaningful to Tuhoe. But I cannot do the things that are meaningful to other people. One of the things, for instance, that is an unbroken law from my own ancestors is that the Tuhoe person must at all times be humble. Humility is one vital aspect of Tuhoetanga. Now I cannot go around telling other people to be humble. That may not be their way. But it is mine. And I say to all Tuhoe young people that they must be humble, because I know them, they're part of my tribal background, they're part of my history, they're part of me.

I can't go round saying because I'm Maori that Maoritanga means this and all Maori have to follow me. That's a lot of hooey. I have a faint suspicion that Maoritanga is a term coined by the Pakeha to bring the tribes together. Because if you cannot divide and rule, then for tribal people all you can do is unite them and rule. Because then they lose everything by losing their own tribal histories and traditions that give them their identity.

Also available from Reed:

Te Ao Marama 2

Regaining Aotearoa: Maori Writers Speak Out

Edited by Witi Ihimaera

In this thought-provoking collection of articles, essays and other writings, Maori speak directly about the issues of concern to them since 1980, including racism, sovereignty, the Treaty, the 1981 Springbok Tour, reclaiming the language and the past, the arts and literature, women's issues and history.

Prominent writers such as Ranginui Walker, Donna Awatere-Huata, Buddy Mikaere, Syd Jackson, Whina Cooper, Tipene O'Regan, Mira Szaszy and Te Arikinui Te Atairangikaahu discuss what it means to be Maori in New Zealand today.

Regaining Aotearoa is the second volume in Witi Ihimaera's monumental anthology of Maori writing since 1980 entitled *Te Ao Marama*. It is indispensable reading for all students of Maori culture, society and thought.